The Kaiser's Lost Kreuzer

The Kaiser's Lost Kreuzer

A History of U-156 *and Germany's Long-Range Submarine Campaign Against North America, 1918*

PAUL N. HODOS

McFarland & Company, Inc., Publishers
Jefferson, North Carolina

Frontispiece: Picture taken from *U-156*'s conning tower towards the bow, with a good view of the sub's principal armament, one of her two 5.9 inch guns (*Lowell Thomas Papers, James A. Cannavino Library, Archives & Special Collections, Marist College, USA*).

LIBRARY OF CONGRESS CATALOGUING-IN-PUBLICATION DATA

Names: Hodos, Paul N., 1980– author.
Title: The Kaiser's lost Kreuzer : a history of U-156 and Germany's long-range submarine campaign against North America, 1918 / Paul N. Hodos.
Other titles: History of U-156 and Germany's long-range submarine campaign against North America, 1918
Description: Jefferson, North Carolina : McFarland & Company, Inc., Publishers, 2018 | Includes bibliographical references and index.
Identifiers: LCCN 2017049565 | ISBN 9781476671628 (softcover : acid free paper) ∞
Subjects: LCSH: U 156 (Submarine)—History. | World War, 1914–1918—Naval operations—Submarine. | World War, 1914–1918—Naval operations, German.
Classification: LCC D591 .H72 2018 | DDC 940.4/5943—dc23
LC record available at https://lccn.loc.gov/2017049565

BRITISH LIBRARY CATALOGUING DATA ARE AVAILABLE

ISBN (print) 978-1-4766-7162-8
ISBN (ebook) 978-1-4766-3040-3

© 2018 Paul N. Hodos. All rights reserved

No part of this book may be reproduced or transmitted in any form or by any means, electronic or mechanical, including photocopying or recording, or by any information storage and retrieval system, without permission in writing from the publisher.

Front cover image of the *U-156* courtesy of the Lowell Thomas Papers Collection, Marist College Archives and Special Collections

Printed in the United States of America

*McFarland & Company, Inc., Publishers
 Box 611, Jefferson, North Carolina 28640
 www.mcfarlandpub.com*

To my wife Renee, thank you,
this never would have happened without you.

Alex and Lila, my children,
hard work and love are the keys to open up the world.

U-Kreuzer (German): In the First World War a U-Kreuzer, in English styled U-cruiser, was a large long-range U-boat fitted with powerful artillery designed to challenge armed merchant ships and small patrol vessels on the surface in areas far removed from Germany's bases of supply. The U-Kreuzers carried more ammunition, fuel, and crew than the average U-boat and could stay on station for months at a time thousands of miles from home. They were called "underwater cruisers" due to their large artillery and ability to wreak havoc on far flung shipping lanes, much like the infamous surface cruiser warships that roamed the oceans hunting for Allied ships earlier in the war. The surface cruisers were quickly sunk by superior Allied sea power. The U-Kreuzers could dive to escape when faced with that same power. The term U-Kreuzer is used throughout this work to describe Germany's long-range submarines in accordance with prior authoritative and primary German works on these vessels like Eberhard Rössler's *Die Deutschen U-Kreuzer und Transport-U-Boote* and the War Diary (Kriegstagebuch) of the *U-156*.

Table of Contents

Acknowledgments   ix
Preface   1
Prologue: The British Are Coming   3

1. The Blockade   9
2. The American Problem   14
3. The Counter-Blockade and the U-Kreuzers   18
4. Room 40   35
5. From Carrying Cargo to Sinking It   38
6. The Great Mirage   47
7. The U-boat Ace   51
8. The Trade War and the Secret War   58
9. U-Kreuzerkrieg   70
10. The Naval Officer   84
11. Targeting North America   89
12. The U-Kreuzer and the Armored Cruiser   105
13. The Battle Off Nauset Beach   113
14. Low Hanging Fruit   120
15. Halifax, Gateway to the East   127
16. Seiner Majestät Schiff Triumph   136
17. U-Kreuzerkrieg Amerika   147
18. Indecision, Loss and a Mystery Solved   162

Epilogue: Deadly Dreams Become Reality   174

Dramatis Personæ 181

Sites of Interest 187

Tables 189
   Ships Sunk or Damaged by U-156 189 • Specifications of
   U-156 191 • The Lost Officers of U-156's Second Cruise 191
   • U-Kreuzer Tonnage Scores Worldwide 192 • U-Kreuzer
   Tonnage Scores for the North American Raids/Campaign 192

Chapter Notes 193

Bibliography 209

Index 217

Acknowledgments

Dwight Messimer is a preeminent researcher, author, retired professor, retired police officer, former soldier, and friend. He has given his time, advice, and repeated help with translations and photographs for this project. He is the top expert on U-Kreuzers and I could not have finished this book without his assistance and wisdom. The U-Boot Archiv at the Deutsches U-Boot-Museum is a great resource for information on U-boats from both World Wars located in Cuxhaven-Altenbruch, Germany. The author would like to thank Horst Bredow (World War II U-boat veteran), sadly recently deceased, and Peter Monte for their selfless dedication to the naval history of their countrymen, and for the primary documents they provided for this work.

Carl-Henrik Ankarberg is a great researcher and has been invaluable to this project due to his access to some of the rarest information about the *U-156*, and his warm and friendly communications. Mr. Ankarberg's connections to the shipwreck diving community and his unquenchable thirst for U-boat history have made him one of the foremost experts on this topic. Robert Grant, renowned U-boat author, also deceased within the last few years, was a huge influence on this work as his book *U-boat Hunters* sparked the fire for the story of the *U-156* that would become my obsession for many years. His loss is sorely felt in the U-boat and Roman history fields.

Dr. Roger Sarty, an excellent Canadian naval historian, professor, and author also contributed much in the later stages of my research. I would also like to thank the University of Victoria Archives and Special Collections for access to their excellent collection of First World War German and Allied documents, the U.S. National Archives staff in College Park, Maryland, and Washington, D.C., the Naval Historical Center and the Naval History and Heritage Command, the staff at the Orleans Historical Society, John Ansley and his staff at the Marist College Archives and Special Collections for the use of their wonderful photos of the *U-156*, and the Provincial Archives of New Brunswick for helping me unearth the story of Heinrich Kamps in their collection of old newspapers. There are many others who assisted me greatly, and without which this book could never have been finished. They have my warmest thanks.

Preface

When I was still in grade school the First World War fascinated me. At that time there were already only a few veterans of the Great War left, so it had an air of mystery around it that had never seemed to surround the Second World War. My grandfather, Paul Hodos, Sr., demystified the second war with his stories about fighting Imperial Japan in the Pacific. The First World War continued to grab my attention into adulthood and I read voraciously about it whenever I could. In several works there were tantalizing references to a little known long-range submarine campaign against North America in the latter part of the war. I could find no details about this sea battle until I began to dig deep into the topic in 2012.

What I found astounded me and led to the completion of this project. I read the Canadian viewpoint on the raids from well written recent academic classics like *Tin Pots and Pirate Ships* and the *Seabound Coast*. I also delved into new American scholarship featuring the U-Kreuzers like *The Baltimore Sabotage Cell*, *The Attack on Orleans*, and *America's U-Boats*. The above works covered some aspects of the U-Kreuzer attacks near the Canary Islands and North America, and are great works on interesting and worthy topics. However, they did not cover the complete U-Kreuzer war, and the focus was never completely on the campaign itself. This work relates the full story from the German viewpoint.

The vehicle for the narrative of this singular campaign that brought World War I to the U.S. and Canada was a no-brainer. By far the most interesting U-Kreuzer of them all is the *U-156*. Her close calls, exciting operations, and the personal stories of her crew and victims make for great reading while still staying true to the overall saga of Germany's first attempt at the deadly game of long-range submarine warfare.

I built the book on the firm foundation of numerous primary source documents from the U.S. National Archives, the Michael Hadley papers at the University of Victoria Archives, the Deutsches U-Boot Museum, the Marist College Archives, and many other places where I obtained useful original material. The documents consist of German, British, American, and Canadian government records and photos that vary from messages to the Emperor of Germany, Kaiser Wilhelm II, down to a submarine captain's notations on what he and his crew did on Christmas Day 1917. Particularly useful was a huge compilation of original British National Archives documents related to the U-boat war under the title *German Submarine Warfare in the Eyes of British Intelligence*. I also used many quality secondary source works from almost every decade of the last 100 years that added much to the strategic background of the story, and also pointed out key details of the war cruises of the *U-156*.

In writing this book I made a solemn promise, over four years in the making, to utilize the best sources available to tell a human story about German strategy, the Allied responses to that strategy, and the real life and death of an extraordinary German vessel and her crew.

Prologue: The British Are Coming

The Bay of Naos is an isolated place near the southernmost tip of the Island of El Hierro in the Spanish controlled Canary Islands. The Canaries consist of seven main islands off of Northwest Africa, well known over the centuries as being a stopover on journeys to the Americas for merchant and military vessels. The islands are still under the control of Spain, despite some autonomy.[1] The waters of El Hierro are clear and blue, and the island itself is a relaxing tourist destination with a small airport, ferry, and a few hotels. According to the official Canary Islands tourism website, El Hierro's crystal clear waters are perfect for diving.

On the early morning of 15 January 1918, the huge Deutschland class ex-merchant U-Kreuzer, Seiner Majestät Unterseeboot 156 (*U-156*), arrived outside Naos Bay to commence urgent engine repairs, and meet with SM *U-157*. They were scheduled to discuss potential joint anti-shipping operations near the Canaries and take part in a daring plan to ship vital war materiel to Germany. *U-157* was not there so the *U-156* departed, and then returned again on 16 January. Once again, the *U-157* did not show and the *U-156* left for a second time.

She stayed in the area, and returned to the tranquil bay sheltered by hills and cliffs close to the shore on the morning of the 17th. At 7 a.m., Kapitänleutnant Konrad Gansser decided to send three of his most trusted officers to land on the beach and take up lookout positions on a hill while the *U-156* underwent repairs. He dispatched Oberleutnant zur see Knöckel, Leutnant Bieberstein, and the U-boat's medical officer, Dr. Minning. A sailor rowed them toward shore in the submarine's dinghy, and dropped them off just before the tumultuous surf.

The three officers swam through the waves, clambered onto the beach soaking wet, and hurriedly ascended the steep hill to begin their watch for any of the vessels of Germany's myriad Allied enemies. The ship's boat returned to the massive profile of the stationary *U-156* bobbing in the bay under anchor.

Eight hours later the men on the hill were likely bored, having taken photographs of themselves and the scenery on the cliffs to pass the time, but hopefully still vigilant. The crew of the *U-156* was dependent on the sharpness of their eyes and the stamina of their brains to remain alert despite the stillness in this remote corner of the world. At the same time, the crew of the *U-156* was also relaxed in the bay below based on posed photos they took of themselves lounging shirtless on the deck.

The three lookout officers were not the first to spot a heavy periscope sticking three feet out of the clear waters about 180 feet off *U-156*'s starboard. The moment this telltale sign of danger appeared it lowered itself back into the depths, and the *U-156*'s crew snapped into action. The two massive 5.9–inch deck guns and multiple machine guns were manned and swung towards the threat within seconds. The anchor was weighed, and

The men of *U-156* relaxing in Naos Bay after their long journey from Germany. This photograph was taken shortly before a British submarine ambushed them and almost sent the crew and their boat to the bottom of the bay. It appears some of the men have been swimming, and the seemingly convivial atmosphere is not what one would expect in a war zone (*Lowell Thomas Papers, James A. Cannavino Library, Archives & Special Collections, Marist College, USA*).

Gansser ordered the ship's boat to land so the three lookout officers could be warned of the presence of an enemy submarine and informed of their commander's plan. Gansser promised to make every attempt to return to the men, and not leave them stranded in this isolated part of paradise, which until now seemed so far from the First World War. The unfortunate reality was that even peaceful Naos Bay could not escape the fury of that war, and just as in the battlefields of Europe, death could strike without much warning during such a terrible conflict.

Two minutes later the periscope appeared again about 1,800 feet from the *U-156*. The gunners immediately opened fire with machine guns and their formidable artillery, and drove the periscope underwater. The anchor was still not off the floor of the bay, although the crew had been pulling up its chain since the periscope was first spotted. An agonizing ten minutes later the anchor was finally up, and the *U-156* immediately turned and headed toward the open sea.

About 1,800 feet into her journey the lookouts spotted the periscope again, this time about 1,500 feet away. Gansser ordered the *U-156* to turn towards the object, and passed the enemy submarine a mere 60 feet away. As the giant U-boat lumbered by and above the submerged enemy submarine, the crystal clear waters revealed the silhouette of the marauding underwater enemy. *U-156* continued on her way towards the open ocean when the crew spotted the periscope again at about 3,000 feet.

Forty-five minutes after weighing anchor, the *U-156* was still changing direction multiple times before finally beginning the return to land. Gansser decided they must have lost the suspected British submarine, and he wanted to pick up his stranded officers. Almost an hour later, the ship's boat retrieved the three relieved officers and loaded them into the *U-156*. Gansser had taken an awful risk, and he would almost pay a terrible price for his loyalty to his men.

Once his officers were aboard, Gansser ordered the submarine to head east while hugging the island's coast. Just as the engines roared to life, the lookouts spotted the enemy periscope at 3,000 feet. At the moment of this terrifying discovery, a surge of bubbles, caused by the air escaping from the enemy's torpedo tubes, was sighted, and the men of the *U-156* opened fire on the periscope. In the hurried desperation only possible when faced with imminent danger, the engines were ordered into full reverse at what was likely record speed to avoid the high explosives hurtling towards the boat and threatening death to the 76 men on board. To the crew's relief, the first two torpedoes passed three ship's lengths off the bow, and exploded near the coast.

Unfortunately for the Imperial German sailors of the *U-156*, a third torpedo, fired right after the first two, was headed straight for their vessel. At first it ran in the exact course of the others, and Gansser thought it might also impact the coast as harmlessly as its predecessors. To the horror of all aboard, the underwater missile curved left suddenly, and went straight for them.

Gansser realized that outmaneuvering the torpedo was no longer possible, and everyone understood this was likely the end of *U-156*—the weapon they hoped would devastate Allied shipping in the area, and their only chance of getting back to Germany alive. Just before the torpedo's impact, four quick thinking and survival minded sailors on the *U-156*'s deck jumped off into the clear water. The torpedo hit the boat with a thud, starboard amidships. All were surprised when no explosion followed. The faulty torpedo popped up about nine feet from the other side of the boat—it had struck the hull, deflected and passed underneath.

The only damage done was a leak in a diving tank, which was easily fixed by counter-flooding. After the torpedo jumped out of the water, it ran on the surface away from the boat, then began curving back toward it again. In an incident that would have been comedic were it not so potentially deadly, *U-156* barely dodged the defective torpedo a second time by accelerating to the submarine's top speed of 11 excruciatingly slow knots.

Of the four men who had jumped into the water, one was pulled aboard, two made it to land, and one drowned.[2] Gansser noted the attack occurred a few hundred meters from the coast in neutral Spanish waters.[3]

U-156 had survived her first brush with death. It would not be the last. She, one of the largest submarines in the Imperial German Navy, was the inevitable outcome of Germany's attempt to create an underwater merchant shipping fleet to service American trade and defeat the British blockade. When that trade ended her peaceful mission did too. Behind the peaceful façade of the merchant boats lurked the looming silhouette of a U-Kreuzer built to attack Germany's far off enemies. The attacks near the Canaries off West Africa were an amazing feat for a U-boat of the age, but the *U-156* would top that achievement during her second cruise to the distant shores of the United States and Canada.

War was coming to North America by a very dramatic and circuitous route. As with most stories worth telling, the journey and decision to do so were not taken or accomplished overnight. The *U-156* was part of a bigger strategic gamble by the German Navy to bring the war to untouched shores with limited resources and forces for the benefit of the main war zone around Europe in an attempt to splinter the Allied defenses and force them to patrol disparate parts of the globe. The U-Kreuzers were also charged with sinking as much merchant, convoy, and warship tonnage as they could manage. The *U-156* and her sisters were pioneers, technologically flawed wonder weapons, statements of German power to distant lands, and the naval high command's forlorn hope to win the war at sea. The chances for success were always slim, but the crew of the *U-156* was ready to take the war to the enemy's distant homeland. The forbidding Atlantic was no longer enough to keep the U.S. and Canada safe.

1

The Blockade

Britain was close to running short of food during the height of the German submarine campaign but never ran out, due to a program designed to increase the acreage of land under tillage, a very efficiently run rationing system, and the largest merchant fleet on earth. France, on the other hand, had basically bankrupted herself since she imported everything. This was especially true after the Germans captured much of her industry and coal producing areas early in the war, and was able to hold onto the conquests for most of the rest of the conflict. France compensated for the loss of her own resources by bulk ordering huge amounts from foreigners.

Britain also borrowed as she had never borrowed before, but watched her consumption. This was especially true during the height of the submarine campaign when civilians were waiting for food in long lines. The entrance of America into the war saved both Britain and France from becoming so indebted to the U.S. that they would have risked the whole of their economies simply to survive the war.

The Germans had no centralized system to control food and the War Ministry's efforts to do so were hampered by the black market and the diffusion of power in the Imperial and state governments who had no strong central force to control them. As a result, the German policy was not unified, but piecemeal and ineffective. Germany, out of the major powers, suffered the most from hunger due to her shoddy system of control and lack of imports from her former oceanic trading partners due to the British blockade.[1] Britain had decided on a policy of blockade in case of war with Germany a few years before the start of World War I. A strategy of close in blockade was abandoned in favor of a distant blockade due to the advent of the torpedo and mine, and their ability to sink large ships without risking one's own capital ships in a large surface engagement.

In short, Britain decided on a policy of confinement rather than encounter with the German High Seas Fleet. Distant blockade was meant to strangle Germany economically rather than tempt the German fleet to fight an engagement, which is what the close blockade may have achieved at great risk to the British ships.

The fleet moved to the outer edges of the North Sea in August 1914 to keep their ever vigilant watch for ships engaged in trade bound for the Reich and her allies. Britain circumvented earlier naval agreements such as the Declarations of Paris and London[2] by engaging in a blockade that would also interrupt neutral trade. In addition, Britain expanded the contraband list to include any goods traveling to Germany even if they were not on accepted pre-war lists of what could be considered the contraband of war. The British quickly realized that for the blockade to be truly crippling these extreme measures against enemy and neutral trade had to be taken.[3] International maritime trade was essential to Germany's survival. In 1912 and 1913, Germany's imports exceeded her exports by 640,000,000 dollars, which was a considerable sum for a nation at the time. The imports consisted mostly of food and raw materials. If Germany lost this influx she could not survive for long. Sixty percent of German trade was conducted by her considerable merchant fleet, which consisted of over 2,000 steamers and almost 300 sailing ships. The Germans anticipated a quick end to the war, and as a result most of her shipping was stranded in foreign or international waters when the fighting began.[4] Germany possessed 5.5 million tons of shipping at the beginning of the war. She had only about 2 million tons of that shipping in home waters in August 1914. The rest would have to be written off as a loss as the war dragged on. In effect, German international trade was destroyed by the end of the first month of the conflict. Germany continued to conduct trade in the Baltic Sea with the Nordic countries, but this was a shadow of what had been a massive trading enterprise.

Germany tried to re-provision herself with neutral shipping since her own ships were all interned or captured. The British attempted to circumvent this by ignoring certain provisions of the Declaration of London, which the British had helped write, and had included provisions from her naval manuals. The British soon discovered the Germans were planning to use the great port of Rotterdam in Holland to funnel neutral trade into their territory. Britain realized this would make the blockade ineffective and essentially give the Germans a merchant fleet flying a different flag.

The British calculated the risks and decided they would ignore the Declaration of London. They also realized they would not need to use neutral shipping exclusively like the Germans since the German fleet wouldn't be able to end British trade as it was locked up in the Baltic by the superior British navy. In public, Britain declared she would follow the Declaration of London, but the government created one key loophole that would allow the navy to stop conditional contraband from being carried to neutral ports. Britain did not aggressively pursue the new policy at first since she did not want to anger neutral countries attempting to trade with both the Allies and the Central Powers like the United States.[5] However, as it became clear that the war would be a long one the British hardened their stance. In October 1914, the British made a rule that a stopped neutral ship would be required to possess paperwork to prove the cargo was not headed for Germany. They also added items to the banned list that were expressly mentioned as not contraband by the Declaration of London. The Declaration of London had become a mere scrap of paper that the Allies would no longer honor.

The British also declared the North Sea a war zone, which meant any ship approaching Germany, Holland, or the other Scandinavian countries would have to go through the control zone of the English Channel and North Sea to undergo inspection by the British. When Germany declared a submarine blockade of Great Britain in February 1915 it actually weakened her trade position since the neutrals now faced more danger from German submarines sinking them without warning rather than the mere inconvenience of British inspections. Destruction was far more terrible than an intrusive inspection in the eyes of most ship crews and neutral governments.[6] The submarine blockade was a direct result of the Germans' suffering under the British blockade. By 1916, the German civilian population was forced to eat only bread and potatoes until the potato crop failed and they became dependent on turnips. The German people, only recently able to bask in the pleasures of modern civilized life, were reduced to thinking only of eating, working, and plotting for their next meal in a fight for survival that echoed a more primal age. The war had taken all of the food and leisure of the population and turned them into animals fighting for their lives at the front and at home. Persons in jails, asylums, and institutions were particularly hard hit and some of these inmates actually starved to death.

The German public had to wait in terribly long lines for hours in the cold for items as small as one egg. In addition, each type of food had its own line so the already tired and malnourished families were in line for food items constantly. George Schreiner, an American newspaper reporter, inspected some of these lines in 1916 in Berlin and found that "In the case of the younger women and children the skin was drawn hard to the bones and bloodless. Eyes had fallen deeper into the sockets. From the lips all color was gone, and the tufts of hair which fell over parchmented foreheads seemed dull and famished."[7] The wealthy and middle class were not immune from hunger either. They suffered as well and had to search for scraps in the night along with the poor. Not many in the civilian world had easy access to food.[8] Rationing in Germany had already begun in earnest by 1915 when authorities nationalized the supplies of flour, wheat, and rye. Meat was also rationed by local governments, and Austria-Hungary enacted food control measures too. The Germans were also hurting for coal, various metals, and nitrates needed for agricultural fertilizer and explosives production. The fall and winter of 1916 made the situation worse in Germany during the infamous "turnip winter." Europe's farms were producing much lower yields than that needed to feed the citizens of the Reich. Ersatz products made from potatoes, powdered milk, and even tree bark were introduced, but these were only stopgap measures, and not nearly as healthy as the old hearty German diet.

The Germans were subsisting on ersatz bread, fatless sausages, a few pounds of potatoes, and the ever-present turnip. The food shortages caused social unrest throughout the Reich and its allied territories. In March 1916, it was reported that lines of from 600 to 800 people showed up when a butter delivery occurred in Hamburg. In April 1916, there were riots and fights over the food supply, which resulted in the deaths of two women in Germany with 16 injured. The protests also spread to Vienna and Budapest.

American entry into the war ended any hope of the end of the blockade and the American Navy soon added its efforts to depriving Germany of any imports. German foreign trade went from a 5.9 billion dollar business in 1913 to a paltry 800 million dollars in 1917. The Germans were subsisting on a meager 1000 calories a day if they were lucky. The hunger was so terrible it weakened German resistance to the influenza pandemic when it came near the end of the war.[9] In addition, the blockade also endangered the stability of the German army, which was running short of food supplies close to the armistice even though it's soldiers had priority for supplies above everyone else in the Reich. An American representative in Germany shortly after the armistice communicated some of his observances of the blockade's effect on German children, and noted the disturbingly detached commentary of a German doctor on the children's plight.

> You think this is a kindergarten for the little ones. No, these are children of seven and eight years, tiny faces with large dull eyes overshadowed by huge, puffed, rickety foreheads, their small arms just skin and bones, and above the crooked legs

with their dislocated joints, the swollen, pointed stomachs of the hunger edema. A doctor treating such children stated, "You see this child here? It consumed an incredible amount of bread and yet it did not get any stronger. I found out that it hid all the bread it received underneath its straw mattress. The fear of hunger was so deeply rooted in the child that it collected the stores instead of eating the food: a misguided animal instinct made the dread of hunger worse than the actual pangs."[10]

The U-Kreuzers, as their merchant U-boat predecessors had attempted to do, were expected to assist Germany in the breaking of the fearful machine of the blockade, and if some German leaders got their way, to attempt to partially initiate such a system on the North American coast so the U.S., Canada, and Great Britain could feel at least a small percentage of the "pangs" felt by Germany's children.

In 1919, after the war had ended and the Paris peace negotiations were in full swing, the French government argued that the Germans should be stopped from buying food to prevent their starvation as it would mean less German money left for reparations. They broached this argument at an Allied meeting to discuss the seizure of German ships. The Germans were to trade their remaining ships for food. Woodrow Wilson rejected this cold argument. Hatred ran deep between the two enemies even after the firing stopped.[11]

2

The American Problem

Prior to the war the U.S. economy was in recession. The period of neutrality for the United States from 1914 to early 1917 resulted in her becoming the primary neutral exporter and supplier for the Allied nations. The export trade boom was the forefront of an American economic resurgence that would last through the whole of the war years. The period of neutrality also served to prepare America's industries for the eventual declaration of war in 1917 since the Allies were ordering the same goods America would need herself when she entered the conflict.[1] From 1914 to 1916 merchandise exports doubled and comprised 12 percent of the U.S. gross national product.[2] The export business had never been more important to the American economy, and the U.S. was one of the few countries left in the world to benefit from this type of trade as it never had before. The Germans faced the same strategic problem while the U.S. was neutral, and later when America was at war with them, how to stop the flow of goods and soldiers to the Allies in Europe?

One of the problems the Americans faced and eventually overcame was their lack of a large merchant navy to transport the men and goods needed to go to France once war was declared. The Germans quite foolishly assumed the United States would not be able to make up for their inherent lack of ships, and even if they did the Reich's leaders thought their submarines would destroy whatever was built.

The U.S. was also asked to build millions of tons of merchant shipping by the British to replace vital tonnage lost to U-boats. The example cited by the Allied powers as illustrative of the problem was the inadequate amount of coal shipments to Italy and France due to lack of shipping to carry the vital mineral.[3]

On 3 August 1917, the U.S. Shipping Board took the first step to take over American shipping and force all shipyards to work exclusively for Uncle Sam.[4] First, they promulgated a requisition order. After this,

2. The American Problem

they commandeered all steel ships over 2,500 tons then under construction in American shipyards. 431 ships totaling 3,068,431 tons were covered by the 3 August order. There were immediate challenges to the directive from shipyards, ship owners, and foreign governments building ships in the U.S. However, they could do nothing to stop the process.[5]

In addition to the seizure of ships under construction, the Americans also gained vast tonnage from enemy ships. Ninety-seven Austro-German vessels of 700,000 gross registered tons were seized in American ports once war was declared. They had been interned since the beginning of the war and included huge passenger liners. The German crews had attempted to sabotage the ships with some success, but most of them could be repaired fairly quickly. The *Leviathan*, formerly the German *Vaterland*,[6] at the time the largest ship on earth, transported approximately 100,000 American troops to France.[7]

The seized ships made a dent in the U.S. need for boats. However, the Americans were so desperate for tonnage they chartered whole neutral fleets for their purposes. The merchant fleets of neutrals played a key role in the Allied effort against Germany as hired hands in the trade war. They would suffer grievous losses to German submarines as the inevitable result of their business deals with the enemies of Germany. By 1 September 1918, Norway had chartered 614,000 tons of steamships and 275,000 tons of sailing vessels to the U.S. 100,000 tons came from Sweden, 265,000 from Denmark, 81,000 for Belgian relief, 533,746 tons from Holland, and 151,000 chartered from Japan.[8]

U.S. Navy manned merchant ships became vessels of the Naval Overseas Transportation Service while the U.S. Shipping Board controlled most of the rest. The U.S. had 7,000,000 gross registered tons of shipping in its service by war's end. About 4.5 million tons were manned by civilian crews while the rest was with the navy. A huge group of men had to be recruited and trained by the U.S. government to man the extra ships. The other Allied powers had much larger pools of experienced seamen in their ranks while the U.S. only had a small number of sailors and merchant crews. Seamen with at least two years service were allowed to enroll in one of twenty schools around the country to become officers or masters of their own ships. Thousands of new sea leaders were trained in this way in a short time.[9]

The question now became how to get the ships across the ocean without having them end up on the bottom after a German torpedo found it's mark. The answer was convoy. The British listed the disadvantages of convoy to their new American partners compared to offensive patrols. If a U-boat found a convoy of ships she would find them a target impossible to miss, convoy communications were poor as not all ships had the equipment needed, and merchant sailors were inexperienced in some of the skills needed to sail in formation due to the best men being inducted into the Allied navies. However, the success of the cross-channel French coal trade convoys showed these arguments were not valid in the long run. The British also opposed convoy based on a lack of destroyers in their home waters. This last argument was scuttled once the Americans pledged their naval forces for duty in British waters.[10]

Convoys headed to Europe congregated off the American coast in the first phase. The next phase was the trip to the submarine zone around the British Isles wherein a convoy was typically escorted by a cruiser and a fast armed merchant ship. The idea for protection the whole way across the ocean came from the man in charge of American naval forces in Europe, Admiral William Sims who suggested the course of action when the fear of long range U-Kreuzers intercepting a convoy in the far flung sea lanes was high.[11] When the U-boat war zone around Great Britain was reached, about 200 miles west of Ireland or France, the escorts were relieved by destroyers at a predetermined time and location. In the European danger zone radios were used as little as possible, smoke was reduced as much as it could be, every ship was darkened at night, and not even a cigarette was allowed to be lit.

In July 1917, Admiral William Benson, overall head of the U.S. Navy, agreed to focus on anti-submarine warfare and destroyer construction to the detriment of capital ship construction despite his grave doubts about that course of action. He was under pressure from the Allies and Admiral Sims in England to fight the current U-boat war and leave future strategic situations and scenarios on the quayside. Later, in November 1917, Benson sent four dreadnoughts to Europe, promised a division of battleships would be attached to the Grand Fleet, and in the spring of 1918 the entire American battle fleet left home for "over there." U.S. Naval cooperation with the Allies was improving.[12]

The effect of all this work is shown in a report published by the Weimar Republic's Reichstag in July 1925 to answer the question of why Germany had collapsed in 1918.[13] The document came to the conclusion that part of the reason for the collapse was the surprise the Germans felt at how quickly the U.S. was able to create a war merchant fleet, and how fast she built up her military presence in Europe because of it.[14]

The U.S. Navy had transported about 45 percent of American troops

(900,000 men) to Europe. They had provided about 27 percent of convoy escorts and 12 percent of the battleship strength of the British Grand Fleet. American sailors maintained 23 naval stations in Europe, manned 368 ships, 128 submarine chasers, and had a total presence in theater of 75,000 enlisted men and officers by the end of the war.[15]

3

The Counter-Blockade and the U-Kreuzers

On 4 August 1914, Great Britain declared war on Imperial Germany after the Reich's forces invaded neutral Belgium on their way to France. Suddenly, Germany's far-flung Kaiserliche Marine units in the Atlantic, Pacific, and Indian oceans found they were at war with the greatest naval power on earth. The commanders of these scattered warships hurriedly prepared to attack the enemy's commerce and cause as much damage to Allied trade as possible before succumbing to the inevitable loss of their bases of supply and freedom of action due to the huge number of ships at Britain's disposal.

The daring captains of Germany's surface cruisers caused a great deal of damage, worry, and shuffling of badly needed naval resources at a time when Britain's fleet was engaged in a constant vigil in the North Sea to keep Germany's huge High Seas Fleet bottled up in its' lair in the Baltic.

However, by March 1915 all of Germany's principal raiders had been destroyed, trapped, or interned. The Kaiser's warships and support craft had been swept from the seas by the Allies. Cruiser warfare, although of some utility in the short term, was the last ditch tactic of a weaker power and could not have the long-term effect of an actual blockade. Once the cruisers had been sent to the bottom, the Germans were reduced to individual forays by disguised surface raiders until the end of the war after 1915.[1]

After the destruction of Germany's ships outside of the Baltic Sea, the Imperial German Navy command had little choice but to look elsewhere to put naval pressure on Great Britain. The High Seas Fleet would make several forays to raid and probe their British jailers, but the result would always be the same, with the German ships running for the safety of home in fear of the superior firepower of the British.

The Germans turned to the U-boat as the weapon that could hurt

3. The Counter-Blockade and the U-Kreuzers

Great Britain and the Allies without risking the destruction of Germany's remaining surface power. Submarines had been used by both sides as scouting vessels, or in attempts to sink warships. A few notable successes were obtained in these endeavors. However, the Germans finally realized the true utility of the U-boat lay in the craft's ability to attack enemy merchant shipping headed to or from Great Britain and the other Allied or neutral countries.[2] The chairman of the U.S. Shipping Board articulated this fact perfectly after the war,

> When the blockade that the Allies declared against German and neutral ports tightened, when it became more difficult to obtain the essentials of life and of war through the aid of merchants in neutral countries, Germany realized that the submarine was her Trump card.[3]

From 1914 to 1917, the Germans flirted with the idea of unrestricted submarine warfare, and sinking enemy and neutral ships trading with the Allies without warning. However, controversial attacks caused them to reinstitute a policy of sinking ships after a warning so the crews had a chance to get away, and the cargo could be inspected and confirmed as contraband headed for an enemy port. As such, the Germans did not take U-boat warfare seriously until the Kaiser, his top advisers, and the navy commanders made the decision to unleash the U-boats on the merchant ships of the world, and attempt to starve Great Britain into submission in 1917.

As we have seen, Britain had also been starving Germany since 1914 when she had instituted a very effective naval blockade of all imports and exports to Germany and her allies. The German people were on the verge of starvation while the German munitions industry lacked some of the essential raw materials necessary for weapons production.[4] Unrestricted warfare, or torpedo attack without warning, was still limited to the declared war zones in European waters due to the Germans' desire not to entirely alienate neutral opinion. The Germans only wanted to sink those neutral ships utilized to supply their enemies. As a result, outside of the declared zones, the Germans were still stopping unarmed vessels and searching them for contraband before sinking them after their crews were allowed to row to safety.[5]

Nonetheless, even the partial unrestricted submarine warfare policy brought Germany into almost immediate conflict with the United States. The U.S. had already protested strongly against German U-boats sinking neutral ships and consequently killing American citizens. The announcement by the Kaiser of unrestricted U-boat warfare in February 1917 caused a diplomatic break with Germany that eventually led to a declaration of war by the United States in April 1917.

At first, the gamble seemed to pay off. German submarines sank over 500,000 tons of shipping in both February and March, 880,000 tons in April, 600,000 in May, and 700,000 in June. However, the success was not to last, and in May and June the British, Americans, and other Allied powers started to convoy ships with warship protection on a regular basis, and after August the loss rate of Allied ships never again reached over 500,000 tons. Losses would remain relatively high compared to rates prior to the announcement of unrestricted submarine warfare, but the Allies had destroyed the ability of the U-boat arm to blockade Great Britain into starvation and surrender.[6]

The convoys cleared the sea-lanes of lone ships, a U-boat's favorite target, and forced the submarines to attack less important vessels traveling alone, or to attack convoys with armed escorts, resulting in higher U-boat contacts with armed enemy ships.[7]

The Germans needed a way to diffuse the number of Allied escort and patrol vessels in the heavily trafficked waters around Great Britain so they could once again attack their victims with impunity. They decided to attempt to get the substantial American naval reinforcements recently sent to the war zone recalled back to their home waters or caught up in patrolling the far flung sea lanes, and they had a weapon on hand to accomplish the mission, the U-Kreuzers.[8]

In addition, it was thought the U-Kreuzers could sink shipping like their surface cruiser cousins had in the early days of the war by using their fairly large artillery guns to engage in firefights with armed merchant ships, and less heavily armed patrol ships. If the Allies did not send in extra protection for their sea lanes outside of the restricted zones then the Germans hoped their U-Kreuzers could send enough tonnage to the bottom to make a real impact on Allied trade. However, the Germans realized this scenario could only play out in the lightly defended waters off West Africa and North America due to the limitations of the ex-merchant U-Kreuzer design.[9]

The plan was a risky one with low odds for success due to the limited resources employed for the mission. Despite that fact, the Germans were experimenting with a naval strategy that would nearly succeed in the next world war. All of this was the inevitable result of Germany's surface fleet strategy formed prior to the beginning of the war. It was a strategy for a bigger navy the Germans thought they would have the opportunity to build. As with so many endeavors, the unexpected arrival of the war a little too soon neutralized Germany's initial plan.

Prior to the beginning of the First World War, the Imperial German

Navy began to form the view that a clash with Great Britain and the United States was inevitable to secure Germany's place as a world power. The Germans saw Great Britain as the more immediate enemy, and the United States as the remaining nation they would have to face in order to have a free hand overseas after the fall or diminishment of the British Empire.

Secretary of State of the Imperial Naval Office, Admiral Alfred von Tirpitz, led the charge in this new quest for world primacy, separate and distinct from actual world conquest which Germany realized would be impossible. Tirpitz and his supporters broke from the traditional European continental power play of the Imperial German army. The German military on land eventually became an instrument of what can be loosely described as a quasi–Napoleonic empire, with Germany taking the lead in Europe minus the focus on overseas acquisitions. This was true at the beginning of the conflict.

When the war in the west began with the invasion of Belgium in August 1914, Tirpitz was against the battle since the Navy did not have the heavy ships he wanted in place before his naval war for world power status was launched. However, the army thought Germany was ready for the conflagration, and knew that time was not on their side as the forces of both Russia and France may have equaled or surpassed their military strength given the growth rate of their forces. Tirpitz had lost his fight to postpone the conflict and the army took the lead in Germany's great struggle.

The British instituted the blockade and neutrals like the U.S. protested, but they could do little to combat such a massive undertaking. The blockade could not be moved by Germany or the neutrals with the resources and diplomatic pressure they had on hand.[10]

As we have seen, the British established a distant blockade of Germany in 1914 from British harbors hundreds of miles from the German controlled coasts. Close in blockade had proven impossible against Germany in the Great War era due to the gigantic German fleet that could attack any close in patrols, the existence of the submarine, and effective defensive minefields. The distance did not diminish the blockade, and German merchant trade effectively ceased to exist in 1914. The British were freed from the dangers of German contested waters while still being in a position to intercept any German ship that dared to leave port.[11]

The first U-boat sinking of a merchant ship was on 20 October 1914, and the first merchant ship sinking without warning was only six days later. Germany realized very quickly that she could not effectively attack the British fleet due to the distant blockade, and so the focus became attacks on British trade. As Admiral von Ingenohl, commander of the High Seas Fleet, stated in reference to attacks on Allied and neutral shipping, "The gravity of the situation demands that we should free ourselves from all scruples which certainly no longer have justification."

Initially unrestricted submarine warfare was rejected by German leaders due to the danger it posed to relations with neutral countries, the lack of submarines available for the job, and the still persistent notion by the Kaiser that his navy should not engage in such an unseemly endeavor. Prewar German research even indicated the Reich would need over 200 submarines in the water to have an impact on British trade. At the time of the first unrestricted debate in late 1914 the Germans had only 28 U-boats.

On 4 February 1915, after much badgering by the German naval leadership, the Germans declared the first blockade zone around the British Isles where ships could be sunk without warning by German U-boats over the objections of the German Chancellor Theobald von Bethmann Hollweg. A quote from the chancellor a month before unrestricted war was declared in 1915 summarized his opinions well.

> Measures like a submarine blockade, which are certain to have a negative effect on the attitude of the neutrals and our supplies, can only be undertaken when our military situation is so secure that the issue is beyond doubt and the danger of the neutrals joining our enemies can be ruled out.[12]

A statement by the German government was made that neutral ships would not be attacked, but this was an impossible promise to keep given the nature of underwater attack, and the difficulty of identifying what type of ship one saw through the limited view of a periscope.[13]

The United States sent Germany a notice stating America would not be bullied into giving up their right to trade on the high seas. The communication inferred military action would follow any attacks on Americans. Several deadly assaults on shipping highlighted the vast gulf between the two powers. The Americans refused to see that trade as usual had ended, and the Germans refused to acknowledge their actions may result in war with the new economic powerhouse of the world.[14]

Just over 20 percent of the attacks by German U-boats in 1915 were without warning despite the leeway given to U-boats by the German government during that part of the year. On 7 May 1915, a U-boat sunk the 32,500-ton British liner *Lusitania* which resulted in the death of 1,197 people out of a total of 1,962 on board. 124 Americans died. Prior to this incident the Americans had protested the British blockade and German submarines equally, after the *Lusitania* American wrath was almost solely focused on the German submarine war.

The *Lusitania* carried 1,250 boxes of field artillery shells and 18 boxes of percussion fuses, which probably ignited after being struck by the single torpedo fired. The on board munitions and coal dust likely contributed to the huge explosion and rupture which made the *Lusitania* sink in a speedy and deadly 18 minutes.[15]

The sinking of the *Lusitania* and other attacks across the seas near Europe and Africa gave the U-boat a mysterious and invincible quality in the eyes of the Allied public. In reality the machines carrying terror to the oceans of the world were frail, imperfect, and uncomfortable as one U-boat crewman related "There was little privacy and little comfort in a U-boat. There was no bath and only one lavatory for the use of all officers and men aboard. Few shaved, no one changed their clothes from the beginning to the end of a voyage. The officers used eau de cologne to mask body odour and the indescribable damp, oil-laden, stale smells of the sweating interior of the boat."[16]

Contrary to popular belief the 1915 campaign did not come to an end due to the *Lusitania*. It continued, but the Germans found themselves operating with a limited force of only three or four submarines per month later in the year. The campaign was slowing down due to the limited number of U-boats, and not a sudden pang of conscience or even fear of the American reaction due to the *Lusitania*.

The Germans called off the first unrestricted submarine war and went back to sinking passenger liners with a warning after the British liner *Arabic* was sunk with the loss of American lives on 30 August 1915. The Kaiser had finally made the decision to curtail the targeting of liners after the public relations disasters of the spring and summer of 1915, and practical military concerns related to the limited number of U-boats available for service.

U-boats sank 1,307,996 tons of shipping in the year 1915. The figure was shocking during that age, but it was also not a catastrophic threat to British or Allied supply of their civilian or military populations.

In the aftermath of this latest row with the United States, a new and influential figure appeared on the scene to take the position of Chief of the Naval Staff. Admiral Henning von Holtzendorff would prove decisive in the formation of the U-boat war, and in particular to the U-Kreuzer concept.

American supplies continued to arm Germany's enemies and enabled the Allies to push the Germans toward eventual defeat. In early 1916, the chief of the Army General Staff, Erich von Falkenhayn, argued the occupation of Serbia and the alliance with Bulgaria had given the Germans a breathing space to mount a large U-boat offensive. Holtzendorff agreed with the powerful general and started to voice his opinion on the subject of an unrestricted U-boat campaign to the Chancellor.[17]

He discounted American involvement in the war against Germany due to the proposed submarine policy as something too insignificant to worry about given the advantages the campaign would give Germany against Great Britain. The conflict with the U.S. was almost guaranteed given what had happened during the last round of unrestricted war with the sinking of seemingly innocent passenger liners. Eventually, Holtzendorff told the foreign office to do all it could to avoid a break with America, but added the unrestricted campaign would have to be waged no matter what the U.S. did. Tirpitz unequivocally stated America's entry would not tip the balance in Europe since in his opinion the U.S. could never build enough merchant ships to provide supplies and troops in sufficient quantities to replace those lost to U-boat attacks.[18] Tirpitz saw the undersea war as the only way to win the conflict in February 1916.

> Immediate and relentless recourse to the submarine weapon is absolutely necessary. Any further delay in the introduction of unrestricted warfare will give England time for further naval and economic measures, cause us greater losses in the end, and endanger quick success. The sooner the campaign be opened, the sooner success will be realized, and the more rapidly and energetically will England's hope of defeating us by a war of exhaustion be destroyed. If we defeat England, we break the backbone of the hostile coalition.[19]

On 6 January 1916, a memorandum from department BIII of the Naval staff to Kaiser Wilhelm was sent "Concerning means for prosecuting an economic war of destruction against England." The letter demanded for the first time that a comprehensive U-boat campaign be carried out to ensure Britain was effectively blockaded. The letter also looked ahead from the current war to a potential future war with Britain alone after Germany had won on the continent.

The memorandum begins with the destruction of the British fleet then strangling Germany.

> Our war aim, apart from destroying the English fleet as the principal means by which Britain controls its Empire, is to reduce its total economy in the quickest possible time, bringing Great Britain to sue for unconditional peace. To achieve this it will be necessary: (a) to cut off all trade routes to and from the British Isles. (b) To cripple in all the seven seas, all ships flying under the British flag and all ships under neutral flag plying to and from Great Britain. (c) To destroy military and economic resources and by means of air attack disrupt the trade and commerce in the British Isles, showing its population quite mercilessly the stark realities of war.[20]

Tirpitz resigned as State Secretary of the Naval Office in March 1916 after he had portrayed the U.S. as an enemy of Germany due to her trade and ties with Great Britain even though the U.S. still had diplomatic relations with the Kaiser's government. On 23 March, shortly after Tirpitz left the scene, Germany resumed unrestricted war for a second time.

It took exactly one day for the new campaign to gain the ire of the Americans, when the French passenger liner *Sussex* was torpedoed without warning and American citizens died when the ship went down. The avowed pacifist, American President Woodrow Wilson, took up the cause and complained to the Germans vociferously. One month after the *Sussex* sank the pressure from Wilson's government forced Imperial Germany to end the second unrestricted war on 24 April 1916. The U-boats were ordered to operate under the prize rules again by boarding and searching their prey. The navy ordered the North Sea flotillas to stay home due to the danger of prize rule warfare to a surfaced U-boat while the smaller boats based in Belgium continued to conduct mine-laying operations. The average sunk during this time period of restricted warfare amounted to a paltry 130,000 tons of shipping sent to the bottom.

The naval leadership was determined to reverse this decision, which they saw as a strategic blunder to ameliorate an America that wasn't at war with Germany but regularly traded war materials with her enemies.[21]

The cancellation did not end the debate in the German public. Political and military leaders in the Reich discussed the issue heatedly throughout the rest of 1916. In August 1916, Holtzendorff came to the decision that only unrestricted U-boat war could save the German military from defeat. He became a staunch proponent of attacks without warning no matter the consequences with regard to America. He shared the view, also held by a Crown Prince of Germany, that "America is not a serious military opponent. It's million-man army exists only on paper, the creation and deployment of this on the continent are only military flights of fantasy accepted by the Anglo-American press alone."

The powerful in Germany were slowly moving towards Holtzendorff's views. None were more blunt than Germany's Minister of the Marine, Eduard von Capelle, when he perfectly stated the completely naive German view of the United States at the time.

> As far as the financial and economic situation is concerned, I have always laid great stress on the importance of America's entrance into the war. But from a military point of view, her entrance means nothing. I repeat: from a military point of view America is as nothing. I am convinced that almost no Americans will volunteer for war service. That is shown by the lack of volunteers for the conflict with Mexico.

And even if many enlist, they must first be trained. This will take time, for America has neither commissioned nor noncommissioned officers enough to train large bodies of troops. And when the men have been trained, how are they to cross the ocean?"

Capelle continued with his flawed line of thought.

America has no transport ships ready for service. And contrary to all appearances, should America be able to provide the necessary transport ships, our submarines could not wish for a better piece of hunting. I repeat, therefore, once more: from a military standpoint, America's entrance is as nothing."

By the end of the war all that Capelle had predicted would never happen would come to pass and more. He and Germany would eat his words even if the country itself had nothing left to eat.[22]

On 29 August 1916, German war hero Field Marshal Paul von Hindenburg became the Chief of Staff of the German Army while Erich Ludendorff was promoted to his First Quartermaster General. The next day the newly minted leaders of Germany's all-powerful military attended a high level conference at the Kaiser's headquarters in Pless in Silesia. The attendees were Chancellor von Bethmann-Hollweg, Karl Helfferich State Secretary for the Interior, Gottlieb von Jagow State Secretary for Foreign Affairs, General Wild von Hohenborn War Minister, Admiral von Capelle Secretary for the Navy, and Admiral von Holtzendorff Chief of the Naval Staff.

All of the attendees were aware of the horrors of the Allied blockade that included the starvation of civilians, and which was slowly sapping the public's will to continue the war. In addition, being military men, they were also aware of the shortages of raw materials affecting munitions production. The conference was called to combat these effects. The leadership was also there to discuss how best to make the same effect on Britain.[23]

At the same meeting, von Holtzendorff read a carefully prepared paper to the assembled leaders which argued unrestricted submarine warfare was the only way to defeat the Allies, and would hit them at their weakest point, their shipping. He said "I do not see a finis Germaniae in the use of a weapon which cripples Great Britain's capacity to support her allies; but rather in the neglect to employ it." The decision of the conference was to table the issue until the Romanians could be dealt with militarily as they had recently joined the Allied cause.

Hindenburg and Ludendorff did not yet feel they completely grasped Germany's strategic situation.[24] However, a representative of the naval staff who visited Ludendorff 11 days after the conference wrote that Ludendorff was completely in favor of the unrestricted war as he believed the conflict could not be won on land alone. This comment may have been referring to the future, after the defeat of Romania.[25]

In the next few months the problems which had held back Hindenburg and Ludendorff from fully endorsing the unrestricted campaign evaporated or were calm enough to be placed on the back burner. The Italian front was holding, the Romanians were defeated by December 1916, and it was clear the Allies would not break through in the west despite heavy attacks against the German lines. The decision was taken to hold strong defensive lines in the west while laying the groundwork for a new offensive, and taking on the issue of unleashing the U-boats to slow the Allies ever increasing material superiority.[26] Ludendorff, as was his style, put it very bluntly when he said "I do not give a damn about America." However, Ludendorff, also an infamous vacillator, was not very dedicated to this point as proven by other statements wherein he expressed fear of American involvement in the war.[27]

As the fall of 1916 dragged on the Germans were still sinking ships without warning due to the British and Allied policy of arming merchant ships. The development of armed merchant vessels became a real danger to U-boats, and made the only viable method of attack, torpedoing a ship without warning, the main survival tactic for those U-boats who were too small to assault an armed ship with deck guns. The arming of Allied merchant ships resulted in fewer U-boat successes against those ships, and was adopted by the British and Allied navies wholeheartedly. By 1918, almost all merchant ships of a certain size were armed with at least one artillery piece.[28]

In December 1916, Holtzendorff made his biggest move yet and counseled Hindenburg to approve of an unrestricted war no matter the consequences. His arguments were a re-hash of what had been said in the past. The Americans could not supply the Allies due to the likelihood of their shipping being destroyed by U-boats, and the inability of American troop transports to get through the German undersea blockade to land in France.[29]

Holtzendorff promised Hindenburg that a start date of 1 February 1917 for unrestricted warfare would result in an Allied peace on German terms by 1 August of that year. Hindenburg agreed with Holtzendorff's views.

The leaders of Germany, the Kaiser, Hindenburg, Ludendorff, the German chancellor Theobald von Bethmann Hollweg, and Holtzendorff came together again on 9 January 1917 and decided once and for all that the U-boats in the declared war zones would resume unrestricted submarine warfare.[30] Outside of those zones ships would still be stopped and searched before a decision was made to destroy the vessel.[31]

The turnip winter of late 1916 into early 1917 had forced the Kaiser's hand along with the constant barrage of arguments from Holtzendorff. He could see the country's morale plummeting and decided to begin unrestricted submarine warfare not only for strategic and tactical wartime reasons, but also to strike back at the increasingly effective British blockade. He wanted to show the people of Germany that they could make Britain suffer too. It was a battle of extreme pragmatism on both sides with Britain using her fleet as a blunt and effective mallet to hammer the Germans into slow submission rather than await a glorious and decisive sea battle with guns blazing as at Trafalgar.[32] The unrestricted campaign and the U-Kreuzers were both born during this desperate time on the German home front.

The German government also reasoned that the U.S., by trading only with the Allies, and by not challenging the British blockade more forcefully had basically become an undeclared enemy of Germany. However, as we have seen, the Germans had made the mistake of underestimating what extra tonnage the Americans would bring to the fray in newly built shipping, and the confiscation of large German vessels in American ports. These acquisitions would more than make good the losses caused by the submarine.

In addition, although American trade was benefiting the Allies greatly, it was a far cry from fresh American armies in the field, which would eventually turn the tide once and for all against Germany. All of this was unknown in February 1917 when unrestricted U-boat war was declared around the British Isles. The ruling would have a long reaching effect since the Germans had basically rejected the chance for a negotiated peace with their enemies and embarked upon an attempt to win all of their war aims and more in their bid to come out of the conflict as the premier power on the European continent and beyond.[33]

Holtzendorff had his new naval war officially declared even though it had been running in some fashion since after the first Pless conference in August 1916 with higher and higher submarine tonnage totals irrefutable evidence of the shift back to the attack.[34]

The U-boat fleet had 111 operational submarines in February 1917 when the much vaunted unrestricted war began. This was only half of what the Germans had thought they needed to blockade Great Britain successfully. Holtzendorff and the other naval hawks thought there were enough to do the job anyway, and their new orders made sure the tonnage would go up for a time at least.[35]

3. The Counter-Blockade and the U-Kreuzers

The U-boats were to go out immediately, as many as possible, so the bottom of the Atlantic would be littered with the ships of Germany's enemies. Minimal time in port for rest and repairs was stressed, and the crews would be right back out into the action again as soon as possible. Germany's 111 operational U-boats present and accounted for at this time were the height of the numbers she would possess during the whole of the war.

In effect, it was the rise in numbers of U-boats put to sea and the "unrestricted" nature of U-boat warfare that increased the tonnage sunk. The Germans were finally taking the U-boat war seriously and providing it with a strategic prominence heretofore lacking. The lowly U-boat had eclipsed the High Seas Fleet as the navy's darling.[36]

Over 500 ships went down in the first two months of the unrestricted campaign. In January 1917 37.5 percent of vessels sunk by U-boats were hit without warning. By April that number had risen to over 60 percent. The naval war was becoming more brutal by leaps and bounds. April 1917 was the apex of the U-boat war with 881,027 gross registered tons sunk spread out over 395 destroyed ships, and only a paltry four percent of this total sunk by weapons other than submarines.[37]

After the decision was taken, Ludendorff advised after the unrestricted war had begun the United States would not be inclined to send troops to Europe due to anti-war attitudes in the U.S. He added a word of caution to his flawed logic, he did not think it wise to send submarines into American territorial waters so as not to arouse a warlike spirit in the country.[38]

Over the next few months the Germans sank many ships, but their diplomatic and military gaffes in relation to the United States were the final nails in the coffin of U.S.–German relations. The Zimmermann telegram promising land to Mexico if she invaded the U.S. combined with German attacks on the high seas were enough to push the almost religious zeal of Wilson's pacifism over the edge and into the dustbin of history. The man who was known in his own time for keeping the U.S. out of World War I would in the end be known for leading the U.S. during the conflict.

The U.S. declared war on 6 April 1917. After the declaration, there were many German officers who wanted to expand the submarine war to the east coast of the U.S. The Kaiser rejected those plans at this time as he thought it would inflame the less warlike parts of the U.S., which he considered to be the Midwest and western sections for unknown reasons. In this sentiment at least Ludendorff and the Kaiser were in agreement for once. As a result of this collective denial of the existence of a state of war between the U.S. and Germany by the high command, there was an odd continuation of special treatment of American shipping by the German Navy.

This occurred in spite of the ever present nagging of Holtzendorff who thought the deployment of submarines across the Atlantic would have an impact on U.S. shipping to the Allies, and advocated for their departure to the eastern American seaboard as early as April 1917.[39]

In the meantime, Admiral Benson, Chief of U.S. Naval Operations, feared a German naval attack on the east coast or in the Caribbean Sea, and continued to hold significant amounts of defensive forces at the ready in these areas for an expected German assault which did not come that year.

By July 1917, the unrestricted war was increasing the amount of tonnage sunk. However, Germany's leaders also began to realize it may not prove to be enough to destroy their primary enemy by itself, Great Britain. Hindenburg's headquarters added more voices to those of Ludendorff and the Kaiser when the Field Marshal ordered no submarines would attack shipping in American waters until a true effort to blockade the coast was possible. He argued the Kaiser's point that single attacks would do nothing but inflame American and neutral opinion into more support for the war against Germany to no appreciable effect for Germany's war effort.[40]

The Royal Navy hit a crossroads in April 1917. Some were still hidebound by the offensive mentality and wanted to rely on more warships to patrol the waters around Great Britain. First Sea Lord John Jellicoe sent a memo to the British government demanding destroyers in British waters from the Americans, more new shipping built, and an increase in the deployment of offensive minefields against German controlled harbors. This was part of a culture that viewed convoy as too defensively minded, and far too difficult given the thousands of ships which sailed into British harbors all of the time.[41]

What First Sea Lord Jellicoe didn't know until later was that most of the ships counted as entering British harbors were smaller vessels making several port calls in a short span of time. The larger vessels, on which the nation's survival depended, numbered only from 120 to 140 port entries per week. This was much more manageable. The convoy system not only denuded the sea of multiple scattered targets more likely to encounter a U-boat patrol by grouping all ships into one area, it also created an opportunity for the destroyers guarding the convoy to attack any marauding U-boats rather than fruitless searches away from the U-boat's favorite targets, merchant ships.[42]

It was in the summer of 1917 that aerial patrols in the North Sea started to garner fruit by keeping the U-boats submerged in the area, attacking them when they could, and genuinely making the area unsafe for surfaced boats. They did not often get to sink or even damage a submarine, but they were another element in the pacification of the hostile waters around Great Britain.[43]

The most important developments in 1917 for the Allies was the introduction of the convoy system, the coordination of defensive measures like direction finding, radio interception and decoding, aircraft, the continuance of patrols, defensive and offensive mining, and an increase in the number of warships due to America's entry into the war. All of these elements started to work together in concert, and very slowly the U-boats' tonnage scores started to fall from their high in April 1917.[44]

The failure of the submarine campaign to end the war with Britain was obvious from Ludendorff on down to the lowest rating in the Kaiser's navy by the fall of 1917. The effect was to make some Germans lose faith in the Imperial government, and rumblings of socialist revolution started to be felt within the old Reich.[45]

September 1917 was the month that convoy started to tell on the U-boats. They were forced to hunt for the convoys rather than wait in their normal operational areas for lone ships. Tonnage scores remained very high, but in essence once the U-boats had to change their tactics to account for the massive number of ships in convoy they had already lost their most vital merchant ship targets. Eighty-three convoys had sailed to safety with a total of 1,306 ships. Out of that total, 12 ships had been sunk while under armed protection. Ships traveling alone were still in grave danger and made up most of the still impressive U-boat scores, but convoy was working only a few months after it was started in May 1917. The most important ships to the Allied cause were punching through the U-boat blockade. Convoys were attacked, but the U-boat often got away with sinking only one ship, or in rare instances two.[46]

The Germans also performed two surface ship raids on convoys plying their trade from Great Britain to Norway. The October and December 1917 raids were local successes with most of the merchant ships and convoy escorts being destroyed. The British were forced to use a Grand Fleet battle squadron to guard the Norwegian convoys, and the German efforts not only resulted in more ships sunk, but used up more Allied naval resources for convoy duties.[47] However, the pressure taken off the U-boats was negligible in the long run.

The failure of these surface attacks to take pressure off of the U-boats were the last straw for the Germans, and some now called for what they viewed as the necessity of sending U-Kreuzers to assault American waters and splinter the forces the High Seas Fleet could not. The thoroughly logical argument posited by Germany's leadership about the numbers of U-Kreuzers then available not being sufficient to cause the damage needed was ignored by these proponents of long range submarine war.[48]

By the end of 1917 the U-boats were no longer hunting out in the approaches to the British Isles, but close inshore where there were still large amounts of unescorted shipping around. The threat the U-boats posed to coastal shipping was real, but the move signaled the defeat of the U-boats out in the open ocean where the largest and most important ships were being convoyed to harbor.

The Germans had lost the most important part of the First Battle of the Atlantic already by the winter of 1917. Nonetheless, the Allies were not universally aware that a turning point had occurred. By the end of January 1918, almost a year since the beginning of the official start of unrestricted war over 6,200,000 tons of Allied shipping had been sent to the bottom. Shipbuilding had not kept up with these losses.[49]

German intelligence estimated correctly that the Americans had six battleships and 36 destroyers in Ireland, twenty cruisers and destroyers in England, and 22 destroyers in France along with multiple smaller squadrons in other ports around the British Isles in the main war zone. The American Admiral Benson, despite his earlier focus on home defense, had sent almost all of his ships to the main war zone to help defeat the submarine threat in 1918, which included hundreds of American battleships, cruisers, destroyers, sub-chasers, and even submarines. In November 1918 the British "Auxiliary Patrol" had 3,000 vessels in service around the British Isles. In January 1917 the British had 283 destroyers in the zone around the British Isles, or over two ships for every submarine the Germans possessed.[50] The German leadership still refused to send U-boats to the American coast for the remainder of 1917 despite the enlargement of the recognized "war zone" out into the Atlantic. The extension did not drift into American waters yet.

Holtzendorff was still predicting the U-boats could sink more tonnage than the Allies could build and thus not be able to arm, equip, and feed their armies in 1918. In February 1918, Ludendorff finally released the needed labor to build more U-boats. The leadership, represented by Ludendorff, was as usual focused on army projects to the detriment of the navy. However, Ludendorff's concession came a little late in the day, and did not affect the U-boat war in any noticeably positive fashion.

The new program only succeeded in delivering 74 submarines, which could just barely replace those U-boats sunk by the Allies in the same period. No net increase was seen before the end of the war despite the Germans' best efforts. Not one loaded American troop transport was sunk on the way to Europe during the war. In July 1917 the U.S. had only been able to deliver 94,000 tons of supplies to Europe. In July 1918 she was able to send 1,753,000 tons.[51]

In April 1918, losses of merchant shipping fell below 300,000 tons for the month. The U-boats would never go over that figure again during the remainder of the Great War. In a double hit to the Central Powers, new Allied shipbuilding exceeded losses for the first time since the unrestricted submarine campaign had been officially announced in February 1917.

The German underwater offensive had clearly failed and now the Allies were finally realizing it too.[52]

Holtzendorff tried to save the campaign and begged the Kaiser to extend unrestricted submarine warfare to the American east coast by mid–May 1918 when two Deutschland class U-Kreuzers would be available for duty in the western Atlantic.

Throughout the spring of 1918, Holtzendorff had called for the blockade of the North American east coast. During this time, Holtzendorff told the secretary of the foreign office that "The military necessity of scattering as much as possible the antisubmarine forces of our enemies makes it necessary to increase the area of the blockade zones." Holtzendorff then specifically stated "the best chance of success lies in an increase of unrestricted submarine warfare to the east coast of the United States. Up to now political considerations and the lack of development in the effectiveness of the U-boats have prevented us from expanding the spheres of operation to the American coast." In Holtzendorff's opinion the political and technical limitations no longer existed in 1918.[53] One detects a hint of desperation in these pleas, and it is possible Holtzendorff was not only trying to save the submarine campaign but also his reputation with the Kaiser. The U-Kreuzers were his last long shot chance to do both.[54]

The State Secretary for the Foreign Office did not agree with the Admiral and told him the German government still did not wish to inflame American public opinion even more than had already occurred. They also continually worried about neutral opinions if their shipping to America was attacked. On the technical side the German leadership did not think much of the U-Kreuzers' ability to get the job of blockade on the east coast done in an efficient enough manner to make the effort worth it.

In 1918, Ludendorff flip-flopped and supported the extension of the war to American waters. The First Quartermaster General's point was that due to the weakness of the anti-war movement in America the political considerations should be disregarded in favor of any chance to sink troop transports. Of course, Ludendorff had missed Holtzendorff's argument that the focus of the navy's effort wasn't so much on sinking troop transports off the east coast, but more an attempted distraction for the overwhelming Allied naval anti-submarine forces then operating around Great Britain.[55] Holtzendorff also wanted the U-Kreuzers to sink troop transports but realized this may not occur given their limited effectiveness against convoyed ships.[56]

On 28 July 1918, Holtzendorff tried yet again and presented a plan to blockade the American east coast to the Kaiser and Chancellor at the Kaiser's headquarters in Spa, Belgium. The Kaiser told Holtzendorff a decision on the blockade zone would have to wait until Holtzendorff's successor, Admiral Reinhard Scheer was consulted. The Kaiser commented on a theme Holtzendorff had heard before, and stated there were not enough long range U-boats to commence anything more than raids against America at that time.[57] Later, on 31 July, Scheer was consulted and tentatively took the Kaiser's side. The Emperor finally had an ally.

> His Majesty received Admiral Scheer and Holtzendorff in audience to discuss the U-boat measures against America. Scheer was against it in principle, but wished to review the whole question of the conduct of U-boat warfare.[58]

Despite repeated badgering by Hindenburg, Ludendorff, and especially Holtzendorff, the Kaiser rejected the unrestricted war off American shores by saying "I am of different opinion and it will remain with that." The U-Kreuzer war off the east coast would stay a restricted and limited one with the U-Kreuzers observing the prize rules when possible. Holtzendorff had his war on American shores, but not the one he particularly wanted.[59] Holtzendorff was forced to resign in August 1918 after his unrestricted war had clearly failed. His chosen and publicly stated date of defeat for Great Britain by the U-boats in October 1917 was a prediction which proved to be utterly wrong.[60]

After the unceremonious departure of Holtzendorff, the Germans attempted to increase the effectiveness of the campaign by building a huge number of submarines, starting in September 1918 with the Scheer program named after the new Admiral in charge, Reinhard Scheer. The army released the labor to work on the project, and it finally took precedence over capital ship production. Although 450 submarines were ordered built the program did not meet expectations before the war ended.[61]

4

Room 40

Of course the Allies knew everything about the Germans' intentions. Unbeknownst to the Germans, the British, and to a lesser the extent the French had broken the German naval codes and read their wireless messages at will.

They had a lot to read since the U-boats began to transmit more frequent radio messages as they patrolled farther out into the Atlantic, which could then be decrypted by the British. The U-boats engaged in more communications due to the need to obtain updated orders from home, and reports from the U-boat back to Germany when engaged in longer cruises. The Germans were surprised by the range of their huge radio station at Nauen,[1] pleasantly so, but its long reach would come to haunt them.[2]

The Germans utilized wireless radio communications for everything from the most mundane movements of the German High Seas Fleet to discussions about the plans for secret operations of the greatest importance. The Germans had complete faith in their communications, and this would be the downfall of some of their most carefully laid plans.

By April 1915, the British had obtained all three German naval codebooks from which all other codes and ciphers were derived. First, the Russians obtained the German warship *Seiner Majestät Schiff (SMS) Magdeburg*'s codebook after the vessel ran aground in some fog while doing a reconnaissance of the Gulf of Finland. The secret codebooks were not destroyed as two Russian cruisers came upon the crippled ship and started to pour fire on her. In the confusion of the attack, the secret papers were forgotten.

The Russians were able to confiscate a German codebook, the key for the codes, the German naval grid system for the Baltic Sea, and the ship's Kriegstagebuch (war diary). The Russians sent the British the codebook in October 1914, and it was well used by them to help win the naval war. The particular book obtained by the Russians, called the Signalbuch der Kaiserlichen Marine, (SKM) was in use until May 1917, which illustrates how long the Germans waited to change their compromised communications.

The British also obtained the Händelschiffsverkehrsbuch (HVB) used by U-boats and zeppelins. The British and the French both managed to utilize the book effectively, and the French read it regularly by the autumn of 1915. The Germans actually knew this code had been compromised by the Allies, but they did not change it until March 1916. The changed code was later obtained by the British after they inspected a zeppelin wreck and multiple U-boat wrecks. Two more books were also obtained from German ships off Holland and Australia early in the war. The British had taken a great prize and they proceeded to use it.[3]

The British created multiple stations to listen in on and capture German naval messages around the clock, and these were forwarded to a Top Secret section in the Old Admiralty building called Room 40. However, by the end of the war the persons who worked on the messages occupied much more than just the one room.

Room 40 was the World War I equivalent of the famous Bletchley Park, which had broken the German Enigma code in World War II with a little luck, hard work, and a lot of help from the Polish government. The Germans re-ciphered their keys often, which was standard practice to stop their enemies from reading their mail. In what would be laughable if it were not so serious, the Germans bungled the re-ciphering and continued to use old ciphers at the same time as the new ones so the British could compare the two and figure out the new set up.[4]

As mentioned above, the British also found clues to new code changes by diving on shallow U-boat wrecks and secretly removing documents. They also searched the wreckage of German naval zeppelins, which were bombing Britain during the war and also carried German codebooks.[5]

The secret of Room 40 would lead to more intelligence coups than any nation could hope for and was closely guarded. As such it can be argued that it was somewhat underused during the war. Eventually it was utilized to re-route convoys around U-boats whose locations could be generally pinpointed through their messages home combined with radio direction finding. The locations were not usually specific enough to send attack ships to destroy the U-boat, but it was enough to send the vital merchant ships around the German marauder.[6] Radio direction finding could also approximate the location of a U-boat from within 20 to 50 miles or more.[7]

The Daily Submarine return was written and compiled by the Intelligence Division of the Admiralty and contained the times, locations, contents of signals, and days on cruise of all U-boats then at sea. This part of the anti-submarine intelligence operation was in evidence from late 1917 to the end of the war and proved to be highly effective.[8]

The U-boats exchanged signals with a few different radio stations depending on their locations and home bases. The main centers were at Nauen, Norddeich, and Neumunster in Germany as well as the light cruiser *Arcona*, and the steamer *Rugia*, who both had radios primed to receive and transmit.[9] Nauen was the link home for the U-Kreuzers most of the time since it outranged all other wireless stations, and was the only radio capable of routine transmissions to far flung operational areas off West Africa and North America.

Room 40's secret was given to the commander of American naval forces in European waters once the U.S. entered the war in 1917, Admiral Sims. Sims kept the secret well while passing very useful intelligence to his own government and explaining the source by omitting it or simply lying that it was obtained from Allied secret agents.[10]

The top German leadership never suspected the truth, and their war effort was severely stunted by their ignorance of the sometimes obvious breach of their communications. Some U-boat commanders came to realize what had happened, but their leaders in the Kaiserliche Marine never took their opinions seriously.

5

From Carrying Cargo to Sinking It

Before the declaration of war against Germany by the U.S., the Allies were reaping the benefits of America's industrial power by buying up raw materials and weapons for their war against the Central powers. The U.S. was not against arms sales to Germany, but the Germans could not pick up the material due to British control of the oceans. This fact angered the Germans who saw the U.S. as an opportunistic neutral power who clearly favored the Allies, and assisted them in the killing of German soldiers for profit.[1]

The Germans came up with two solutions to address the trade imbalance with the U.S. created by the British blockade. The first was an undeclared and extremely savage war waged by German spies and saboteurs in America in an attempt to slow the munitions trade to the Allies through explosives and sabotage. The second was the employment of a cargo carrying U-boat with no weapons, and a crew with no overt ties to the German Navy.

Germany hoped the cargo submarines could start a meaningful trade with the U.S., and allow the Central Powers to utilize the seemingly endless stream of war materials flowing out of America to the Allies. No thought was given to importing foodstuffs with the underwater merchantmen since despite the desperation of the German people the government's primary goal was to win the war. Also the small cargo capacity of the merchant U-boats would have made the transport of food to the homeland a drop in the bucket of what was actually needed.[2]

The Germans built and commissioned two cargo U-boats of 213 feet in length with a 29 foot beam, and a surface displacement of 1,575 tons. The boats could carry about 900 tons of cargo.[3] Both would be available for transatlantic trips by 1916. Certainly not huge quanties of items could be carried out of or into Germany. However, the boats would fulfill a need for critical war industry materials like nickel, which Germany could not obtain in great quantity from continental supplies within the lands controlled or occupied by her and her allies.[4]

The *U-Deutschland* left German waters in June 1916 on her maiden and unprecedented voyage to America. Her Captain, Paul König, complained of her slow diving time, poor handling capabilities, and tendency to drop to the bottom during routine diving operations. The boat also had a slow speed, and could only make eleven knots on the surface while she could manage a paltry five knots underwater.[5]

Luckily for the crew, as with most U-boats of this time, the *U-Deutschland*'s cruise would take place mostly on the surface. However, during storms, the hatches would have to be closed and the boat had a habit of wildly pitching about, causing the hardened seamen aboard to vomit due to seasickness like they were new sailors. The interior also became incredibly hot once the boat entered the warmer waters of the Gulf Stream.

Despite British patrols, terrible weather, and their untried boat, the crew of the *Deutschland* made it into Baltimore harbor to great acclaim and fanfare from the U.S. press. König went ashore and hobnobbed with local politicians, German American groups, and a German spy ring headquartered in Baltimore.

The ring was engaged in secret sabotage operations against the U.S. munitions industry, but in this case they provided protection for the *Deutschland* while she was docked in the U.S. The boat unloaded it's cargo of coveted German dyes and loaded 400 tons of nickel, 400 tons of rubber, and 90 tons of tin for the return trip. On 1 August 1916, the *Deutschland* headed out to sea and arrived in German waters on 23 August to a great celebration. The Kaiser himself bestowed civilian medals on all the crew.[6]

A cargo submarine named the *Bremen* was the second boat commissioned and the first sent on a run to New London, Connecticut in September 1916. Her outbound voyage from the American port was to be covered by a specially modified combat U-boat with extra fuel for the trip, SM *U-53* under Kapitänleutnant Hans Rose. However, when Rose arrived in North American waters he heard radio reports that the *Bremen* was missing and presumed lost. The *Bremen* was never heard from, and the wreck has not been discovered to this day.

Rose's principal mission was to scatter any waiting Allied warships from the *Bremen*'s departure route, which was a real worry during the *Deutschland*'s exit from Baltimore harbor earlier in the year. Rose also had two secondary directives, which he proceeded to carry out.

Rose made a short port call at the American naval base in Newport,

Rhode Island to the astonishment of the American authorities. He received many curious guests from the American Navy on his boat during his whirlwind visit. After only a few hours, Rose left and carried out the second part of his mission, the sinking of Allied ships just beyond neutral American waters. Rose sank a few ships within sight of several American destroyers who could do nothing but watch and rescue the fleeing passengers and seamen in their lifeboats.[7] The only casualties during Rose's attacks were a lost baby doll and a mother's injured hand. As the mother and daughter evacuated the British passenger ship *Stephano* the daughter dropped her doll, and as the mother reached out to retrieve it, to assuage the crying girl, a wave hit the rowboat and crushed her hand in between the lifeboat and the doomed ship.

Despite the humane manner with which Rose carried out his duty, the incident strained American relations with Germany just a little further than they had been.[8]

In the meantime, the *Deutschland* was making her second voyage across the Atlantic to America. She had a miserable journey over caused by leaks and the terrible handling qualities of the boat in a storm, but the *Deutschland* made it to New London, Connecticut in late October 1916. The reception in the small port city was ecstatic as the Mayor and local politicians imagined they would become the hub of a new North American trade with Germany. König was feted at a party attended by 4,000 people and given a commemorative gold watch. It was the last show of goodwill between the Imperial German government and the U.S. for a while. During the merchant U-boat's departure she collided with a tugboat resulting in the loss of five lives on the ship. The incident served as a chill wind for New London's misplaced enthusiasm for the potential new trade boom they expected.[9] In November 1916, König and crew returned to Germany with their cargo for the last time.[10]

No other cargo U-boats would make the trip to America. In December 1916 and February 1917, after the Kaiser had decided to unleash unrestricted U-boat warfare, the remaining seven cargo U-boats were overtly taken over by the German Navy and changed into combat vessels.

The boats had really always been under the control of the navy, but to allay American fears that the boats would be armed or associated with the same ilk that had sunk the *Lusitania* and other ships with American casualties, a civilian shell company was created to own the boats until the navy openly claimed them once war with the U.S. was imminent. Six of the boats had never even been used as merchant vessels, and the conversions to warships were carried out as quickly as possible.[11]

5. From Carrying Cargo to Sinking It

While the conversion of the boats fulfilled an immediate need the German Navy had for long range U-boats, it also created a weapon with a lot of technical problems which the crews would curse in the months to come. The preceding was caused by the urgency attending the merchant U-Kreuzer project, which meant engines and other aspects of the boats could not be invented for specialty use in a U-Kreuzer. Instead the engines and other parts would be from already existing designs, which contributed to the clumsy handling and equipment failures so common in the merchant boats, and in the later converted U-Kreuzers.[12] The policy of peaceful underwater trade had failed, and the *Deutschland* class cargo boats would soon bring war to North American shores.[13]

In 1914 and 1915, the German cruisers and raiders busy protecting German overseas colonies and trade were spread throughout the Atlantic and the Pacific. As stated earlier, they attempted to wage a war against Allied shipping until they ran out of ammunition or were cornered by a superior force and destroyed. The romantic and exciting episodes in the short lives of the surface cruisers were immortalized in the media of the day until the Allied and German militaries had an inflated view of their actual strategic utility. In fact, the eight principal raiders had sunk only a little over 280,000 tons of shipping.

Arguably, the most famous of the raiders was the *SMS Emden*. She sank over 66,000 tons of shipping, bombarded oil tanks in the Indian port of Madras, attacked Allied ships in Penang harbor, and captured a British wireless station on a Pacific island before being destroyed in battle. The cruisers had caused havoc with Allied plans and shipping in the early part of the war. However, their real impact on the wider war was minimal, and their often violent ends served as a perfect lesson in Britain's absolute mastery of the world's oceans.[14]

In late summer 1916, the German Navy commissioned a study to ascertain what type of wartime roles the planned seven merchant U-boats would play if they were converted from their purely cargo carrying role. The navy envisioned three possibilities, which included conversion to an oil tanker and combat U-boat re-supply ship, conversion to a large mine laying U-boat, and lastly transforming the awkward U-boats into U-Kreuzers with heavy artillery. The oil tanker role would be rejected this time around, but would serve the German Navy well in the next war as the Milchkuh (Milk cow) concept. The mine laying U-boat idea would be adopted in part since the converted cargo submarines would carry mines for placement outside far-flung Allied harbors. However, the U-Kreuzer concept was the main role decided upon in reference to the ex-merchant U-boats.[15]

A U-Kreuzer would have a long cruising range, very heavy deck guns capable of engaging armed Allied escort vessels if needed, and hopefully be able to re-create the panic and damage the original cruisers had caused in far flung Allied enclaves without the fear of being caught in a duel to the death. The U-Kreuzers could submerge when faced with overwhelming odds and escape unlike their surface counterparts.

One more revolutionary idea put forth was the utilization of the converted merchant boats as radio command posts and convoy surveillance platforms, which could direct other U-boats for coordinated attacks on the grouped Allied ships. While attacking a convoy could be suicidal for a single U-boat, a group coordinated by a command boat could theoretically overwhelm the convoy's defenses and sink more ships.

Kommodore Hermann Bauer, commander in chief of the U-boat arm (Führer der Unterseeboote) at that time, proposed this departure from the U-Kreuzer concept in April 1917. He even added the Milchkuh concept to his radical idea since the command boats could also carry extra fuel and ammunition for the smaller combat U-boats so they could stay on patrol longer after refueling and rearming from a U-Kreuzer.[16]

However, this truly strategic use of the ex-merchant boats was not taken up by the German naval high command, and a potential war winning combination known as the wolf pack in World War II was lost to the Imperial German Navy in that first submarine war.[17]

The Germans set up a U-Kreuzer command to direct the operations of these new far flung submarines. The U-boats eventually placed under this designation were the ex-merchant boats *U-151* to *U-157*, the new mine laying and U-Kreuzer boats *U-117* and *U-139* to *U-141*, and a few of the regular ocean going boats represented by *U-35*, *U-38*, *U-62*, and *U-91*. Bauer's successor, Andreas Michelsen, inherited the leadership over the U-boat arm and the U-Kreuzer program from 1917 until the end of the war.

The new unit had fifteen U-boats at their disposal, and much was expected from their mission to take the war beyond the already recognized zones around the British Isles and the Mediterranean.[18] As the author of a British intelligence report put it, the Germans had the potential of creating a "New Race of Emden's" with all the possible damage that entailed. In the same report, British intelligence surmised the U-Kreuzers had arrived too late to be effective. The report goes further by stating if the U-Kreuzers had started to operate in 1916 they could have made "shipping a perilous business along the whole length of the trade routes."[19] What British intelligence failed to take into account in this instance is the small number of U-Kreuzers built by Germany regardless of when they started using them.

Despite their optimism, the navy immediately noted the major drawback that the boats were painfully slow on the surface. However, they surmised the underpowered nature of their engines would be offset by the overpowered nature of their guns.

Two 5.9-inch guns were strapped to the decks of the long-range U-boats. The artillery would theoretically allow them to outrange and outpunch any armed Allied merchant vessel then on the oceans, and would even let them challenge smaller Allied patrol vessels on the surface if they chose. The guns were of the type principally used to arm large U-boats, torpedo boats, and anti-aircraft batteries.[20] An immediate drawback of the big guns was their tendency to shake the whole boat when fired with the potential to loosen their deck supports.[21] They were just a little too big to be perfectly effective deck guns for a U-boat of this type.[22]

The other armament carried in the boats consisted of two internal bow torpedo tubes with 18 torpedoes, the two aforementioned cannons on deck with 1,672 rounds of ammunition in storage, and for *U-151* to *U-154*, an extra two 3.5-inch cannons close to and on either side of the conning tower. *U-155* to *U-157* would never be fitted with the extra 3.5-inch guns due to concerns about their weight. The boats also carried at least one heavy machine gun, and sometimes one or two 2-inch quick firing guns for installation on captured prize vessels used as temporary surface raiders or supply ships for the U-Kreuzer while on station.[23] They could also carry a varying number of explosive mines to deploy in wait for Allied and neutral ships once the U-Kreuzer had left the scene.[24]

At the beginning of and throughout the war, both powers utilized their surface ships to cut underwater communications cables that were used for secure telegraph messages. The British were much more successful in this endeavor since they commanded the surface of the Atlantic Ocean.[25] The German naval command placed great importance on the cutting of cables, and the destruction of land bound cable stations by gunfire.[26]

The U-Kreuzer's big guns were particularly suited to the last mission. The cable stations were the nerve centers of Allied oceanic communications, and without them the Germans imagined a dramatic break in Allied messages back and forth, with a subsequent increase in Allied wireless traffic. The Germans reliance on wireless radio messages, which could be intercepted and decoded, was a great lesson in the benefits to an enemy of forcing the use of the airwaves when all of the main submarine cables were cut.[27]

However, how could the Germans cut the Allied cables with almost no surface presence in the Atlantic? The Kaiser's men came up with a specially designed and installed cable cutter mechanism for U-Kreuzers. The rare device is described in some detail in this excerpt from an American Office of Naval Intelligence report authored in 1918 from information provided by British authorities.

> It has been stated that the converted mercantile submarines of the Deutschland class are being fitted with mechanical cable cutters that consist of a heavy shaft, a revolving spur, and two prongs or arms that take up the position of the flukes of a patent anchor. The spur, which is a very strong circular-toothed cutter, extends below the arms and its cutting edges pass between the shank and the arm. When the cutter is dragged along the seabed the teeth also engage in the bottom, causing the cutter to rotate. If a cable is picked up, it is forced into the cutting knives by the position of the arms or prongs. It is claimed that this appliance will cut cables up to 6.3 inches.[28]

Bauer and Michelsen both thought cable cutting was a waste of time but they must have been overruled.[29] Bauer stated the cables had to be cut close to the coast where they could be easily repaired rather than in deep water where it would be more difficult. Michelsen rightly thought that cable cutting stopped submarines from performing their real mission, which was to sink as much shipping as possible.

Michelsen commented that many cables had to be cut "simultaneously and permanently" for cable cutting to be a worthy endeavor. Michelsen also claimed he knew of only one U-boat to achieve such success, the *U-156*, which he credited with cutting five cables off North America. However, this was Michelsen's misreading of one of the *U-156*'s radio signals. In essence, it appears the captain of the U-Kreuzer thought he had cut one cable off North America and no more. Information from Room 40 had indicated the Germans would make a "special effort" to cut cables to South and North America.[30] This was proven correct.

The U-Kreuzers also had two 30-foot retractable radio masts to send and receive messages from other U-boats, and from the previously mentioned Nauen in Germany. The large radio masts on board made it possible for the U-Kreuzer's 2-kilowatt radio to communicate or at least receive messages while operating as far away as the North American coast.[31] Photographic evidence also indicates the crew used the radio masts as lookout towers to get a better view of the horizon for enemies or victims. The submarines also carried a smaller portable wireless set to be fitted out in any prize vessel the U-Kreuzer may capture, and work in tandem with against shipping.[32]

The ex-merchant U-Kreuzers were essentially a jack of all trades when it came to undersea warfare due to their ability to cut cables, attack ships from underwater with torpedoes, bombard targets with their big guns, and lay mines in Allied shipping lanes. The Germans were also building purposely built U-Kreuzers meant to be warships from the very beginning. These new U-boats did have advantages over the ex-merchant boats. However, they were not ready until later on in 1918 and had a minimal role in the war.

The ex-merchant U-Kreuzers long haul surface propulsion came from two fairly underpowered diesel engines of 400 horsepower each, and two electric battery powered engines of the same horsepower for underwater propulsion. The surface range was an impressive 15,200 nautical miles at cruising speed, while the submerged range was a paltry 70 nautical miles at 4.5 knots. The fuel capacity was much larger than that of a normal ocean going U-boat, and was about 250 tons with the option to carry more in the U-Kreuzers' large storage spaces.[33] The extra fuel allowed a U-Kreuzer to stay on station longer than the smaller boats like that captained by Hans Rose off the American coast in 1916.

The crew consisted of 56 men and officers with an additional 20-man prize crew added for boarding ships and manning captured prizes if necessary.[34] At times, there was also a second Kapitänleutnant on board, serving as first officer to the sub's captain, and learning the trade of submarine warfare in anticipation of a command of his own once the boat returned to Germany.[35] This was standard operating procedure in the U-boat arm although some men took command of their own U-boat right after their training in Kiel[36] ended.[37]

An average ex-merchant U-Kreuzer crew with the addition of a prize crew would typically come to 76 or 77 men and officers onboard.[38] The living spaces for the crew were larger than a typical U-boat due to the large interior spaces in the former cargo carrying boats. This feature was important since the crew would be asked to go on patrols for months rather than the weeks typical of smaller U-boat cruises, and U-Kreuzer crews were much larger than their smaller submarine cousins. Despite this the living conditions were still extremely cramped and uncomfortable.

The keel of the *U-156* herself was laid on 7 September 1916 in the Atlas Werke shipyard. She was launched on 15 April 1917, and the final touches done in the port of Kiel at Germaniawerft, and in Wilhelmshaven where the deck guns were mounted. In May 1917 the navy announced delays in the conversion of some of the boats due to labor and material shortages. *U-156* and *U-157*'s final completion dates were moved back to July.[39]

A German who worked in Kiel during the war, and was a spy for British intelligence reported that the workers at the shipping yards were prone to strike despite the illegality of such actions during a time of war. He described one such strike where the workers stopped construction on new submarines and ships due to the sentencing of a leftist political leader. The strike leaders were careful to say that was not the reason for the strike, and instead claimed the work stoppage was for higher pay. After a few days they received their extra pay and went back to work. The same spy also reported on the construction of the U-Kreuzers and new surface craft at the port in some detail.[40]

6

The Great Mirage

Despite the false nature of the belief, the Allied and neutral governments at large could be forgiven for seeing the German army and nation as an inexhaustible and completely militaristic foe with a seemingly endless supply of men, weapons, drive, and spiked helmets. No matter how many times the Allies assailed the enemy in France, Russia, Italy, the Balkans, and the Middle East, they kept coming back for more. As the U-Kreuzers came on the scene in 1917 and 1918 the Germans and their allies were particularly busy for countries actually on the brink of collapse at home.

In the Balkans the Bulgarians, Austrians, and Germans continued to occupy Serbia, Montenegro, Albania, Romania, and parts of northern Greece while also tying down and containing a multi-national Allied force of hundreds of thousands of men in the Allied camp at Salonika. The Allies would not begin the liberation of the Balkans until September 1918 when the Central Powers were already collapsing on more important fronts. On 7 May 1918 the Central Powers signed the Treaty of Bucharest with the defeated Romanians. The treaty was a sign of what those conquered by the Germans and their allies could expect, and included territorial concessions to Bulgaria and Austria-Hungary while the Germans obtained a 90 year lease on the Romanian oil wells and mineral rights for resources within the country.[1]

In the Middle East the Ottoman Turks, Germans, and even a few Austrians fought a losing defensive battle against General Sir Edmund Allenby's Allied forces and Arab rebels under Sharif Faisal accompanied by the famous Lawrence of Arabia. In 1917 and early 1918 resistance was kept up against the British enemy, although plans for the recapture of Baghdad had to be canceled due to alarming Allied gains in Palestine, which included the capture of Jerusalem in December 1917. The Middle Eastern fronts were the only truly bright spot for the Allies on land in

1917 and the first half of 1918. Nonetheless, they would not obtain a truly decisive victory over the Central Powers in Palestine until September 1918.[2] In addition, the Caucasus front between the Ottoman Empire and Russia was in complete chaos with German and Turkish forces making a serious bid to control the valuable oil fields in the area late in 1918 after the complete collapse of the Russian army.

The German leadership in 1917 and 1918 could see the Balkans and the Middle East were holding, if losing some ground, for the Central Powers throughout most of 1917 and the first half of 1918. As a result they focused on other more critical areas. In Italy, the Austrians and Germans were able to engineer spectacular success. In the north of the country the Italian army had been hammering at the Austrians since that nation entered the war on the Allied side in 1915. The Italians had gained little territory and suffered horrible casualties, but they also inflicted grievous losses on the Austrians.

Finally, in 1917, the Austrians asked for German assistance. On 24 October of that year over 4,000 artillery pieces fired explosive, gas, and smoke shells into the Italian lines for six hours. After the bombardment the Austro-German forces launched an overwhelming attack. The Italian front crumbled under the weight of the assault and the Austro-Germans were soon wreaking havoc in the Italian rear areas. On 3 November the Central Powers forced the Tagliamento River line and the Italians retreated to the Piave River.[3] The Italians finally held the enemy in check there. The battle of Caporetto, as it came to be known, had cost Italy 320,000 casualties, 3,152 artillery pieces, and hundreds of thousands of rifles and machine guns lost. In addition, the enemy now occupied northeast Italy.[4]

In Russia the news was even worse for the Allies. The Russian army slowly collapsed after the fall of the Tsarist regime in March 1917, and the subsequent overthrow of the Kerensky government in October. The Germans, in order to assist a government they knew would sue for peace, facilitated Vladimir Lenin's travel back to Russia from Switzerland. The plan worked, Lenin came to power, and soon the Bolshevik delegates were at the negotiating table in Brest–Litovsk in German occupied Poland. However, the first round of negotiations failed when Leon Trotsky refused to give in to the German demands and simply stated he considered the war at an end.

The Germans did not agree and promptly invaded the Ukraine, and delved deeper into other parts of Russia's heartland while they met little to no resistance. The Bolsheviks returned to the table with even less to bargain with and signed a treaty that ranks as one of the harshest in world history. The Russians agreed to give up Finland, the Baltic states, Ukraine, Poland, the Crimea, and the Caucasus territories to the Central Powers. Germany and Austria-Hungary dreamed of the rich grain harvest in the Ukraine to feed their starving people while Turkey and Germany coveted the Russian oil fields near Baku.[5] It was all a very temporary mirage but the German boots marching in to occupy these vast lands seemed to presage victory.[6] Victory on the Eastern front meant one last chance for triumph in France before the American army arrived in large numbers. Ludendorff hoped the German troops freed up for service in the west would be enough to tip the balance in the Reich's favor.

Ludendorff made his preparations for what he hoped would be the final blow in the west. Elite German storm troops, thousands of artillery pieces, fighter and bomber planes, and the last hopes of the German people were all put into one last gamble starting in March and ending in July 1918 just as the U-Kreuzer attacks off North America were heating up. It seemed the Allies were close to defeat although the almost victorious German armies were not what they appeared to be.

In reality Germany was scraping the bottom of the barrel with this last series of offensives.[7] She was using up the last and best of her men and officers while also placing young boys into the line to replace those lost in the great attacks of 1918. This fact was noted by an American lieutenant who came across two wounded German "soldiers" in the rear.

> At the road where the litters were taken, we came upon two other stretcher cases just brought down the north slope ... a couple of German lads. One had taken a piece of HE (high explosive) in the lungs. The other had a machine gun bullet through his guts. The boy with the belly wound was about 13 years old. He was jabbering to anyone who would talk to him. "This other boy is my brother," he said. "His name is Rudolph. We haven't been in this war very long.... Only about a month.... And the Red Cross man says we are going where there aren't any shells." There was something pathetic about this baby and his eager interest in the strange country that lay back of the lines. Somebody translated for the benefit of the Medical Corps lieutenant who had examined our wounded. He shook his head. "I guess there won't be any shells where that kid is going," he admitted. "He probably won't live til they get him to the dressing station." The boy, who could not understand, seemed to think that the lieutenant was agreeing with him in the matter of safety from shells. He pulled out of his blouse a thick nickel watch. Spare wheels and corners of brass fell out of it through a jagged hole. A bullet had gone clean through it. "Do you think I can get my watch fixed in this country?" he asked me. I gulped. "I think so," I said. "The French are very good at fixing watches." "I hope so, he said. "My mother gave it to me just before I came into this war and I shouldn't want her to think I had been careless with it." I tried damn hard not to bawl at that. I don't believe I succeeded. The kid was still smiling when they loaded him into the ambulance.[8]

The short-lived victories, daily sacrifices, and hunger at home all pointed to eventual defeat. Germany was deluding itself into thinking it could overcome the material superiority of the Allies and the fresh divisions of Americans arriving every day in France despite the German submarines lurking off the coasts of Europe.

The U-Kreuzers themselves were a delusion in a way. A precursor to the wunderwaffe (wonder weapons) of Hitler's day when the Nazi German government tried to reassure an uncertain populace that despite the dark times and strategic defeats they had experienced the war could still be won by some long shot weapon right out of a sci-fi movie. The V2 rockets, fighter jets, and super heavy tanks came too little and too late in that war. The World War I German government and public had the same tendencies with their U-Kreuzers, super long range artillery that bombarded Paris for a time, Zeppelin bombers, and long range airplane bombers that struck the great city of London.

The Germans in both world wars convinced themselves into thinking that small numbers of technological curiosities could save them from defeat, occupation, or starvation, and reverse the courses of battles already long decided. The U-Kreuzers had some propaganda value in this regard since photos and stories of their exploits could be shown to the public, and their far off adventures trumpeted as a distraction for a war weary populace. The Battles in the North Sea, the Atlantic, and the Mediterranean were lost by the time the U-Kreuzers arrived, and there was little that could be done to change that fact.

The wonder weapons captured the German and Allied imaginations while they sent their children to fight in the most terrible battles the world had yet seen. The U-Kreuzers were born into a time when Germany was falsely confident, and thought she could win it all with what little she had left. The U-Kreuzer battles were real and had an impact beyond their small numbers, but the war was won and lost on the home front where German families fought each other for food, and on muddy fields in France that were stained by the blood of children like Rudolph and his brother.

7

The U-boat Ace

On 13 March 1882, Konrad Gansser was born to Wilhelm and Josephine Gansser in Baden-Württemberg, a kingdom under the aegis of the German Empire created in 1871. He was baptized less than a month later in Stuttgart, located in southwest Germany.[1] Stuttgart is about as far as one can get from the sea in Germany, and had about 170,000 inhabitants then. Gansser moved away from his landlocked roots, and joined the Imperial German Navy on 1 April 1900.[2]

He became a Kapitänleutnant on 19 November 1910, had a short stint at a post on land at the beginning of the war in August 1914, and then entered the U-boat school in September 1914. During training, he commanded the obsolete U-boat SM U-8 until he was given command of SM U-33 later on in 1914. Gansser would command the U-33 until March 1917, during which time he used his boat to ravage the Mediterranean, Adriatic, and Black Seas from his two bases at Pola on the Adriatic and Constantinople in modern day Istanbul, Turkey.[3]

Gansser was one of the top U-boat aces of World War I. He sank 41 ships while he commanded U-33 for a total of 126,596 tons of shipping sent to the bottom before spring 1917. Gansser was awarded the Iron Cross First and Second Class, and received the prestigious Royal House Order of Hohenzollern medal for his U-boat exploits. The medal was second only to the coveted Prussian order Pour le Mérite, and was a great honor for any officer to receive.[4]

To the Germans, Gansser was a hero. To the Allies, he was an unscrupulous villain. The British especially painted Gansser as a merciless proponent of unrestricted submarine warfare who had purposely sunk a marked hospital ship, and then callously bombarded a Russian village onshore.

On 30 March 1916, the *Portugal*, a French hospital ship under charter to the Imperial Russian government was towing several flat bottomed boats off the northern Turkish coast to carry wounded from the shore to

Gansser (center), flanked by two Austro-Hungarian officers on the deck of U-33. Gansser became a submarine ace while he commanded this smaller U-boat in the Mediterranean, and had a reputation in Allied circles for being merciless during his attacks on enemy shipping prior to his command of *U-156* (*Lowell Thomas Papers, James A. Cannavino Library, Archives & Special Collections, Marist College, USA*).

the ship. One of the boats started to sink so the *Portugal* stopped while repairs were made. The crew spotted *U-33*'s periscope but did not take evasive action as hospital ships were not considered legitimate military targets under the Hague Convention. Gansser's submarine fired one torpedo and missed, and then reportedly fired another from a very short distance away. The result was devastation and the *Portugal* split in two. Approximately 90 doctors, nurses, and crew died in the attack. No patients were killed as the *Portugal* had not picked them up yet. The ship was reportedly painted white with multiple large red crosses and flags plainly visible at the short distance of the submarine from the ship.[5]

In addition to his destruction of the hospital ship, Gansser had started out his submarine career with an incident that would go down in the annals of infamy alongside the execution of British nurse Edith Cavell.[6] On 28 March 1915, Captain Charles Fryatt was the master of the SS *Brussels*, a passenger ferry with regular service between Harwich, England and Rotterdam, Holland. On that day, Gansser, commander of *U-33* at the time, spotted the ship and ordered her to stop. Fryatt, following a practice that was sanctioned by the British government, and which was used throughout the war, attempted to run from *U-33* and then went to ram her when Gansser appeared to be lining up for a torpedo shot. Gansser was forced to dive to escape. Gansser was a novice commander and had not even sunk his first enemy ship at the time.

One year later, in June 1916, Fryatt was leading the *Brussels* on another run back to England and was leaving Dutch waters. He was immediately captured by a group of German destroyers and his ship taken as a prize. Fryatt was given a trial in occupied Bruges, Belgium for attacking *U-33* as a civilian, which was supposedly illegal under German law at the time.[7]

Essentially the Germans argued Fryatt was a "franc-tireur" of the sea.[8] They attempted to portray him as the equivalent of a civilian sniper behind the lines in occupied Belgium or France killing German soldiers without the sanction or direction of an enemy government, and without a uniform. In reality Fryatt was just protecting his ship's passengers and crew from a potentially deadly fate in open lifeboats, or a watery grave if torpedoed by *U-33*. Fryatt followed Admiralty protocol when dealing with a submarine, and was even given a gold watch and honored in Parliament after his encounter with Gansser. The accolades he received in England were all cited as additional evidence by the Germans that he had committed a crime against *U-33*. Gansser did not appear at Fryatt's trial, but submitted a written statement that outlined the facts of the encounter as he witnessed them.[9]

Fryatt was tried, found guilty, and executed on the same day. The outrage in Allied and neutral countries was palpable. The Germans had martyred Fryatt, murdered an innocent civilian, and made a foolish foreign policy blunder yet again. The war crime was never avenged, and those who so hastily and harshly judged Fryatt for an action taken in wartime were never brought to justice. His seven children and wife were left without a father and husband, but at least Mrs. Fryatt was given a monthly check to help her huge family survive. Gansser was listed as a war criminal by the British.[10]

War criminal or not, the fact remained that he was experienced, daring, and successful in war. The German naval command hoped he was the right man to take the *U-156* out on her maiden voyage against shipping in the lightly defended waters off the Azores and Canary Islands.[11]

Oberleutnant zur see Paul Richard Knöckel was the *U-156*'s talented prize officer who commanded the 20 men designated as those who would board enemy vessels to sink them with bombs, outfit them as prize vessels for commerce raiding, or as U-boat supply ships during both of the *U-156*'s war cruises. The job was dangerous, for if a hazard appeared on the horizon the U-boat may have had to leave the boarders to their fate. Also, if the crew of a ship resisted capture then the prize crew would be in the line of fire.[12] The former had happened before when the prize crews from the *U-49* and *U-50* were captured by the British while they manned their prize vessels. The British did not find their home U-boats in the area.[13]

Knöckel was born on 18 July 1887, and was baptized two months later in Oberkirch, Baden, Germany in the same state as Gansser.[14] The captain of a ship captured by the *U-156* in August 1918 described Knöckel as a short man with brown hair, four days growth on his beard, and who wore a brown leather jacket with a blue cap and spoke English. Allied intelligence described him as a line officer in the German reserves who was commissioned as a Leutnant in January 1915. They state he was from Lubeck, Germany, and was awarded the Iron Cross 1st Class and the Officer's Military Cross 4th class with swords. Knöckel's name was often on the receipts given to the captains of sunken vessels by the *U-156*, and he was mistakenly thought of as the commander of the U-boat several times by the crews of those ships.[15]

In late 1916, the navy decided to extend submarine warfare to the area near the Azores in the Central Atlantic and the Canary Islands off West Africa and Spain in order to disrupt Allied supply ships coming from South America and other parts of Africa. The Azores were controlled by Germany's enemy, Portugal, and the Canaries by neutral Spain. Germany's first forays into this area were carried out by smaller U-boats which could only stay on station, once they finally arrived, for about two weeks. The Germans wanted to create a more substantial presence in the area, especially after the United States entered the war in April 1917. They anticipated more U.S. ships would be transiting the waters off West Africa and in the Central Atlantic on their way to Mediterranean ports, and the earlier patrols had not found a substantial Allied or neutral defensive presence in the area.

The Germans even considered making this area a part of their expected future naval empire after the war ended as outlined in an excerpt from a Kaiserliche Marine memorandum "One cannot tell at this point in time whether, when peace is declared, the Faeroes and the Azores may be acquired and whether in the next war it will be possible to obtain the use of Spanish ports for our purposes: all this will depend completely on future political alignments."[16]

The navy realized the U-Kreuzers, whose slow speed denied them the chance to effectively operate in the vital war zone around Great Britain, may be able to make a big impact on Allied trade in the less heavily defended waters around the Canary Islands. Furthermore, they could stay on station there for months due to their ability to carry large amounts of food supplies, ammunition, and fuel. The Spanish had a paltry patrol force, and could not maintain a vigilant watch over their principal harbors, let alone the more remote islands in the Canary chain. The Azores and Madeira were also not heavily defended, and both island territories essentially depended on passing British and French cruisers for the protection of Allied and neutral trade in the area. Essentially, the waters off West Africa were thought by the Germans to be the perfect testing and operating ground for the new U-Kreuzers.[17]

The Germans, in an attempt to keep Spain from treating with the Allies due to anger about submarine operations near or in their waters, ordered the U-Kreuzers to conduct their attacks in this area under the prize regulation rules when possible. The rules as the Germans interpreted them specified a U-boat must stop any unarmed ship, inspect her cargo to see if it was contraband bound for an Allied port, and then sink her after allowing the crew to escape to a place of safety in their lifeboats if contraband was discovered.[18]

Among the commanders and crews chosen to man the U-Kreuzers for their initial war cruises were some experienced men who had served in U-boats prior to this mission. There were also some experienced surface naval officers who were in command of their first U-boat. They had a

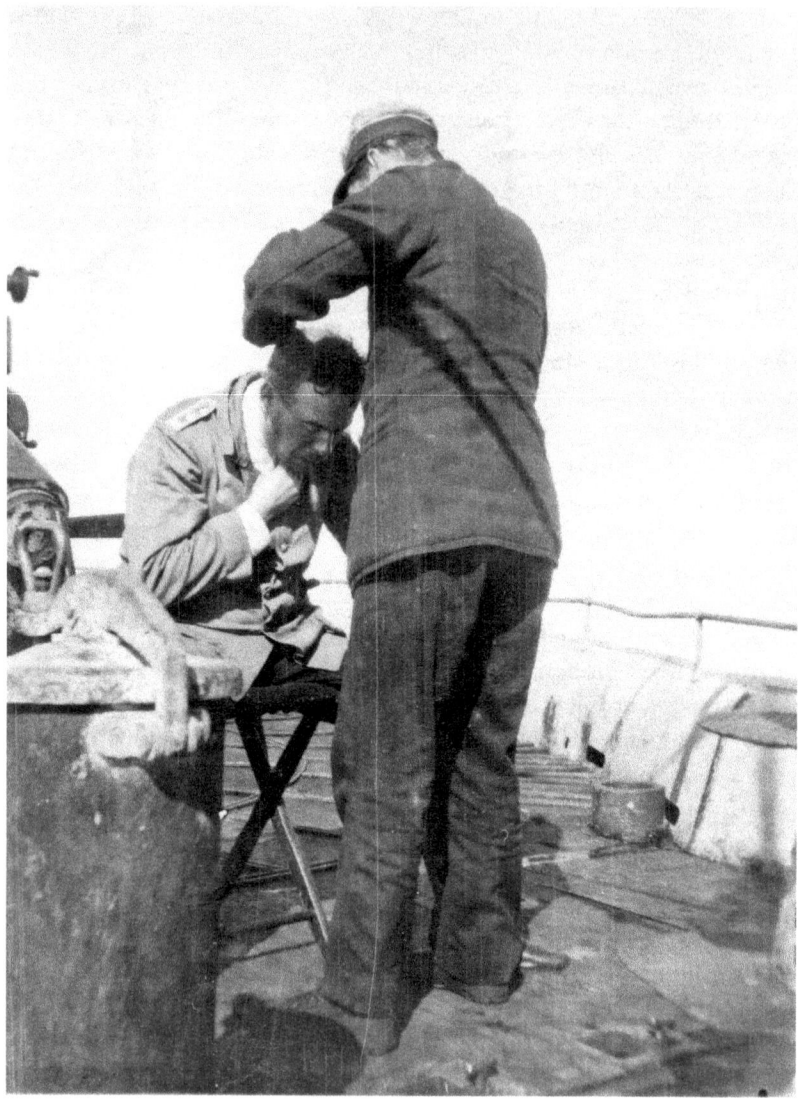

Gansser, in a tropical uniform jacket, gets his hair cut on the deck of *U-156* (*Lowell Thomas Papers, James A. Cannavino Library, Archives & Special Collections, Marist College, USA*).

great deal of naval experience, but only time would tell if they could handle the clumsy new submarines. U-Kreuzer command and the German naval leadership clearly expected results from their best captains, and likely wanted their veterans to excel with the unstable new boats while the new men would have been accompanied by veteran crews and officers to help them along.

Finally, on 28 August 1917, the *U-156* was commissioned under Gansser's experienced command. He took his boat through the sea trials, which included dive, speed, engine, and torpedo firing tests. On 14 September 1917, the *U-156* did her deep dive test, which took her below 90 feet underwater. This was not even close to her rated 150 foot diving limit, and may say something about how reliable the crew thought the boat actually was. Having passed her tests, the *U-156*, Gansser, and his crew prepared for war.[19]

On 16 October 1917, Gansser sailed *U-156* out from Kiel expecting to engage in the "U-Kreuzer war in the North Atlantic." However, the voyage was doomed from the beginning. Gansser had to dodge torpedoes from British patrol submarines on two separate days right at the start of his cruise.[20] This was apparently not an uncommon problem as a declassified American memorandum from the British marked "Very Secret" from 14 June 1918 mentions that British submarine L15 was on patrol and spotted a total of five German submarines. She attacked two without effect. The report goes on to note that sightings are much more common than successful attacks. The British patrols may have scared the Germans, and sunk a fair number of U-boats over time, but they were an obstacle most U-boats overcame.[21]

On the fourth day, raging storms off the coast of Norway flooded the *U-156*'s control room. On 24 October, Gansser called off the mission with a radio message noting severe leaks while diving, jammed equipment, and on the return trip a damaged rudder was reported.[22] Gansser returned to Kiel after several days of doing nothing but keeping the *U-156* afloat. The failure of his first foray in the new boat likely pushed Gansser to do everything in his power to make the next cruise a grand success.[23] The new mission was to take the war to the hoped for U-Kreuzer' promised land near the Canary Islands to pick up a valuable cargo and use his prize crew to capture a vessel to work in tandem with against shipping.[24] Gansser departed for his destination on 14 November 1917. Only time, chance, and Room 40 could decide how much failure or triumph he would experience while there.

8

The Trade War and the Secret War

Gansser started out his shipping war off West Africa with a small catch. On 7 December the Canadian flagged sailing and fishing vessel *W.C. McKay* of 147 tons traveling from Newfoundland to Genoa, Italy with a cargo of fish was spotted and stopped.[1] In Gansser's log the sinking is relegated to a simple explanation worthy of such a small prize. Gansser states the *McKay* was spotted on the horizon, stopped and boarded, the seven-man crew put into lifeboats, and the boat sunk with explosives placed on board.[2]

12 December found Gansser gunning for an Allied port. Funchal, Madeira[3] was Portuguese, isolated on an island off West Africa, and host to some Allied convoys in the area during the war. The town had land based artillery batteries and some protection from a patrol boat in the harbor. However, if no Allied warships were present the *U-156*'s guns were at least a match for the defender's artillery.

Gansser's intention was to go south of Madeira in the favorable weather, and then head for the outer harbor of Funchal in the dark of night. As the *U-156* approached the harbor the crew had a little scare and the diving alarm was sounded when a dimmed-out vessel was suddenly spotted in the darkness in close proximity to the U-Kreuzer. At the last moment before closing the conning tower hatch, the vessel, which passed close to the *U-156*'s stern, was made out to be a steamer running completely dark. Gansser noted the possibility of attack was non-existent due to his own low speed.

After the near miss with the steamer, Gansser received a radio transmission from Nauen, which ordered him to hunt ships in a known steamer route in the area after his bombardment of Funchal. The navy brass apparently knew about Gansser's planned attack on Funchal according to this message, which would become relevant later when they did their after action report on his cruise.

8. The Trade War and the Secret War

A merchant captain, his motionless steamer seen in the distance, brings his papers over to Gansser's *U-156* for inspection (*Lowell Thomas Papers, James A. Cannavino Library, Archives & Special Collections, Marist College, USA*).

Gansser and the *U-156* silently slipped closer to Funchal's outer harbor, and noted the bright lights of the city shone all the way up the mountains as if the little port did not know there was a war on. They should have known better as Funchal had felt the wrath of German U-boat guns only a year before. As the *U-156* lay quietly in the middle of the outer harbor, Gansser scanned the town and the inner harbor. He noted the beach was clearly seen, but no steamers or other vessels were visible. The *U-156* then turned away from land in order to reach an already chosen position for bombardment of the town.

Before the *U-156*'s guns could fire their first shot, the Portuguese Fort Santiago opened fire with her artillery, and shattered the calm morning. The *U-156* then started the bombardment of the defensive forts and town in earnest.[4] Four Portuguese forts and a patrol vessel returned fire and started a lively exchange with Gansser. The *U-156*'s gunners were not able to hit the patrol boat although their shots splashed to within 15 feet of the target. After firing 52 shells into the forts, town, and at the patrol vessel, Gansser broke off the action and started out to sea. He observed a low cloud of smoke over the center of the city where several hits were observed.

According to the Allies, some civilians were killed during the bombardment, which had also damaged the 15th century Santa Clara Church and Convent. The people of Madeira later created a monument to the victims of both U-boat bombardments of Funchal during World War I. The point of the whole episode was likely an attempt to destroy whatever ships were in the harbor, and to destroy the cable communications station in town. The cable station was not destroyed, and Gansser found no merchant ships near Funchal so the mission was in the end a useless diversion of the U-Kreuzer's time on station.

The civilians, as is so often the case in war, were caught in the middle of the attack. U-boats targeting land based facilities was a fairly rare event. However, it did happen multiple times over the years during the Great War. In 1916, a German U-boat bombarded what it thought was a military target near Seaham, England, and instead hit a civilian house and two cousins taking a walk. One woman, who had endured several Zeppelin bomber attacks on her hometown moved to Seaham to avoid the danger from the air. She and her cousin left to take a walk together, and as it turned out the stroll was the last for one of them.[5]

On the night of 13 December, Nauen informed Gansser that a convoy would arrive in Funchal on 20 December. Gansser decided not to return to attack the convoy due to bad weather, and instead headed for the shipping route detailed in an earlier transmission from Germany.[6]

On the same day as the attack on Funchal, the *U-156* stopped the Greek steamer *Joannina* of 4,191 tons. The vessel was carrying a large quantity of opium and tobacco to New York. Before the *U-156* could get to her she radioed "SOS" and "come quick." No help arrived in time. Gansser's men boarded her, placed a bomb on the ship, and sunk her. 63 men in three boats were set adrift.

Five days later on 17 December the *U-156* stopped the Portuguese sailing vessel *Accoriano* of 312 tons. The small prize was sunk by explosives while carrying a cargo of copra and animal hides from Portuguese Guinea in Africa to Marseille, France. 12 men set off in lifeboats from the doomed vessel.

On 25 December, Gansser and his men were delighted to receive a Christmas message from Nauen to the *U-156*, which was then the farthest submarine from Germany in the world according to Gansser's notations. Germans are still well known for their love of the Christmas holiday, and it was no different when they were stuck on a U-boat in 1917. Nauen read out a Christmas message from the Kaiser, and the crew of the *U-156* gave three hurrahs in response. Gansser wrote that the Christian festival was celebrated in the midst of calm blue skies followed by a bright moonlit night overhead.

On 30 December, Gansser captured the Spanish Steamer *Joaquin Mumbru* of 2,703 tons carrying animal hides and a cargo of food from Spain to New York. Despite Spain's neutrality in the conflict and the vehement protestations of the captain, Gansser ruled the cargo contraband heading to an Allied port and sank the offending vessel. In the same time frame, Gansser had stopped two small Spanish vessels and released them due to no connections found to trade with the enemy.

On 10 January 1918, east of the Canary Islands, the Germans stopped and boarded the Dutch owned steamer *Atlas* of 1,813 tons. She was carrying peanuts for a Dutch-French company for France. Gansser decided that

U-156 stops a steamer in the Atlantic. The ship is not displaying a name and is painted in dark nondescript colors due to the war. However, a careful comparison of this ship with a prewar photograph reveals she is likely the *Atlas*, sunk by *U-156* on 11 January 1918 after she was rejected as a potential prize vessel by boarding officer Oberleutnant zur see Paul Knöckel (*Lowell Thomas Papers, James A. Cannavino Library, Archives & Special Collections, Marist College, USA*).

despite the neutral status of the Dutch, the ship would be destroyed due to the foodstuffs the vessel carried for an Allied nation. The *Atlas* was blown up by explosives placed on board on 11 January after Knöckel and a 10 man boarding party realized the *Atlas* was unsuitable as a prize vessel. Apparently, Gansser and Knöckel had hoped to utilize the *Atlas* in tandem with the *U-156* in their war against shipping.[7]

Prior to Gansser's departure for West Africa the German government began a search for a new source of a vital war material. Tungsten, also known as wolfram ore, is a high-density chemical element, which has a particular usefulness in the manufacture of projectiles. The material is also very rare and was coveted by both sides for their arms industries.

In July 1917, the German ambassador to Madrid suggested Germany secretly purchase wolfram ore from neutral Spain by utilizing two former merchant U-boats to ship the element to the Fatherland. The navy and the naval attaché in Madrid discussed the secret plan to obtain the ore via wireless radio transmissions from Nauen in a code the British and French had both broken.[8]

The British tracked the ore from the very beginning by utilizing one of their agents in Spain by the name of Commander Maurice Mitchell. In September 1917, Mitchell reported that Spain had arranged to sell 50 tons of ore to Germany. Mitchell had a network of spies in country and had the wolfram mines under constant covert surveillance. Mitchell used his agents to confirm the presence of the wolfram, and gave the British the missing pieces of the plot not gleaned from the German communications. One of Mitchell's agents had even infiltrated the warehouse where the wolfram was stored by pretending he was looking for a lost dog.[9]

In October, Nauen asked Madrid about using a U-boat to ship the ore from the Canary Islands to Germany in November 1917. The German ambassador to Spain was busy arranging for a Spanish boat to take the wolfram to the Canaries, and Mitchell was keeping a close watch on land. Admiral William Reginald Hall ordered the British naval forces at Gibraltar to use every means possible to prevent the wolfram from getting into German hands. The plan to defeat the German scheme was more than just an operation against one ship and two submarines, it was the enforcement of the British blockade against a clever German attempt to circumvent it.

The ship chosen to take the ore to the U-boats was the *Erri Berro*, a sailing ship of 170 tons with the Spanish flag painted on both sides of the vessel out of Bilbao, Spain. The ship would be easily recognizable at the proposed rendezvous. In November 1917, the *U-156* and *U-157* were des-

8. The Trade War and the Secret War

A profile shot of *U-156* while she waited in Naos Bay for her planned meeting with *U-157* and the *Erri Berro*. Note the laundry hanging out while the crew lounges on deck (*Lowell Thomas Papers, James A. Cannavino Library, Archives & Special Collections, Marist College, USA*).

ignated as the ore carriers who would meet the *Erri Berro* in the Canary Islands and take 40 tons of ore apiece. The amount of ore had apparently been increased since the reported 50 tons had been discussed.

The *U-157* was commanded by the very successful U-boat captain Max Valentiner. Valentiner had been to the area off West Africa before in a smaller U-boat and had bombarded Funchal, Madeira for the first time in December 1916.

It seemed the converted merchant boats would finally get the chance to act in their original roles and carry important war cargo for their Fatherland. In late November 1917, Berlin wired Madrid that the U-boats would meet the *Berro* in U-Platz 130. However, Madrid appears not to have known the location of U-Platz 130, so Berlin answered that it was on the southwest side of Hierro Island, and the meet should occur by 25 December. Of course now the British had the exact place, and a general time the meeting would occur in the Canaries. Unfortunately for the Germans not only was their operation completely compromised, but Berlin also notified Madrid the U-Kreuzers would be late to the meet and would not be at Hierro before 15 January.

Madrid informed Berlin that the *Berro* had already left and could not be recalled. Prior to this, Mitchell informed his superiors that the wolfram was being loaded into 50-pound sacks. The Admiralty sent two submarines to Gibraltar to intercept the U-Kreuzers and await their arrival off the Canary meeting place. His Majesty's Submarines (HMS) *E35* and *E48* left to get to the area on 10 and 12 November respectively.

The E class submarines were principally utilized for defensive and offensive patrols, anti U-boat operations, and operations with the British fleet. Weaponry wise, the E class boats had a stern torpedo tube, forward tubes, and one deck gun of varied calibers. They were probably the best all around submarines used by the British in the war, and could manage a relatively speedy 16 knots on the surface and 10 knots underwater with a crew of 31. They were half the size of the U-Kreuzers, but much more suited for a successful underwater attack.[10]

The *Erri Berro* left Bilbao on 31 December with a cargo of "cement" when a little after midnight she encountered the British warship HMS *Duke of Clarence*. The *Clarence* captured the *Berro*, her crew of five Spanish seamen, and one German who had been on an interned ship in Spain for years, and had hoped to get back to Germany to see his family after the mission was over. The British towed the *Berro*, but before they could reach England the ship went down due to sabotage by the crew prior to capture, or damage to the ship sustained during the operation. The German and the Spanish crew were placed in custody in Britain and not allowed to have contact with anyone until the operation had ended. All of this was unknown to the Germans for a while, and the *U-156* and *U-157* were not aware they were headed to a rendezvous with a British submarine rather than the *Erri Berro* in Naos Bay.[11]

On 18 January, after the unsuccessful torpedo attack on the *U-156*, Gansser moved out of the area and radioed the *U-157*: "U-Platz compromised, danger for U-boats."[12] A day earlier, prior to dawn on 17 January, the British submarine E48 submerged before she approached Naos Bay. Lieutenant Commander F.H. Taylor sighted the *U-156* on the surface, and lined up for an attack, but was apparently spotted when the *U-156* moved rapidly toward him. Taylor dived deep as quick as he could and chased the *U-156* for as long as his submerged speed would keep up before the *U-156* returned to pick up the three lookout officers on land. Taylor saw his chance and attacked with both bow torpedo tubes at about 2,100 feet away. One broke the surface and ran towards the target. The other became stuck in the tube with the propeller going. Taylor turned the boat so he could fire from the stern tube, and when he did the stuck torpedo in the bow tube flew out and headed in the general direction of *U-156* before it broke the surface too. *E48* was only 15 feet below the bay and came under Gansser's fire.

Taylor then had *U-156* in his sights again and fired the stern tube. The underwater missile also broke the surface and Taylor thought the torpedo had either gone under the U-boat or had just missed. *U-156* ran and lost E48 when the British gave up the chase after dark.

The naval command in England was angry about Taylor's report, and despite the fact that Taylor had sunk another enemy submarine prior to his attack on the *U-156* he and two other officers on E48 were relieved of command.

On 23 June 1915, the then Lieutenant Taylor was part of an ingenious submarine trap, along with the trawler *Taranaki* off the coast of Scotland. Taylor's submarine, HMS *C24*, was connected by a towline and telephone cable to *Taranaki* during the mission. The telephone was in place so the disguised trawler could communicate with the submerged Taylor whenever a German U-boat may appear to attack the seemingly helpless target.

Around 9:30 in the morning the *Taranaki* called Taylor to report a submarine about 3,000 feet astern. The tow was thought to have been disconnected and Taylor moved to attack. Once the line was let go the submarine made a sudden jerk downward and it took Taylor a little time to right his submarine again. Once Taylor started to move, he realized the towline and telephone wire were still attached to his ship, and this made his movements much more difficult. In spite of this Taylor moved to within 1,500 feet of the Germans and saw the *U-40*'s gun and conning tower.

The sailors on the *Taranaki* pretended to panic at the sight of the U-boat and started to play-act at abandoning ship. At 9:55 a.m. Taylor's torpedo sliced through the calm sea and hit the U-boat's conning tower directly. *U-40* sank immediately, and the only survivors were the Kapitänleutnant, an Oberleutnant, and a petty officer. *U-40*'s short career under Gerhardt Fürbringer was cut short by this amazing military operation, and the novice German commander went into Allied captivity with no ships sunk by his command. He had thought the *Taranaki* would be his first victim, but it ended up being the death of his crew and vessel.[13]

Despite Taylor's bad luck the second time around, he knew for certain that his torpedo had hit *U-156* and failed to explode by 9 March 1918. Taylor's career had been saved by the code breakers in Room 40 who were reading Gansser's post encounter transmissions. They had read his 20 February description of the ambush to Nauen, which included the fact that a torpedo had struck the *U-156* amidships.[14] Taylor was in command of another submarine by May 1918.

In the meantime, Gansser and Valentiner continued to radio each other after the drama of 17 January. They also constantly and intelligently changed their radio ciphers in fear of British decryption. On 19 January, Valentiner and Gansser rendezvoused their two boats in person southwest of the Canary Islands. Valentiner was convinced the wolfram ore scheme had been betrayed and agreed to meet Gansser 100 miles from Hierro Island before 23 January.[15]

The ever-present Nauen instructed the pair to meet with *U-152* as well. On 20 January, Valentiner went back on the plan and stated combined operations would not be prudent given the bad weather conditions and the fact that he thought the British had broken the German codes, which of course was completely correct. He told Gansser to work with a captured prize vessel as a partner for resupply purposes during the cruise if possible.[16] Valentiner had successfully captured a small steamer, which he used in the manner described from January to March.[17] Valentiner returned to Germany after a cruise of 135 days and a paltry total of only

U-157 and *U-156* eventually met up away from land after *U-156* was ambushed in Naos Bay. Valentiner's *U-157* took this shot of *U-156* bobbing up and down in the Altantic just before the meeting took place (*Lowell Thomas Papers, James A. Cannavino Library, Archives & Special Collections, Marist College, USA*).

10,000 tons of shipping sunk. Valentiner was given sick leave when he came home.

As Gansser and Valentiner came to the realization that their codes were compromised, the two men who had jumped overboard during *E48*'s failed attack swam ashore on Hierro Island. As stated earlier, four men had jumped off the deck at that dramatic moment on 17 January when the dud torpedo struck. Two of them swam to shore and were stranded when *U-156* was forced to run for open water.

On 24 January, the Madrid naval attaché sent a message to Nauen which informed them the *Erri Berro* had been captured, and that the German consul at Tenerife was made aware that two seamen from the *U-156* had been discovered on Hierro.[18] The message went on to state the German agent on board the *Berro* was completely trustworthy and that the communications on land were completely secure. Also, that the rendezvous instructions were to be thrown overboard if the ship was in danger. Once again the Germans missed the point, and the very method they were using to discuss the potential leak was actually the leak itself.

The whole exchange was decoded and read by the British who continued to study with interest as Tenerife informed Nauen and Madrid of further developments. On 31 January, Madrid informed Nauen that the two *U-156* sailors were interned at Tenerife, and had jumped overboard after the *E48*'s attack. The stranded sailors told the German consul they had remained in the area of Naos Bay until 21 January when hunger forced them to seek an inhabited area. Madrid added that a torpedo had been found on the beach, which was likely one of those fired from the *E48*. The Germans suspected treachery but were still clueless about their massive communications breach.[19]

On 23 January, Gansser stopped the Spanish steamer *Urkiola Mendi* that was traveling from Bahia Blanca to Cette in France with barley for the Swiss government. Her papers were in order and the ship was released.

On 25 January, a Norwegian steamer was stopped without cargo on a voyage from Spain to South America where it was to await further orders from Montevideo. Gansser let the ship go since no contraband was found. After this last disappointing stop, Gansser decided to begin the slow return north toward home due to concerns about his fuel.

On 27 January, Gansser mentioned he made a patriotic speech on the occasion of the Kaiser's birthday to the crew. Neither he nor the crew could possibly imagine this would be the last birthday the Kaiser celebrated as the reigning German Emperor.

On 8 February the Germans had a very busy day west of Gibraltar starting with their capture of the English tanker *Artesia* of 2,762 tons traveling in ballast from Marseilles, France to New York. They also captured the Greek steamer *Chariton* of 3,023 tons in ballast from Athens to Philadelphia. The third ship captured on the same day was the Italian sailing vessel *Nuzza* of 1,102 tons on a voyage from Porto Ferraio in Italy to Pensacola, Florida. All three ships were blown up by boarding parties on the 8th and 9th. The *U-156* took a 3-inch defensive gun from the *Artesia* on board the submarine as a prize before sinking the ship.[20]

On 9 February the *U-156* attacked two steamers traveling close to each other heading west in the same area as the prior captures to the west of Gibraltar. The travelers were identified as the English steamer *Pensilva* of 4,316 tons and the Italian *Atlantide* of 5,431 tons. The *Atlantide* engaged in a short firefight with the Germans before she raised the white flag and surrendered. At the same time the *Pensilva* let loose with a smokescreen, put on steam, and ran as fast as she could to freedom. The *Atlantide* was found to be in ballast from Genoa, Italy to New Orleans and was destroyed by explosives placed on board. The *U-156* also took her defensive 3-inch artillery piece as a prize.

On 10 February Gansser spotted a juicy target consisting of four steamers headed west off Gibraltar. The convoy spotted Gansser before he could get in effective gun range and escaped through speed and a change of direction to the south. Gansser was tenacious and followed the small convoy for days trying to get off a torpedo shot or artillery round. Each time he was frustrated by the ships' high speed in relation to his tortuously slow U-boat. The ships also used other measures to thwart the U-Kreuzer and laid down smokescreens, fired off a few shots from their defensive guns, and eventually forced the *U-156* to give up the chase. This scenario had happened several times already, and could be blamed on the slow speed of the U-Kreuzers in relation to their prey. Gansser had lost chances to sink the English steamer *Cranley* of 4,544 tons, the English *Pensilva*, the *Farnworth* of 5,964 tons, *Ariadne* of 2,000 tons, and two ships by the names of *Mirita* and *Tibet* in fruitless chases.

Finally on 16 February Gansser headed home for good. By 4 March he was rounding the Shetlands and seven days later he was back in Kiel. The cruise had lasted 117 days and the *U-156* had a respectable score of 21,484 tons of enemy shipping sent to the bottom. As Gansser pulled into port he could at least be satisfied with the two 3-inch guns he had captured from the armed merchant ships he had sunk. It was not enough to justify the Canary U-boat campaign but Gansser had done something of note after his near death experience in Naos Bay.

8. The Trade War and the Secret War

However, back in Germany, Gansser was relieved of his command of the *U-156*. The code breakers of Room 40 could look with pride on a job well done, and the Germans could only scratch their heads and wonder what went wrong. A German staff report compiled after the fact blamed Gansser for the ambush in Naos Bay, and cited that his escape was completely due to luck, and postulated his misfortune could have been caused by his "strong aversion to cruising submerged."[21]

They also thought the British had possibly sent the E class submarines to the area after Gansser's high profile attack on Funchal. The head of U-Kreuzer command, Fregattenkapitän Koch, even scolded Gansser for attacking Funchal when there were no ships at anchor. This was despite the fact that German naval leadership clearly knew and approved of the Funchal attack based on radio transmissions received by *U-156* just before and after the bombardment. Gansser was also criticized for his decision not to use a prize steamer to attack shipping. Koch thought this would have increased his success against Allied traffic despite the failure of this same tactic when utilized by Valentiner only a short time before.[22] In opposition to this criticism, Gansser was also touted by his superiors for his past successes despite the somewhat disappointing cruise in the *U-156*.[23]

The German naval brass did not come to the same correct conclusion as Valentiner and Gansser had. They ignored the obvious signs that the German codes were broken, and ignored the fact that their U-Kreuzer captains had done nothing wrong. In fact, they had actually given the Germans a chance to correct the flaws in their code system. In the event, the leadership did nothing, and the Germans continued to operate with radio messages that could be read at will.

The German naval command had made an unforgiveable error, and put more of their loyal men in peril. Gansser was apparently forgiven for his alleged mistakes and promoted to Korvettenkapitän in 1919 after he had served in the "U-boot Inspection" and as liaison officer to the U-boat flotilla in Pola[24] in 1918. He retired from the navy in 1919, and died in 1937.

9

U-Kreuzerkrieg

During, before, and after Gansser's brush with death, the other ex-merchant U-Kreuzers and their new warship U-Kreuzer cousins attempted to add to his and Valentiner's modest tonnage scores off the Azores and Canary Islands as well as the busy shipping lanes west of Gibraltar. They had some successes in the midst of great hardships.

The SM *U-151* was one of these attackers, and under Korvettenkapitän Waldemar Kophamel left for the balmy waters of the Azores from Germany on 4 September 1917.

Northeast of Madeira the *U-151* sank two steamers and one sailing vessel. On 18 October, Nauen informed the *U-151* that heavy steamer traffic had been reported between the coaling station of Dakar and Gibraltar. She worked jointly with a 2,868-ton Norwegian prize she captured named the SS *Bygdones*. Nauen reported *U-151* was working with this prize ship near the Canary Islands on 24 October 1917.

Earlier, on 12 October the *U-151* was rammed and slightly damaged by HMS *Parthian*, a British destroyer. *U-151* then sank two Brazilian steamers named *Acary* and *Guahyba* in São Vicente Harbor in the Cape Verde Islands on 2 November. Both ships were carrying non-contraband cargoes of hides and coffee.[1] The *Acary* was torpedoed and beached, but was still a total loss.[2]

The *U-151* was depth charged by the British armed merchant cruiser HMS *Marmora* west of Madeira on 14 November.[3] On 22 November she captured the Norwegian SS *Johan Mjelde* close to the Azores, and on 23 and 24 November unloaded 22 tons of copper from her with forced help from another captured ship's crew.[4] On 26 November the ship was scuttled with explosives.[5]

On 9 December 1917, Nauen radioed the *U-156* and told her to make contact with *U-151* for an unknown reason. On 11 December *U-151* reported to Nauen about the repairs that would need to be made to the

U-boat on arrival in Germany, which included a deck gun damaged by shellfire, and water cooling pumps and air cooling pumps which were apparently underpowered. *U-151* ended the cruise after sinking three more steamers and one sailing vessel.

She made her way back to Germany on Christmas Eve 1917 after sinking 36,785 tons of Allied shipping and 5,909 tons of neutral shipping for a grand total of 42,694 gross registered tons spread out over nine steamships and four sailing ships. After *U-151*'s arrival home she apparently made a report on shipping in the area, which was relayed by Nauen to the *U-156* and *U-157* to advise them of where the *U-151* had seen the most traffic along the West African coast.[6]

The *U-152* was under the command of Kapitänleutnant Constantin Kolbe for her first cruise. Kolbe was a veteran U-boat commander. The *U-152* left Kiel right before Christmas, on 23 December 1917, a cruel departure time for the holiday loving Germans. On 16 January 1918 the *U-152* reported to Nauen that she had observed a convoy rendezvous in the early morning hours. However, she stated she could not use any of her weaponry due to bad storms in the area, which included heavy snow.[7] The *U-152*'s luck would change after this first disappointment.

On 25 January 1918 the *U-152* found herself near the Portuguese coast. She stopped the Spanish steamer *Giralda* of 2,194 tons and sank her after declaring her cargo contraband headed to an enemy port. The next day two small Portuguese steamers, the *Germana* of 236 tons and *Serra do Gerez* of 257 tons, were sunk. On 27 January the 183-ton American sailing ship *Julia Frances* was sunk with gunfire from the 5.9-inch deck guns. On 28 January the *U-152* sank the tiny 321-ton Portuguese steamer *Neptuno*.

The next month on 5 February, the *U-152* was hunting northwest of the Canary Islands when she spotted and sunk the Spanish steamer *Sebastina* of 2,563 tons with a torpedo after she was stopped. The *Sebastina* was carrying salt from Spain to New York. South of the Canary Islands on 8 February the Spanish steamer *Seserino* of 3,647 tons was found to be under charter to the British and Americans. She was sunk the next day.

On 15 February the Spanish steamer *Neguri* of 1,859 tons was stopped with contraband from New York to Marseille and sunk. One day later the *U-152* was northwest of the Canary Islands and stopped and sunk the Spanish steamer *Mar Caspio* of 2,723 tons with cannon fire. The *Mar Caspio* was heading from Marseille through Gibraltar to New York. On 16 February the *U-152* received a transmission from the German Admiralty Staff to carry out a "blockade" in the waters off West Africa. The above order was given despite the small number of boats operating off West Africa and Spain in the Canaries and Azores Islands.

Nonetheless the *U-152* did her best to carry out the lofty orders and sunk the Italian steamer *Gaetana Costanzo* of 1,005 tons with a cargo from Nigeria to Genoa off West Africa on 24 February. The next day the Norwegian steamer *Giliestad* of 4,298 tons under an English charter was in ballast from Genoa through Gibraltar to Montevideo when the *U-152* encountered her. She was sunk.

On 6 March off the coast of Spanish West Africa a 134-ton Portuguese sailing ship named the *Elector* was stopped and sunk. On 7 March the *U-152* encountered a challenge she had to chase, bombard, and finally sink. The Italian steamer *Luigi* of 3,549 tons went down due to an accurate artillery bombardment. On 8 March a short skirmish occurred with a French commercial vessel armed with defensive artillery. The *U-152* ended up breaking off the engagement and the steamer escaped.

On 12 March the *U-152* met with the *U-157* by prior arrangement via radio and exchanged experiences. The next day the *U-152* stopped the American sailing ship *UG Myrland* of 130 tons traveling from Cape Verde to the Canary Islands. The *Myrland* was sunk. On 16 March the U-152 was once again northwest of the Canary Islands when she met and engaged in an artillery duel with the English steamer *Claston* of 3,192 tons, which was in the service of the British Admiralty. The *Claston* was carrying about 4,000 tons of coal from Cardiff to Sierra Leone and Cuba. She was sunk with a torpedo. The captain of the *Claston* was captured and taken on board while the 3-inch gun from the ship was confiscated.

On 18 March a convoy headed north was spotted but could not be caught due to the slow speed of the *U-152*. On 24 March the *U-152* started to head home. On 31 March she came upon the Danish steamer *Indien* of 4,199 tons. The *Indien* was traveling in ballast from St. Nazaire to Hampton Roads, Virginia. Kolbe decided she was in the service of the French, British, and Americans, and so she was sunk. On 3 April near Cape Finisterre the English sailing ship *Elsie Birdett* of 90 tons was stopped.[8] She was headed from Porto to Newfoundland, Canada, and was sunk.[9] The *U-152* had sent 13 steamers and 4 sailing ships to the bottom on this cruise for a total of 30,580 gross registered tons of shipping.[10]

U-153's cruise to the Azores under Korvettenkapitän Gernot Goetting from February to June 1918 was hampered by a lack of successful attacks on shipping right from the start. On 1 March on the way to her area of operations Goetting spotted a 20,000-ton and a 5,000-ton steamer but could not successfully attack. On 2 March the *U-153* attacked the English

9. U-Kreuzerkrieg 73

steamer *Petroleine* of 4,217 tons. The *Petroleine* fired back with a defensive gun and was able to get away. Later the *U-153* spotted a few steamers in a fast convoy. *U-153* could not catch up due to her own slow speed.

On 5 March the *U-154* contacted *U-153* with orders to link up and work together near the Portuguese coast. On 8 March the *U-153* spotted another convoy of nine steamers but it slipped away. West of Madeira the Italian sailing vessel *Alessandra* of 2,394 tons in ballast from Gibraltar to New York was sunk by the *U-153*'s artillery fire.

On 6 April, south of Dakar, the *U-153* had an artillery fight with the English steamer *Headcliffe* of 2,654 tons. In a depressingly familiar scenario for the crew of the *U-153* the ship got away. On 9 April the *U-153* laid six mines off Dakar.

On 14 April the *U-153* was finally able to fire a torpedo and engaged in an artillery attack on the British steamer *Santa Isabel* of 2,023 tons with a cargo of coal headed from Cardiff to Dakar. The torpedo missed and then *U-153* engaged the armed steamer in a short surface fight before patrol ships arrived on the scene. The *Santa Isabel* later succumbed to her wounds and sank.

On 20 April the *U-153* started to work in tandem with *U-154* after radio contact. On 25 April they both engaged and sank the British *Bombala* of 3,314 tons, which they mistakenly believed to be a Q ship. Q ships were Allied warships disguised as merchant vessels to lure submarines into a false sense of security before they attacked with their hidden guns. The vessel was sunk by torpedo after a long and lopsided artillery duel. She was carrying coal and another cargo from Gibraltar to Sierra Leone.

On 8 May a message was received from the naval high command via Nauen that ordered *U-153* and *U-154* to meet with *U-62*. On 9 May the Italian steamer *Enrichetta* of 5,011 tons was sunk by torpedo and artillery. On 11 May the *U-153* witnessed the *U-154* explode after the torpedoes of a British submarine hit her at the meeting place set up by radio with *U-62*. On 13 May the *U-153* started to head home and by 3 June had returned to Kiel. Goetting had sunk a disappointing four ships for a total of 12,742 tons.[11]

In spite of the disastrous meeting set up by radio with *U-62*, *U-154*, and *U-153*, Nauen was still very busy contacting the unlucky *U-153*. In April Nauen contacted the U-boat to let Goetting know about an alleged Brazilian troop transport, an important convoy traveling from Dakar to Marseille, and another large convoy carrying wheat to Great Britain. Nauen also knew that American torpedo boats and a gunboat had arrived at Dakar, and that a minefield was close to U-153's route home based on reports from a Swedish fisherman.[12] None of this did *U-153* any good and Goetting was not able to attack any convoys during his lengthy time on station.[13]

In March 1918 the British would have another chance to prove the effectiveness of Room 40. Kapitänleutnant Hermann Gercke was the commander of the U-Kreuzer *U-154*. Gercke was new to the command of a U-boat, but he was also aggressive and daring as later events would prove.

Gercke's mission involved operations off the coast of Morocco, and he appears to have been very active in seeking out his merchant ship prey.[14]

On 20 March 1918 *U-154* sent an urgent message reporting she had sunk 10,000 tons so far and had stopped the Spanish passenger steamer *Montevideo* and sent her back to Cadiz, Spain as she was carrying contraband. An unusual gesture of mercy likely created by the fact that the vessel was neutral, Spanish, and carrying civilian passengers. Gercke also reported he had on board about 27 tons of rubber and five tons of wax he had apparently taken from a ship he had sunk.[15]

Gercke laid six mines off of Freetown on 7 April, and attempted to cut cables in tandem with *U-153*, but all they achieved was the loss of their cable cutting apparatus. The minefield later claimed a Japanese steamer of over 5,000 tons.[16] Gercke then headed south toward the small African nation of Liberia, which had been a great friend of Germany's before the war.[17] However, due to increased Allied pressure, the government of Liberia had declared war on Germany in August 1917. The capital of Liberia, Monrovia, was situated on the sea, and was dangerously exposed to a potential German attack. Monrovia was about to get a taste of German wartime diplomacy, and *U-154* was to be the first and last U-boat to intimidate the government of an entire Allied nation directly.[18]

U-154 cruised into view off Monrovia on the night of 9 April. She sunk the token vessel owned by the Liberian government, and then Gercke sent his ship's boat into the Liberian capital to deliver his ultimatum. Gercke informed the President of Liberia that Monrovia was "helpless under German guns," all cable stations must immediately cease transmissions, and if they wished to avoid the Germans shelling the cable stations they should come over in a boat under a flag of truce to tell Gercke the stations would be shut down.

The Liberian President eventually decided to shut down the stations and informed Gercke of his decision. However, Gercke must not have believed him since his reply indicated he would destroy the cable station by an artillery bombardment. Gercke bombarded Monrovia for one hour and reportedly killed three children and wounded three adults.[19] He apparently believed he had destroyed the station.

However, both of the cable stations in town were back in operation within two months, if not sooner. He ceased his attack when a steamer appeared on the horizon and he gave chase out to sea. Gercke failed to permanently damage the cable stations, but he had brutally humbled a whole country with one U-boat. This singular event would be the zenith of his modest successes. The steamer he chased was able to get away despite having taken severe damage from a vigorous bombardment by Gercke.

As stated in the account of the *U-153*, on 25 April, *U-153* and *U-154* hunted together and jointly destroyed an armed Allied freighter named *Bombala* after a long fight. Three German sailors died and five were wounded when a mistake was made in loading one of the artillery pieces on *U-154* and it exploded on deck. On 5 May 1918 the Spanish steamer *Achmi* landed two of the wounded crew from the *U-154* at Las Palmas in the Canary Islands so they could be treated for wounds at the military hospital there. They were luckier than they knew.[20] In May 1918, Nauen informed Gercke he had been promoted to Korvettenkapitän. Later, Nauen arranged for *U-153* to meet with the incoming *U-62*. All three submarines would rendezvous west of Cape St. Vincent.[21]

The commander of *U-153* made the British party to the meeting when he signaled the exact coordinates for the exchange of supplies to the *U-62*. British submarine E35 was told to patrol in the area of the meet on 11 May, and spotted *U-154*. She fired one torpedo at the U-Kreuzer and missed, the shot going under the big U-boat. Gercke must have heard the miss since he started to move. At this point E35 lined up perfectly for a twin shot and fired two torpedoes. Both warheads sailed directly for the guns on either side of the *U-154*'s conning tower and exploded. The effect was absolute devastation. *U-154* evaporated in the smoke and fire, and her wrecked hull slipped beneath the waves immediately.

U-62 and *U-153* had witnessed the hit from a few miles away and stumbled upon E35 trying to rescue three German survivors of *U-154*'s sinking. E35 and the other two German boats got away unmolested. The captain of *U-62*, much like Valentiner and Gansser before him, thought that the German codes were broken. The German naval command was not convinced, and tried to study the methods utilized by British submarines that attacked German U-boats during the war so far. The Liberians and British were able to have the last laugh at the expense of the Germans.

In June 1918, a British admiral suggested the government of Liberia should be given the news that *U-154* had met her end so they could rest easy that the Allies were at work to protect their tiny ally.[22] Gercke and his crew had sunk five ships for a total of 8,132 tons sent to the bottom while they damaged four more ships for a total of 18,220 tons sent to the repair dock.[23]

The cruise of the *U-155*, the former *Deutschland*, is very instructive as it illustrates what can be accomplished by an aggressive commander on the first test of a U-Kreuzer on patrol. Despite extensive technical problems her commander succeeded where others would fail. Kapitänleutnant Karl Meusel was chosen to command *U-155* even though he had never led a U-boat before. His mission was to test the long-range U-Kreuzer concept and determine if the ex-merchant boats were up to the challenge.

Meusel complained of the many technical failures of the ex-merchant U-Kreuzers and was a competent commander despite his inexperience in submarines. He was thirty-six when he took over *U-155* as a Kapitänleutnant. On the second day of the first cruise Meusel experienced the first of many technical problems. The motor for the main compressor blew out on 24 May 1917. The compressor was a needed component as it supplied the compressed air to blow the tanks in order to surface the U-boat. The repairs took over a full day and overheated the engine when the auxiliary compressors started to run to compensate for the broken main compressor.

The bad luck would continue. On 26 May, south of Norway, the *U-155* spotted a steamer, ran at full speed and then one of the two diesel engines quit due to a design flaw caused by the overly quick conversion of the U-boat from an underwater merchant vessel to a warship. Meusel did not turn back but marched on with one engine while the engine crew worked constantly to repair the damage to the second engine.

Meusel had to stop for three hours each day on the surface in order to recharge his electric batteries due to the limited engine power he had. This slowed his progress temporarily. On 27 May, SM *U-19* spotted the *U-155* on the surface off Norway and almost made a submerged torpedo attack on her until her commander, Johannes Spiess, consulted with his officers and they deduced they were looking at a large German submarine. *U-19* surfaced close to the *U-155* to the surprise of the U-Kreuzer crew, and both commanders exchanged information. Spiess informed Meusel of the new Allied convoy system, which was just then taking effect although it was not fully implemented yet.

On 28 May, the *U-155* was still heading north on one engine to go around the Faroe Islands to avoid British patrols when she was spotted by a British destroyer and two depth charges were dropped on her. The crew was scared during the attack as this was their first encounter with the relatively new Allied weapon. Luckily for them the ship only carried four charges and the other two were dropped far away from *U-155*. Even though the *U-155* was a severely damaged ship during this time, Meusel stopped three Dutch steamers and an American ship named the SS *Texel*. He released all of them after an inspection. Releasing the Dutch steamers is understandable due to their neutrality, but the release of the *Texel* is a head scratcher since she was a Dutch ship seized by the Americans for war service against the Germans. Nonetheless, the ships were allowed to go on their way.

On 30 May the second engine was fixed and *U-155* resumed her normal surface cruising speed of 8 or 9 knots. On 2 June, Meusel stopped the SS *Hafursfjord* and sank the 1,699 ton steamer carrying salt from Spain to Norway with charges and his deck guns. The ship was involved in completely neutral shipping from one neutral nation to another so it is hard to understand why Meusel sank the vessel. The crews were placed at the mercy of the North Atlantic for absolutely no legitimate reason, but were luckily picked up a short time later.

After the puzzling sinking, Meusel discovered that the shoddy work of the German shipyards in Kiel, combined with the rough seas he had encountered, had caused his externally welded torpedo tubes to become partially detached so that they were now moving with the current. It was a ridiculous situation which proved the U-boat's design was clearly inferior. No other U-Kreuzers would be fitted with external torpedo tubes after the horrible failures of the design on this cruise.

On 10 June, a few hundred miles west of the Bay of Biscay, Meusel attacked the Canadian oil tanker SS *Scottish Hero* carrying oil from Canada to Australia. The ship had a defensive gun which she fired at the *U-155* and then ran from the U-boat at 12 knots. After a short fight the *U-155* scored a hit on the *Scottish Hero*'s engine and the crew abandoned ship. The *U-155* had finally sunk her first enemy vessel.

Over the next few days of June, Meusel would chase multiple ships only to have them outrun him and get away. On 14 June, Meusel attacked the SS *Aysgarth*, which was carrying iron ore from Spain to Great Britain. The *Aysgarth* was armed with two defensive artillery pieces which she used to fight the *U-155* for about an hour. The *U-155* had about 15 hits on the merchant ship, while the *Aysgarth* hit an oil tank on the *U-155*. The hit severely crippled the U-boat and Meusel had to run slow while the oil was transferred to other tanks. The 3,118-ton *Aysgarth* was sunk with charges after she stopped.

A short time later, the *U-155* captured the 4,612-ton Norwegian SS *Benguela* in ballast from Great Britain to New York. Meusel decided to take the vessel as a prize, which was manned by his 20 man prize crew with a Leutnant zur See in command. Meusel and his prize crew used the ship to hold prisoners, house the prize crew, hold stores needed for the U-boat, and even to tow the wounded U-boat to conserve fuel. The *Benguela* was also outfitted with a radio so she could keep in contact with the *U-155*.

On 17 June, the *U-155* left the *Benguela* to hunt for shipping. By 25 June, all of the major repairs needed to make the *U-155* fully operational again were finished and Meusel found a target to attack as well. The *U-155* dived and then surfaced broadside of a ship to attack with both deck guns. The ship's captain was brave and turned toward the U-boat instead of away as it fired a defensive gun. The *U-155* made three direct hits but the ship had one more surprise, a second defensive gun of a larger caliber than the first (5 inches). The gun fired a few shots and opened a hole in another fuel tank, which quickly emptied into the ocean. The steamer ran, put on a smokescreen, and fired her guns. Meusel chased her for three hours, fired one hundred rounds without a hit, and then decided to end the chase. He returned to the *Benguela* defeated.

The *U-155*, as with the other ex-merchant U-Kreuzers, had a very low top speed and rarely achieved the 12 knots she was rated for during her trials. Mostly it was 8 or 9 knots. The bulkheads put in place to strengthen the gun decks slowed the U-boat considerably. The engines were also too low powered to be effective for such a large boat.[24]

By 29 June, the *U-155* was just north of the Azores and stopped and sunk the 1,938-ton iron hulled sailing ship *Siraa* on a trip from Buenos Aires to France with a cargo of materials bound to be used in the leather industry. The *U-155* then stopped the 2,701-ton Spanish SS *Joaquin Mumbru* bound for New York with a varied cargo. The *U-155* disgorged her prisoners on to the ship and sent the neutral steamer on her way. Of course the *Mumbru* wouldn't last long as the *U-156* under Gansser would sink the unlucky ship within six months. On 30 June, Meusel sunk the *Benguela* as she had outlived her usefulness to the *U-155*.

On 4 July 1917, Meusel attacked the harbor at Ponta Delgada on Portuguese São Miguel in the Azores. He wanted to sink any ships he found in harbor but discovered the attack route for his torpedoes blocked by a large stone mole which shielded the ships within. He shelled the harbor for a short period of time instead but did little damage as the Portuguese Fort São Brás started to fire back and forced the *U-155* to retreat. Meusel tried to approach again but lost control of the boat while submerged and the *U-155* unintentionally surfaced before it was time. Meusel gave up his bombardment plan and headed out to hunt more shipping.

After this Meusel chased and lost two more ships due to his slow speed. Finally on 8 July he torpedoed and sank the 3,583-ton British SS *Ruelle* which was working for the French government to bring coal from Great Britain to Algiers. On 12 July the *U-155* torpedoed and sank the 2,883-ton British SS *Calliope* carrying ore from Spain to Montreal. Meusel's torpedo split her in two and she sank in five minutes with the loss of all 27 crew. Meusel had attempted to look for survivors in the floating wreckage but found none.

In the next few days the *U-155* sank a Greek freighter, a Norwegian steamer, and then fired a torpedo at an armed merchantman which missed. The *U-155* surfaced but broke off the attack since she now faced a foe ready for a fight. The U-Kreuzer's guns were supposed to be too big for any merchant vessel's armament, but *U-155* was already a greatly weakened vessel due to her multiple technical problems and Meusel probably made the right decision when he exited the engagement.

On 20 July the *U-155* sank a Norwegian steamer, the next day an American cargo schooner, a Canadian cargo schooner, and an Italian sailing vessel carrying wheat to Gibraltar. *U-155* continued to have technical problems but Meusel's dogged determination ensured ships would still be sunk.

On 31 July, Meusel fired a warning shot at the French steel hulled sailing vessel *Madeleine* when he was met with the retort of the ship's two 3.5-inch defensive guns. The French vessel had left Bordeaux and was heading to Sydney in ballast. The *U-155* had a surprisingly long fight with the ship for about 90 minutes before one of the *U-155*'s shells hit the French ammunition storage area which exploded and the ship caught fire. Only two lifeboats got away and 11 of the French crew died during the fighting.

Shortly thereafter, the *U-155* attacked and sank three more vessels, but not before capturing and taking on board five of their defensive artillery pieces. On 7 August, Meusel used his last good torpedo, one was defective due to saltwater damage in the external torpedo tube, and sunk the British SS *Iran* heading from Calcutta to London with 10,000 tons of sugar, tea, rice, and corn. Meusel then sank one more tiny American vessel. He ended his cruise with a score of 21 ships sunk and 52,370 gross registered tons sent to the bottom.

Despite the technical flaws of his weapons and U-boat, and the *U-155*'s slow speed, Meusel had achieved a respectable score for the first U-Kreuzer test run. One can imagine he would have had an outstanding score had his boat worked as it was supposed to. The faulty external torpedo tubes were moved inside the pressure hull by the engineers back in Kiel and no U-Kreuzer would ever operate with the *U-155*'s original set up again.[25]

U-155's second cruise was guided by another U-boat newcomer, thirty-eight-year old Korvettenkapitän Erich Eckelmann was chosen to command the new and improved *U-155*. She now had internal torpedo tubes and better designed 5.9-inch artillery guns on her deck. The smaller *U-Deutschland* boat propellers were also placed back on the boat as the larger ones installed for the first cruise were less fuel efficient, and did not add any speed to the U-boat. The *U-155* also received one of the new cable cutters. The cutter was meant to be operated from inside although some U-Kreuzers controlled the cutter from the deck.

On 14 January 1918, the *U-155* again went north around Scotland and down towards the Azores. Eckelmann and his crew hit a storm just as they came out into the North Sea and endured the horrible weather for 18 days straight. The *U-155* experienced some of the same problems that daunted Meusel, which included engine failures, unreliable torpedoes, and the slow speed of the underpowered U-Kreuzer.

Eckelmann's first kill was the 5,395-ton Italian steamer SS *Tea* which he hit with a submerged torpedo attack. The ship was carrying grain and flour from Maine to Gibraltar, and did not immediately sink due to the torpedo explosion. Eckelmann finished her off with a boarding party and charges. On 13 February 1918 the *U-155* reported to Nauen that she had cut cables from Lisbon to Gibraltar and Madeira. She elaborated that both of her cable cutters had broken during the operation.[26] On 18 February the *U-155* attacked and sunk the paltry 105-ton British sailing vessel *Cecil L. Shave* with gunfire. No members of the twelve-man crew survived.

On 23 February he sank a neutral Spanish steamer heading with a cargo meant for the neutral Swiss government. Eckelmann clearly should have let the ship go due to its purely neutral cargo, but he sunk her with charges after the crew abandoned ship. Shortly after this, Eckelmann released two Spanish steamers, one of which clearly contained goods meant for wartime France. Eckelmann and his crew threw the cargo overboard but did not sink the Spanish ship. On 2 March Nauen sent a message to *U-155* based on a "Spanish report from Casablanca," which stated little traffic was piloted near the French African harbor, defensive mines had been placed, and a French battleship and destroyer are moving between Casablanca, Mogador, and Mozagan.[27]

On 10 March, after sinking another Italian steamer a few days earlier, the *U-155* captured the 4,271-ton Norwegian steamer SS *Wegadesk* with a large cargo of brass bound from Baltimore to Gibraltar. Brass was a critical element for Germany's war production, and one she was in short supply of. Like some other ex-merchant U-Kreuzers, the *U-155* was about to utilize her extra storage space to benefit the war industries of the Fatherland. For three days, the *U-155* transferred brass from the doomed Norwegian vessel to her hold. The *U-155* obtained forty tons in this manner before charges were set and the *Wegadesk* was sunk.

The seizure of valuable cargoes for the Fatherland was part of a U-Kreuzer's ancillary mission. Small cargoes of rubber, copper, brass, wax, and leather were obtained for German industry in this way by several U-Kreuzers. The seizures were a way to beat the blockade, sink enemy shipping, and deprive the Allies of their own supplies all at the same time.

A few days later the *U-155* attacked the Italian tanker *Prometeo* carrying a cargo of flammable naphtha. The Italians fired a 3.5-inch gun at *U-155* until the U-boat made a hit on their volatile cargo and the ship became engulfed in flames. Eckelmann showed the wounded crew members mercy and took ten of them on board. The rest of the uninjured crew was left in their lifeboats.

The *U-155* returned to Kiel on 4 May and claimed the destruction of sixteen ships for a total of 50,522 gross registered tons.[28] The convoy system had been introduced by the time of Eckelmann's patrol, which had severely reduced the number of large steamers traveling alone in the area as they were during Meusel's cruise. Despite convoy, Eckelmann's foray resulted in very respectable results for the *U-155*.[29]

The *U-157*, under Valentiner, left Kiel on 1 December 1917. The U-boat started her cruise out with a small success in the form of the Portuguese sailing ship *Lidia* of 302 tons bound from New Orleans to Oporto. On 1 January she stopped the French steamer *Oued Gebou* of 1,540 tons carrying 133 Senegalese soldiers from Marseille to Dakar. Valentiner confiscated a 3-inch gun from the prize.

Next on the list was the Danish steamer *Hulda Maerst* of 1,566 tons on her way from Senegal to Marseille on 10 January. On 11 January the *U-157* captured and turned the Norwegian steamer *Norefos* of 1,788 tons into a prize vessel. The *Norefos* was on a trip from Dakar to Marseilles. The *U-157* took 27 tons of rubber from *Norefos* for German war industry use.

On 17 February the Portuguese sailing vessel *Estrella da Bissae* of 129 tons was sunk. On 20 February the 2,240-ton Greek steamer *Kithira* was fired at and stopped. The *Kithira* was carrying a cargo of copra and cotton from West Africa to Marseille. Valentiner sank her and took the ship's 3.5-inch gun as a prize. On 1 March the prize vessel *Norefos* was finally sunk. On 14 March, the *U-157* stopped the Spanish steamer *Urpillao* of 2,768 tons in ballast from Barcelona to Tenerife. She was sent to the bottom by a torpedo on 15 March.

On 19 March the Spanish steamer *Montevideo* was stopped with contraband from Cadiz to New York. 60 female passengers on board saved the ship from destruction. Valentiner decided to show mercy to the neutral ship. The ship's master also agreed to turn back around to Cadiz, and not transport any items to the United States without the express permission of the German Embassy in Spain. Two days later Valentiner was west of Gibraltar in a gunfight with a 6,400 ton American steamer. Three of his

A view of *U-157*'s conning tower from the stern of the U-Kreuzer. Notice the mix of uniforms worn on this cruise to the Canaries. One officer, identified as Kapitänleutnant Max Valentiner, has a pith helmet with a white or tan tropical uniform, while another officer sitting to the right wears the standard uniform common in the colder climates of the North Atlantic (*Lowell Thomas Papers, James A. Cannavino Library, Archives & Special Collections, Marist College, USA*).

men died during the battle and the ship got away. The *U-157* returned to Kiel with a disappointing total of 10,333 gross registered tons sunk spread out among five steamships and two sailing vessels.³⁰

The *U-157*'s next commander had even less luck than Valentiner. Korvettenkapitän Ortwin Rave was in charge of the *U-157* from 21 July 1918 to the end of the war. The *U-157* sunk a pitiful 5,572 tons off the Azores and Canaries spread out over eight ships. The U-Kreuzer then interned herself in Norway on 30 November. Rave had received the 21 October 1918 message that the U-boat war was over and proceeded into internment rather than risk a return to a turbulent Germany.³¹ Rave's cruise was a pathetic end to the war in the Azores and Canaries that claimed the lives of six more Allied and neutral sailors to no effect.

10

The Naval Officer

Münster is a mid-sized German city. According to the town's website it had a population of almost 300,000 persons in 2013. The picturesque downtown has that distinctly old European look, complete with an open market and festivals in the main central area called the Prinzipalmarkt. Münster was home to the noted Anti-Nazi Cardinal and Catholic Saint, Clemens August Graf von Galen, aka "the Lion of Münster," and 19th century German poet Annette von Droste-Hülshoff. It is unlikely anyone now living in the town of Münster knows that Richard Feldt was also born in their beautiful city on 24 September 1882.

In 1899, when Feldt was 16 and 17 years old, the Dortmund-Ems Canal was finally finished, and ships started to ply their trade up and down the new waterway and right through the formerly landlocked Münster. Münster now had direct access to the sea, and became an inland port of under 100,000 people at the time. It is unknown if the building and opening of the canal had any impact on young Feldt's decision to join the Imperial German Navy. Nonetheless, Feldt joined that navy one year after the canal's completion on 7 April 1900 in the same cadet class as Konrad Gansser.

Feldt rose through the ranks slowly, which was normal in peacetime. He became a Leutnant Zur See in 1903, an Oberleutnant in 1905, and a Kapitänleutnant on 21 August 1910. He served on small torpedo boats from 1904 to 1911. His first commands were the torpedo boats S 117 and S 119 from 1909 to 1911. He then graduated to first officer of the small surface cruiser, *SMS Cormoran* in 1912 and 1913.

In the first half of 1914, Feldt found himself on Marine inspection duty. When the war started later that year Feldt was assigned to the cruiser *SMS Graudenz* as the navigation officer from 1914 to April 1916 based out of the principal Baltic German port of Kiel. Feldt likely participated in the *Graudenz*'s actions against Allied naval forces during the raids on Scarborough and Whitby in Britain, the Battle of Dogger Bank, and the Battle of the Gulf of Riga. He was then moved to the navigation officer position on the cruiser SMS *Frankfurt* from April to May 1916 before a quick transfer back to the *Graudenz* from May to July of the same year. Feldt was then moved to the cruiser SMS *Königsberg II* from July 1916 to September 1917 as the ship's navigation officer and first officer. Feldt may have served aboard the *Königsberg II* when she participated in Operation Albion in September 1917, when the German army conducted a successful large-scale amphibious landing to capture Russian held islands in the Gulf of Riga.

However, Feldt apparently wanted more action and the command of his own vessel. The best opportunities for officers with a need to move up to command of their own warship in 1917 and 1918 was the U-boat arm. In addition, Room 40 had intercepted transmissions that indicated the navy specifically wanted reliable surface navy officers to transfer to the U-boat arm.[1]

At the time, the U-boat arm was the only truly offensive wing of the German Navy, and the only real chance a novice commander had of engaging the enemy, and affecting the outcome of the war. This was due to the continued inability of the German surface fleet to break out and engage the British without being destroyed by their superior firepower.

Kapitänleutnant Richard Feldt commanded *U-156* on her cruise to North America. Feldt was a U-boat novice when he took over the unwieldy submarine and her veteran crew, but soon showed a knack for daring exploits despite a tendency to hesitate when important decisions were needed (*author's collection*).

By 1917 and 1918, the U-boat flotilla's training and operations even took precedence over the movements of the once vaunted High Seas Fleet. Feldt had experience with the big guns utilized on Germany's surface cruisers, and had seen combat multiple times. Feldt's experience with a cruiser's guns, and in torpedo firing during his time on a torpedo boat could have recommended him for the command of a U-Kreuzer whose combat performance depended so much on their two massive 5.9-inch cannons, and to a lesser extent on their torpedoes.

Feldt also already held the prestigious Lifesaving Award from his prewar service, and had obtained the coveted Iron Cross First and Second Class after the war had begun. He had no U-boat experience, but that would change. He had the right amount of daring and naval warfare experience for a U-boat captain, but would he be able to perform under pressure, and make the right decisions quickly?[2]

Feldt attended the U-boat school for officers from September 1917 to January 1918. He likely attended class with 15 to 20 other officers, and studied submarine tactics, methods of attack, periscope use, torpedo firing exercises, and depth keeping in Kiel. Great emphasis was placed on torpedo firing since unrestricted submarine warfare had already been declared, and underwater attack was more important than ever due to Allied countermeasures like convoys, armed merchant vessels, and even aircraft.

Feldt may have even had to attack a fake convoy set up by his instructors for practice. The point of the exercise was to attack without being seen by the lookouts on the ships until it was too late. The final trials involved Feldt commanding the training U-boat SM *U-30* for a little while. *U-30* had sunk about 48,000 tons of shipping during its relatively long career from 1914 to 1917. The boat was given to the U-boat school at Kiel for training purposes in November 1917 after it had been deemed obsolete. Feldt is listed in the *U-30*'s logbook for just a few short pages while he commanded her during exercises.[3]

After Feldt successfully completed his training, his former fellow cadet classmate, Gansser, was removed from command of the *U-156* and Feldt soon learned he was Gansser's replacement to lead the boat and the veteran crew. The Germans often mixed new officers in with an experienced U-boat crew so the old hands could advise the new man on the intricacies of U-boat operations not apparent from U-boat school. A prisoner on board the *U-156* for six days would describe Feldt as a thirty something man of 5 ft. 7 in., about 170 pounds with a "fresh" complexion, blue eyes, and of a "very military appearance." Apparently, Feldt knew some English but could not speak it well.

Feldt's new first officer would also have been introduced to him by this point, Thirty-two-year old Kapitänleutnant Arnold Vorkampff-Laue was described as thinner than Feldt, of the same height with a healthy tanned look, and a little mustache. Vorkampff-Laue could apparently speak English well. He also had a family back home, which included a wife and at least one daughter. Vorkampff-Laue was training with Feldt so he could take command of his own U-boat after the cruise. This was common practice in the U-boat arm. In the crew list of the *U-156* Vorkampff-Laue is listed as a "Kmdt. Schüler," which translates roughly as "commander's school" or "commander student." This judgment is bolstered by the fact that the *U-156* had 77 men on board during this cruise while a standard ex-merchant U-Kreuzer crew had 76. This indicates there was one extra person who I believe was Mr. Vorkampff-Laue.

During the mission, Feldt and his officers indulged in the more relaxed military dress code of a U-boat. According to a captive British captain, they wore what was described as American style dungarees with insignia on their navy caps as the only indication of their military rank.

Feldt is also described in another prisoner's report as having worn a white uniform with stripes to indicate rank. Gansser had worn a similar tropical uniform during his cruise in the hotter southern climates, which would have been appropriate off the North American coast in summer as well. The prisoner also said the crew and officers had disagreements, and that Feldt's discipline was lax, but unfortunately he does not elaborate on what that means. Feldt apparently did not mingle with his crew too much, and was only seen with them when he wanted to waste a little time during the quiet moments.

Quiet moments aside, the new commander's target for his first cruise would have made even an experienced U-boat officer wince since Feldt was directed to prepare his boat and crew for attacks off the faraway coast of North America.[4]

Feldt and his sailors loaded their weapons on board in Kiel bound for American and Canadian shores with a veritable arsenal of about 1,500 rounds of 5.9-inch shells, 18 torpedoes, two 2-inch quick firing guns for mounting on a captured prize, likely a few heavy machine guns, a number of hand carried explosive charges for placing aboard captured vessels marked for destruction, a cable cutter, and at least 7 or 8 German naval mines.[5] The U-boat itself was apparently painted grey and black for this cruise, had a short railing around the raised gun decks, and sported a small German battle ensign on a pole near the conning tower.[6] These details were noted by several victims who witnessed the vessel after she stopped their ships.

The *U-156* also still had her tall radio masts for contacting home and other U-boats. In addition, she carried another smaller radio set for installation on captured vessels.[7] The same prisoner who had described Feldt and his officers also gave a rare look into what the crew had for provisions on their mission. He described a happy crew who sometimes disagreed with their officers, but had plenty to eat and drink including tea, coffee, bread, butter, and marmalade in tins. The *U-156* was ready for war and Feldt was likely eager to prove himself as a commander.[8]

11

Targeting North America

The first U-Kreuzer to arrive off the coast of North America was the SM *U-151* in May 1918 a little over a year after the United States had declared war on Germany. Allied naval minds at the time may have asked why the Germans had not attacked sooner since it was clear German submarines could reach the U.S. based on the visits of the *Deutschland* and *U-53*'s short American war patrol. In fact, the Germans had many good reasons to hold off U-Kreuzer operations in U.S. and Canadian waters until the summer of 1918.

First, in 1917, the Germans wanted most of the available boats to operate around Great Britain or in the Mediterranean until the U-Kreuzers played a losing hand in the ill-fated West African campaign in late 1917 and early 1918. Once it became clear that Allied convoys, the increased naval resources from the U.S., and the continued dominance of the Royal Navy had destroyed any chance the primary unrestricted campaign could win the war and starve Great Britain into submission on its' own, the Germans began to look for more fruitful areas of operation.

In 1917 and into early 1918, the German leadership had hoped to keep the U-boat war against American shipping limited to the unrestricted war zone around the British Isles since America was not a traditional enemy of Germany, and the Germans wanted to preserve some semblance of a relationship with the neutral countries, and especially South America for trade purposes after the Germans' expected defeat of Britain and France that year.

The Kaiser did not want to unleash even a limited U-boat war against America outside the main war zone until later in 1918 when the last ditch German offensives on the western front were in motion, and even still he declined to create the conditions necessary for a full blockade of the American coast as proposed by the top brass in the German Navy. Holtzendorff,

This 1918 newspaper cartoon illustrates the awareness the American public had of the U-Kreuzer raids off their coast (*author's collection, Homer Stinson cartoon originally appeared in the* Dayton News *and Volume 8 of* Cartoons *Magazine under the title "Waking Him Up"*).

as we have seen, was the main proponent of strategic unrestricted U-boat warfare, and one of the Kaiser's closest naval advisers. He vehemently opposed a limited war. Holtzendorff was the principal champion of the idea to establish a blockade zone on the east coast of North America.[1] The Kaiser and the German Foreign Office overruled him based on the above concerns and the fact that only a few U-Kreuzers were available. They were hardly enough to institute something so grand as a German "Sperrgebiet" (*blockade zone*).

The U-boat war against the Canadians and Americans would be fought under specific rules unless the attacked vessel was armed then an unannounced torpedo attack would be acceptable. Otherwise the Germans would have to stop, search the cargo of the ship to confirm enemy ownership or the presence of contraband, and only sink it when the crew's basic safety was assured.

The third reason the Reich delayed their battle in North American waters was that German U-boats did not have long on station when traveling the distances needed to the American coast. The *U-53*'s trip in 1916 had illustrated this problem perfectly when Hans Rose had only one day to sink ships before he had to return to Germany.

However, the U-Kreuzers allowed this limitation to become a thing of the past. A U-Kreuzer could stay on station for months, even after the long voyage from Germany as they had done in the Canaries. The final nail in the coffin was the necessity to attempt to draw Allied naval resources away from patrolling and protecting convoys and the main war zone around Britain, and involve those warships in the hunt for the U-Kreuzers off the North American east coast. This would give the U-boats patrolling the more important European waters a break, which could lead to more Allied tonnage sunk. Admiral Sims, in London, had predicted that this would be the Germans next goal in January 1918.[2]

This eventuality depended on the U-Kreuzers wreaking havoc by sinking ships, causing outrage and outcry for naval protection from the Canadian and American public, and handling the costal defenses already in place.[3]

The American and Canadian east coasts are huge and the two navies were operating without the advantage of the technological advancements available in the next war like radar and longer-range planes. The German submarines headed to the well over 2,000 miles of coastline would have to be countered through vigorous sea and air patrols, convoys, minesweepers, harbor defenses, and information from U-boat victims and Room 40.

The sheer size of the area that needed to be patrolled was daunting with the few naval resources on hand. However, the Americans were as ready as they could be given the primacy of the European theater and transatlantic convoys for the allocation of naval assets. The Canadians were worse off since they had less patrol vessels available, with much less firepower and no aerial assets until later in 1918.

Submarine hunting in the First World War was a combination of luck, resources, and timely intelligence, which was a difficult business even in the U-boat crowded waters of the North Sea. The expanse of ocean next to the American coast made the job of finding, let alone destroying a U-boat, seemingly impossible. Although the defenses were stretched thin the United States was prepared for the U-boat threat in a way they would not be at the start of World War II, and the Germans would have to be more cautious than they had been in the comparatively defenseless waters off West Africa.

This time there were organized defenses instead of the odd passing Allied warship, or token Spanish or Portuguese gunboats and forts which had defended the Canaries, Madeira, and the Azores. The American defensive scheme started to gain steam on 29 August 1916 when Congress authorized the President through the powers of the Naval Appropriation Act to build ten battleships, six battle cruisers, 60 destroyers and torpedo boats, and 67 submarines by July 1919. The fleet was built with surface actions in mind even though by the summer of 1916 it was clear an American entry into the war would need a massive antisubmarine force.

The U.S. was thinking beyond the emergency of the moment to a potential need for a large surface navy to challenge that of a victorious Germany, or to rein in the still feared Royal Navy after the war with Germany was over. In short, the U.S. did not want to lose their ambitious international trade program to an even more strident Britain after they slapped the Kaiser's navy down. This plan was put forth despite the fact that hundreds of American lives had been lost in U-boat attacks like that on the *Lusitania*.[4]

The US ship protection committee also studied proposals for protecting ships from U-boats. The committee approved several protective methods then already in use. Arming merchantmen with navy guns and gun crews was the most effective. Smoke screens were also approved although their effectiveness was not certain when used by ships traveling alone. Smokeless coal was also adopted since it made a steamer's position harder to detect from long distance.[5]

Sailing ships were purposely removed from the eastern Atlantic sea lanes since they were easy prey for U-boats. The frail craft were redirected by the US government to South American and North American coastal trade as this was safer for them.[6] The U-Kreuzers would come in contact with many of these easy targets when they ventured to North America.[7]

Admiral Benson, overall commander of the American fleet, decided to detach destroyers and other patrol craft to combat the expected submarine threat in American waters on 4 February 1917. On 6 April 1917, with the declaration of war, some of these assets were sent to the waters around Great Britain to fight the U-boats in the main theater of operations.

Admiral Sims, commander of American naval forces in Europe, started to change minds when he told the brass back home that the Allies were losing the war in the eastern Atlantic, and that if something was not done grave consequences could be expected. He urged more naval assets be sent east. As we have seen, the American coast eventually became a naval backwater after no enemy appeared there for over a year after the U.S. declared war on Germany.[8]

The Americans also had 272 Coast Guard lifesaving stations equipped with rescue boats, and sometimes telephone communications to call for help. The telephone communication network on the coast was organized after Woodrow Wilson ordered it improved in 1916. Once the war broke out the work continued, and soon the coast had a reliable network capable of quick communications from Maine to Florida.[9]

The U.S. Weather Bureau stations and navy wireless radio stations were also hooked in to the same net.[10] Sixty percent of the lifesaving stations in the U.S. were on the east coast and the brave men who manned these stations acted as a surveillance platform to watch out for U-boat victims and the U-boats themselves, in addition to their normal lifesaving duties. The surfmen would patrol the beaches for the enemy, for distressed ships and sailors, and man the watchtower at their station.

The United States Coast Guard had been folded into the navy on the outbreak of war so these lifesavers were also officially a part of America's national security apparatus from April 1917. This had been put forth as a possibility since the Coast Guard's inception in 1915, and plans for the placement of the Coast Guard with the navy were already spelled out.

Small Coast Guard vessels and cutters were outfitted with guns and depth charges throughout the war so they could begin coastal patrols and convoy duty. The Americans also had all major ports fitted with anti-submarine nets with gaps protected by guard ships and harbors protected by naval guns.[11] The coastal guns were not always fully manned since some of the talented gunners were sent to Europe to operate heavy railroad artillery fired at German land positions.[12] In the event, the Germans were not foolish or daring enough to attempt to enter the inner sanctum of an American or Canadian harbor.

The U.S. also set up minesweepers to counteract the expected mining of harbor entrances and approaches by the U-Kreuzers. The little sweepers would see a lot of action in the summer of 1918. The Lighthouse Service was also transferred to the navy at the outbreak of war and brought their 46 lighthouse tender ships, four light vessels, and 21 lighthouses to the war effort. They patrolled harbor entrance areas, laid defensive mines, and acted as coastal surveillance platforms much like the Coast Guard surfmen did.[13]

The Coast Guard was also authorized by the Naval Appropriation Act of 29 August 1916 to construct and maintain air stations to patrol the coasts of the United States. Before any could be built the war began and the navy hurriedly started work on the first of the naval air stations charged with defending the eastern frontier of America.

The Naval Air Stations were equipped with HS-1L and HS-2L flying boat biplanes and Curtiss R-9 seaplane biplanes for patrolling and attack. The planes were usually armed with one Mark IV bomb, which unfortunately had a bad habit of not blowing up during training bomb runs. The planes also had a Lewis machine gun or light artillery called a Davis gun attached later in the war. The stations also sometimes had telephone links with the coast watchers on the shore and utilized patrol blimps and kite balloons to see far out to sea in an attempt to find the elusive Germans off the coast or rescue sailors in trouble.[14]

The first Naval Air Stations were established in Chatham, Massachusetts, Montauk and Rockaway, New York, Cape May, New Jersey, Hampton Roads, Virginia, and Key West, Florida.[15] By the time the U-boats arrived in 1918 all of these stations were operational. In January 1918, the Americans convened a special naval board to decide how the east coast would be defended and how destroyers could be used for that role. The board agreed the transatlantic convoys were first in line for naval resources, then the strategic campaign against the U-boats in European waters, and then the defense of the coast.

The board recommended at least nine destroyers remain on the coast at any one time while they were undergoing their "shakedown after commissioning" for one month before potentially moving on to convoy or European duty. Four were assigned to the Third Naval District in New York, four to the Fifth Naval District at Hampton Roads, and one new destroyer to the First Naval District in Boston. The bulk of the destroyers undergoing their shakedown were of the new type with four 4-inch guns main armament, four smoke funnels, 1,284 tons displacement, and a complement of over 100 sailors and officers. They were extremely fast at 35 knots and some were equipped with depth charges. They were the only vessels assigned to the coast that could challenge a U-Kreuzer and hold their own in the process.

New York and Hampton Roads were also assigned at least five submarines apiece, which would be available while they underwent a two-month shakedown. Submarines were of dubious value in anti-submarine patrols at this time since they could be fired on by friendly vessels and scare shipping away from their patrol areas due to the understandable but mistaken notion by many merchant mariners that all submarines were German.

New York and Hampton Roads, being the designated U.S. convoy departure ports were also given about 30 sub chasers each for convoy and anti-submarine duties. The sub chasers were made of wood, 110 feet long, had a respectable top speed of 16 knots, one 3-inch gun, and depth charges. A sub chaser by itself would be cannon fodder for a U-Kreuzer captain with guts, but it could potentially scare a U-Kreuzer underwater, or attack in a pack and overwhelm a solitary U-boat. However, in practice the sub chasers did not have much success despite great efforts in the First World War. They also had hydrophones, basically underwater microphones, in order to listen for submarine motors underwater. The hydrophones, much like the sub chasers themselves, were not very successful in combat.

The U.S. also kept about a dozen older destroyers and torpedo boats on the coast for anti-submarine patrol in addition to the nine or so new "shakedown" boats. The U.S. drafted many private yachts and boats into government service, outfitted them with weaponry and navy crews, and turned them into auxiliary patrol vessels. The USS *Jouett*,[16] an older destroyer, was the head of a special "naval hunt squadron" which was focused on offensive anti-submarine patrols along with a group of from six to eighteen submarine chasers for backup.[17] All of these forces would face their first real operational test in May 1918.

The *U-151* was equipped with two 5.9-inch deck guns, two 3.5-inch guns, fourteen mines, and a hold full of torpedoes for its America cruise. Prisoners of the submarine during this time state the *U-151* had three gramophones for entertainment purposes too, and the *U-156* may have had a similar setup for those long hours of boredom.[18] *U-151*'s orders included instructions to sink ships, and then move to a completely different area in order to create the illusion of more U-boats on the east coast than there really were. Of course Room 40's information negated all of those efforts, but the Germans could not know their deceptions were not fooling the U.S. Navy.

From April to June Nauen sent the *U-151* a steady stream of messages consisting of tips about her mission to the American coast. On 22 April Nauen sent the *U-151* information that the patrols on the American coast were strong, troop transports left from Newport News on Mondays, and the New York transports left on the same day although New York was said to have departures on other days. According to Nauen, New York outbound transports also had destroyer and cruiser escorts until 80 miles out from the coast when the cruisers took over and handled the convoy until it reached the Azores. On 27 April Nauen clarified that New York convoys are mostly for troops while convoys out to Bermuda and the Azores consist of goods and materials.

On 14 May Nauen informed *U-151* that a barrier patrol existed off all American harbors. However, the Delaware Bay harbor pilots took large ships south of the *Five Fathom Bank Lightship*. Nauen indicated *U-151* should place some of her mines here as there would likely be "success" in this area. On 6 June Nauen recommended an attack on the Halifax shipping route if circumstances allowed for such an operation.[19]

Korvettenkapitän Heinrich von Nostitz und Jänckendorff left Germany on 18 April to attack the as yet untouched American home waters. Sims sent a message to the U.S. government about *U-151*'s likely destination and a summary of her decoded signals so far on 1 May. Sims cabled Washington the next day to drive home the need for secrecy as to the source of the information, but also warned the government of the *U-151*'s potential mining operation. A short time later one of the *U-151*'s torpedoes missed the British steamer *Huntress* by only six feet, and the intended victim called Bermuda to report the submarine. The U.S. Navy department issued an alert based on the *Huntress'* information, which was the perfect gift as it protected the secret of decryption. A story on the *Huntress'* incident ran in the New York Times of 1 June 1918.[20]

On 24 May, Nostitz and his crew laid mines at the mouth of the Chesapeake Bay near the Cape Charles lightship. Under the cover of night, Nostitz and his men began the preparations to push the mines over the side of their ex-merchant boat. The *U-151* was in a very busy shipping lane and astonishingly all of the ships had their lights on as in peacetime. The *U-151* was thus able to avoid any uncomfortable encounters. As the crew got ready to lay the first mine a U.S. cruiser warship came up to the *U-151*'s position and they were forced to dive. However, the ship had not seen them and they continued with their business once it had passed. The *U-151* laid six mines in the small field meant to scare shipping in the area rather than blockade the entrance to one of the biggest avenues for shipping on the North American coast.

The *U-151* then busied herself with damaging and sinking a few small schooners with boarding parties and explosives in the time honored fashion of prize rule warfare. The Germans took many prisoners on board the U-boat during this time as they thought their presence was still a secret although the Americans knew all about them due to continued information dumps from Room 40. However, the American government had decided to try to hide the U-boat's presence from the American people despite the fact that some public confirmation about a U-boat in the area had come from the attack on the *Huntress*.

On the night of 26 May, von Nostitz laid his final eight mines in Delaware Bay and barely avoided the death of his U-boat. The currents underwater tossed the *U-151* around and made her strike the bottom of the ocean. The crew hurriedly surfaced only to dive again when the heavy ship traffic in the area came close to being able to see them. Von Nostitz then traveled out of the area on the surface in the fog while blowing his warning siren to warn away any ships who got close. He must have been mistaken for just another merchant ship by those nearest to him.

During the cruise, Leutnant Robert Kohler of the *U-151* sent two letters to German relatives he had in the United States. He gave the letters to one of the captains of a smaller ship sunk by the German submarine and expected the enemy captain to mail them. Of course they made their way into the hands of Allied intelligence. Kohler wrote that the conditions in Germany were bad but bearable, and hinted that people were having a hard time getting food, especially in the cities. In the second letter he admits he is off the coast sinking ships on a U-boat and hoped to be back in Germany by September. He also bragged about the German offensives that started in March 1918, and talked about the status of some of his relatives in Germany.[21]

Allied or neutral crews temporarily taken onto the *U-151* as prisoners were treated well. They described feeling more like guests than prisoners. The captured usually ate with the crew of the submarine and had tea, bread, stew, potatoes, canned beef, soup, fruits, coffee, marmalade, and corned beef. The food was described as well cooked and somewhat tasty. The officer prisoners ate with the German officers. U-boat officers were supplied with liquors, wines, and fine cigars. German officers on the *U-151* also had plenty of water for bathing and washing while the crew only had a limited supply for such niceties. Prisoners were allowed on deck to exercise and smoke twice a day.[22]

Later, the *U-151* attacked and sunk the SS *Texel*, a merchant ship in the service of the American government carrying a cargo of sugar, which had earlier been spared by the *U-155* under Meusel. However, the boat was also used to carry railroad guns to France, and due to her sinking by artillery and explosives placed on board this vital cargo was delayed for a few weeks. On 29 May the American passenger ship *Carolina* was stopped by von Nostitz with a warning shot across her bow. The ship was carrying 217 passengers and 113 crew on this voyage. The passenger ship was a regular on a route from Puerto Rico to New York City. The radioman on board the *Carolina* had sent a few distress calls but these were stopped when the *U-151* warned her to cease communications and fired another warning shot. The Germans were merciful, allowed the crew and passengers, which also included children, to get to their lifeboats and row towards the not too distant shore. The *U-151* shelled the empty *Carolina* until she sank. The boats of the survivors separated and one group was caught in a storm. Thirteen men, women, and children died when one of the boats was separated completely from the others.

The survivors of the *Carolina* hit shore at different points but some washed up right in Atlantic City, New Jersey as a small parade of Shriners was in the middle of a march on the boardwalk. The beachgoers, Shriners, and lifesavers on the beach rushed into the water to help the survivors and hear their tale of being on the wrong end of a German gun. The Shriners' band also started to play the "Star Spangled Banner" to welcome their unexpected guests. One of the survivors who washed up in Atlantic City that day was Mario Rodriguez who was coming to the continental U.S. from Puerto Rico for a better life. In an ironic twist, his son, U.S. District Judge Joseph Rodriguez, heard a court case for salvage rights related to a sunken ship in 1996 and was shocked to learn the diver who placed the petition before him had found his father's sunken ride to the mainland U.S., the *Carolina*.[23]

On 3 June, the 7,145-ton oil tanker *Herbert L. Pratt* struck one of *U-151*'s mines in Delaware Bay. Although considered lost at first she was salvaged and eventually repaired since the crew had managed to get her into shallow water before she partially sank.[24]

On 8 June, von Nostitz had the second to last significant victory of the cruise when he spotted and stopped the Norwegian *Vindeggan* on a trip from South America to New York with a cargo of copper after a shot across the bow. Copper was a metal needed for German war industry so the Korvettenkapitän decided to transfer some of it to the *U-151* before sinking the neutral ship engaged in trade with the enemy. The ex-merchant U-Kreuzer's large storage spaces were going to come in handy once again. Von Nostitz acquired 77 tons of the vital material for Germany in a daring open ocean transfer of the cargo from the doomed ship to the *U-151*. The *U-151* towed the survivors of this boat and one other towards land until she forced a Danish ship to take them to shore. The Danish ship complied as this duty was better than being sunk.[25]

The last significant vessel sunk by the *U-151* was the 8,173-ton British steamer *Dwinsk* which was returning from taking American troops to France. The ship had two British artillery pieces on board manned by Royal Navy crews. The *U-151* attacked her without warning with a torpedo shot on 18 June. The ship did not immediately sink and the U-boat had to finish her off with her guns after the crew abandoned ship.[26]

On 15 June Nauen informed the *U-151* that the former German Minister to neutral Argentina Count Luxburg would return on the Swedish ship SS *Suecia* from Buenos Aires and put in at Halifax for inspection.[27] The message is basically a warning for *U-151* not to sink the ship. This message also highlights that information was being passed to Nauen from Buenos Aires despite herculean American and British efforts to cut German diplomatic personnel off from communications to Germany. On 9 July, Nauen warned that the Allies had worked out the position of *U-151* by dead reckoning. Late in the cruise the *U-151* was attacked twice by marauding British submarines on patrol in European waters. She dodged two torpedoes and made it past the danger. Nauen told the *U-151* to be careful, which seems a bit of an understatement. On 19 July Nauen reported a message to the U-boats still at sea that the *U-151* had reported enemy naval craft off of Baltimore and New York. The *U-151* had a celebrated homecoming and a visit from one of the Kaiser's own sons on arrival.[28]

The *U-151* had accomplished much for one U-boat including mines laid off of the Chesapeake and Delaware Bays, two small submerged telegraph cables cut off New York harbor, she had also forced the U.S. Navy to institute coastal convoys, and to finally admit a U-boat was off the coast, which the Navy had somewhat weakly denied earlier.[29] The *U-151* did its job well and caused panic in the American press and public, and sank 23 ships for a total of 58,028 tons.[30] Still, despite the success of the raid, no significant naval forces had been diverted to protect the American coast to the detriment of the war zone around Britain, or to the all important convoys. The Kaiser's lack of enthusiasm for the U-Kreuzer campaign and the *U-151* in particular can be seen in the below anecdote.

> On 25 July 1918, while at the Imperial German Headquarters in Spa, Belgium "His majesty was very depressed at lunch. I had recommended him to receive tomorrow the brilliant commander of *U-151*, Korvettenkapitän von Nostitz und Jänckendorff, who has just returned from a trip to the North American coast. His majesty refused on the plea that he must have rest and that his house was not a hotel, but later he somewhat surlily consented."[31]

However, *U-151* did help stretch the defenses on the coast since the Americans had instituted coastal convoys from between Rhode Island and

Cape Hatteras under the protection of the numerous but relatively slow sub chasers so the destroyers could focus on anti-submarine patrols.[32] Feldt would attempt to augment *U-151*'s efforts and stretch the American defenses until they broke. The *U-151* would venture out one more time before the war ended only to be recalled a few days later before she had reached her designated hunting ground due to the end of the U-boat war on 21 October.[33]

On 16 June 1918 the *U-156* left Kiel later than expected after engine problems were detected and a complete overhaul carried out in port.[34] Once the engine was deemed safe the *U-156* headed north around the Shetland Islands and Scotland. Feldt's orders were to cut underwater communications cables off Canso in Nova Scotia, lay a minefield off New York Harbor, gather intelligence about enemy dispositions, and turn a captured prize into an auxiliary warship while carrying out cruiser warfare by the prize rules from the Canadian coast south to New York. In mid–July, Feldt's boat was to be the first to institute Holtzendorff's unapproved blockade zone on the east coast of North America before the Kaiser rejected the idea.[35]

On 20 June, Feldt's boat attacked and exchanged artillery salvoes with two armed trawlers guarding fishing boats near the Faroe Islands, which British and American intelligence called the "Iceland Fishing Fleet." No ships were sunk.[36]

Unfortunately, not much is known about this early leg of the voyage due to the lack of records given later events in the cruise. According to decrypts from Room 40 information, Feldt informed Nauen the *U-156* was suffering from "frequent oil explosions" early in the mission. Despite this, the *U-156* told U-Kreuzer command she could continue.

Also, Feldt was not overly concerned about keeping his American destination secret since he attacked more shipping on the way over the Atlantic. The U.S. Navy was immediately notified by Admiral Sims about the approach of the enemy based on the ever reliable, but still Top Secret information from Room 40 and by Feldt's own brazen attacks.[37] On 22 June Nauen informed Feldt that steamers from New York proceeded close to the coast of Long Island until they reached Montauk Point. Nauen also told Feldt regular airplane patrols occurred from Long Island, and that a reliable source had informed them Nantucket Island is fortified and pilot service from there is continued until an escort ship is reached.[38] In addition, Nauen reported trawlers proceeded to Cape Breton and Halifax along the coast.[39]

Four days after the messages from Nauen, on 26 June, Feldt torpedoed the defensively armed British merchant ship *Tortuguero* of 4,175 tons without warning over 200 miles from the northwest coast of Ireland.[40] The *Tortuguero* was traveling from Liverpool, England to Kingston, Jamaica in ballast. Twelve men died in the attack, the largest loss of life for any of the *U-156*'s victims.

Eighteen-year old Arthur Harold Turner of Darwen, England was one of those victims. He was the only child of his parents, and had just joined the British Mercantile Marine in March 1918 as the *Tortuguero*'s wireless radio operator. His body washed up north of Scotland on 1 September 1918 over two months after his death. The U-boat war in 1918 provided many cruel ends for brave young men such as Arthur.[41]

By this time the U.S. Navy had learned that their withholding of news about the *U-151* had actually created more panic and groundless speculation in the American press. This time they took the opportunity of the *Tortuguero*'s sinking to warn that a U-Kreuzer would be on the coast within weeks. From 1–3 July, the *U-151* attempted to reach out to Feldt by radio multiple times. However, Feldt appears to have not heard these transmissions. Radio problems would plague the *U-156*'s operations in North American waters.

On 5 July the naval cargo ship USS *Lake Bridge* engaged in a half hour artillery duel with the *U-156*, during which she was splattered by shrapnel.[42] The U-Kreuzer's notoriously slow speed allowed the U.S. Navy ship to escape and spread the alarm after Feldt opened fire from the considerable distance of 30,000 feet. The *Lake Bridge* reported the *U-156* was disguised as a small steamer with a collapsible funnel, although no other evidence exists that the *U-156* had actually utilized this ruse, which had started with a questionable story about the *U-Deutschland*'s trip to Baltimore. The *Lake Bridge* was returning from a trip carrying naval mines to the great North Sea barrage, a mine barrier laid by the Americans and British in an attempt to block the northern passage around Scotland to U-boats, which had been used by Feldt in June.[43] The barrage, which *Lake Bridge* helped to build, would come to play a very important part in the story of the *U-156*.[44]

On 7 July, Feldt made his first capture, the Norwegian ship *Marosa* of 1,987 tons carrying coal to Montevideo after a warning shot splashed the deck with shrapnel.[45] As the crew was loading two lifeboats with provisions, the U-boat approached until a half mile away and then sent five men over with revolvers to take possession of their prize a few hundred miles south of Cape Race.[46] The boarding party gave the *Marosa*'s crew 20 minutes to get their supplies and possessions before they ransacked the ship. All the while, one of the five German U-boat men was stationed on a mast of the captured ship with powerful binoculars.

The *U-156* did not give the *Marosa*'s crew any directions to the nearest terra firma. However, someone from the submarine shouted at them in English "Good trip and God bless you; you are eight hundred miles from land." One can imagine this comment was not appreciated by the *Marosa*'s crew. On 8 July, the crew of the *Marosa* saw a sailing vessel on the horizon, and then witnessed their hope and the ship slip beneath the waves.[47] The ship was the Norwegian *Manx King* of 1,729 tons, which was carrying a varied cargo from New York to Rio de Janeiro.

The captain of the *Manx King* argued vehemently that his was a neutral ship, sailing to a neutral port, and as such he should be released. However, Feldt ruled the cargo of oil, cotton, barbed wire, sheet iron, and shoes as contraband and ordered the ship destroyed with bombs brought on board. The survivors of the *Manx King* were picked up by a British vessel, which reported the U-boat in the area. The men from the *Marosa* were finally picked up by another Norwegian vessel, which then proceeded to drop them off 200 miles from the coast of Nova Scotia where they finally landed on 16 July.[48]

Nothing is known about Feldt's movements for certain for the next nine days. In mid-July, Nauen estimated *U-156* was off the coast of the United States and sent Feldt information about landmarks and coastal shipping. Nauen was oddly concerned with information about Cape May and Cape Hatteras, which was farther south than the *U-156*'s operational area appeared to be.[49] On 14 July, Nauen sent *U-156* intelligence that the Americans had laid defensive minefields close to the coast near Martha's Vineyard, and that transports leaving New York took a route through Nantucket Sound.[50]

Feldt's mission on arrival in American waters was to sow at least seven and possibly more mines in the approaches to New York Harbor, probably on the night of 18 July, Knöckel's 31st birthday. Although they could have laid the mines earlier since the USS *Harrisburg* had reported sighting a surfaced U-Kreuzer south of Nantucket before the above date. However, this alleged sighting was not confirmed.[51] In addition, a British Admiralty report stated the mines were thought to have been very recently placed.[52]

Feldt chose a spot off the southern coast of Long Island for his mines, which is about eight miles from Fire Island. Feldt's men could simply push the mines over the side of the surfaced U-boat from the deck at night using a specially designed rail system and chute attached to the stern. The

A German postcard depicting an ex-merchant U-Kreuzer on the surface. The 5.9 inch guns can be clearly seen on either side of the conning tower, along with the ship's boat lashed to the deck toward the stern. Note the large deck around the conning tower which served as the gun platform for the outsized artillery carried by these submarines (*author's collection*).

U-151 had done the same thing and claimed this method was much easier and more accurate than a launch from inside.[53]

In late May 1918, the prize officer for the *U-151* described the sight of New York from the area of Fire Island where their U-boat was busy attempting to cut submarine telegraph cables weeks before Feldt visited the same area.

> On May 28, 1918, we arrived off New York, and now began our angling. We moved back and forth on the surface with a long line played out. Our cable cutting mechanism dragging on the bottom. We waited patiently for a bite, that feel of the line which would indicate that we had caught hold of the cable. Then our mechanism at the bottom was set going to cut it. Every time a ship hove in sight we would close our hatches and submerge. This happened many times and grew somewhat exasperating. That night we had our first sight of the bright lights of Broadway, the great glow that hangs over New York City after dark. The glow and splendour of the western metropolis filled us with a restless longing. A wild idea came of stealing into the harbour and up the Hudson, of landing at some obscure place and taking a night off along the Great White Way. But then, we were hardly so romantic as all that, except in fancy. Fire Island Beach, which we could often see in the course of our trolling for the cables, was also a temptation, with its pretty houses, long beach, and white surf. A stroll on the sand and dip in the breakers, wouldn't that have been fine? Ah yes, but there would be no welcome there for us.[54]

There are no records of what Feldt and his men thought about while in the presence of the massive port of New York. Based on conversations the sailors of the *U-156* had with their prisoners and victims we know that some of them worked for German shipping firms like Norddeutscher Lloyd, which meant stops in places like New York during those bygone days of peaceful trade and luxury passenger liners.[55] In fact the crew was probably picked due to their earlier experiences in these waters. In reality, on that night they probably just wanted to get their mines off the deck and into the water as quickly as possible. The approaches to New York Harbor were heavily traveled by ships of all types, including armed patrol and convoy vessels. The area also had aerial patrol assets, formidable shore defenses, and closer to the actual harbor, anti-submarine nets and mines. The risk was great for the Germans and so was the reward.[56]

12

The U-Kreuzer and the Armored Cruiser

The USS *San Diego* was a 13,680-ton armored cruiser launched in 1904 with a length of 503 feet, armed with four 8-inch guns, and fourteen 6-inch guns. The cruiser had two coal fired steam engines that pushed her massive 37,000-pound bronze propellers. She was at the fleet review in San Francisco in 1908, traveled to Samoa, and then represented American interests in Asia for a few years. *San Diego* had also been the first naval vessel to enter Pearl Harbor after it had become a navy base in 1911.[1] In August 1912 the *San Diego* went to Nicaragua where she protected American persons and property during an uncertain time in that country. She did the same in Mexico afterwards when that country was embroiled in revolution after revolution. The *San Diego* was known as the USS *California* until September 1914 when state names were declared as reserved for battleships by the U.S. Congress. She was the on and off flagship of the U.S. Pacific Fleet until February 1917, and then flagship of the Atlantic cruiser escort force until September of that same year. Captain Harley H. Christy was her commander with a complement of 1,189 officers and men under his care in July 1918.[2]

In 1915, two Medals of Honor had been bestowed on two crew members of the *San Diego* for their heroic actions during a steam boiler explosion that year.[3] On 21 January 1915 an Ensign read the steam and air pressure on one of the boilers as part of his routine duties. He left the room and the boilers suddenly exploded. The Ensign, named Robert Cary, Jr., held the watertight door open so the engine crew could get out of the way of the danger. The doors were controlled from the bridge, and it took great stamina and strength to prevent them from shutting. The steam was red hot and all around him from the damaged boilers, but he remained to save his fellow sailors. Telesforo Trinidad, a U.S. Navy Fireman from the Philippines, rescued two men from the deadly situation despite being

The USS *San Diego* was the largest U.S. warship sunk in World War I. She met her end at the hands of one of *U-156*'s mines on 19 July 1918 off Long Island, New York. This photograph is from happier times, on the day after Christmas in 1915. Note the tree on the bow (*U.S. Naval History and Heritage Command*).

wounded by the hot steam himself. Trinidad and Cary were both awarded the well-deserved highest honor their country could bestow.

On 18 July 1917 the *San Diego* was ordered to the Atlantic for escort duties after having convoyed an interned German ship in the Pacific.

The *San Diego* was one of the types of convoy escort vessels Feldt was trying to avoid contact with the night before during his mining operation. She had the important job of escorting convoys out of the vital ports of New York and Halifax, Nova Scotia. On 19 July she was steaming into New York harbor to pick up yet another convoy.

The *San Diego* had originally been designed for general surface fleet actions, but her class would have proven to be less than satisfactory in gun duels with sizeable surface warships in World War I. However, the *San Diego*'s powerful guns were more than a match for any U-boat the Germans had, which made her the perfect speedy escort for convoys leaving the American and Canadian coasts. A U-Kreuzer could have never hoped to challenge her on the surface.

The *San Diego*'s sailors, much like the German sailors may have been the night before, were thinking about New York, and preparing their best uniforms to show off for a night on the town. Christy was not one to take chances, and he was not as distracted by the imminent port of call as some of his men may have been. He was aware of the coastal U-boat threat and was traveling at a speed of 15 knots while zigzagging to avoid torpedo

This view of the bow and sides of the USS *San Diego* illustrates the heavy guns she had available against any surfaced enemy craft that came her way. Unfortunately for the ship and crew, the guns were little protection against the underwater threats of mines and torpedoes (*U.S. Naval History and Heritage Command*).

strikes during that hazy but calm morning. Christy had even inspected the coal loaded on his vessel in Portsmouth, New Hampshire in an attempt to detect any explosives hidden among the black lumps. He was aware that the placement of hidden explosives and incendiary devices was a tactic utilized by a since dismantled German sabotage cell to sink ships while America was still neutral.[4]

A little after eleven in the morning the tranquil scene of men getting ready for shore leave was shattered by a massive explosion that tore open the port side near the number eight fire room, killing at least two men. The water flooded in quickly and Christy's men could do nothing to stop it despite heroic efforts. The captain ordered the engines to full speed in an attempt to ground his ship in low water where it could be salvaged. The attempt failed when the engines did, due to flooding.

Christy also ordered his sailors to battle stations, and told them to fire at any sign of a submarine. They fired their guns until the water lapped up to the casements and began to pour into the ports for the guns. One crewman stated an officer threatened to shoot any man who abandoned ship before the order was given.

The explosion and subsequent flooding had already disabled the ship's power system and radio so the *San Diego* could not call for help. The gun crews fired at the non-existent enemy. This was the last use of the *San Diego*'s guns in anger. Ironically, the *San Diego*'s guns had their first use in wartime one hour earlier when a lookout had sighted a small object moving on the water, which they thought could be a periscope. The gun crews fired a few rounds at the item until it was out of sight. The mind wonders if the object was a German mine that had floated away from its mooring.

Feldt and his crew were likely far away by the time the *San Diego* struck the mine. Long after the event, when some of the *San Diego*'s sailors recounted their ordeal, some would still claim they had been torpedoed. Christy ordered all hands to abandon ship once he realized the situation was hopeless. The mighty ship went down 28 minutes after she struck the mine, which had also exploded a boiler and likely the ship's magazine. The two subsequent explosions probably accelerated the sinking of a ship that had cruised the waves of both the Atlantic and the Pacific for over 14 years.

Besides the two men lost during the initial explosion, four more men died while the ship was sinking. One was lost when the ship's smoke funnels hit the water and the unlucky sailor was crushed, one was never seen again after he was observed oiling the port propeller shaft, one died after a falling lifeboat hit him in the head, and the last drowned in horrific fashion while trapped in the crow's nest. The dead were later identified as James Rochet of California, Clyde Blaine of California, Paul Harris of Ohio, Thomas Davis of Louisiana, Andrew Munson of Minnesota, and Thomas Frazier of Minnesota.

Christy, in grand naval tradition, was the last to leave his ship. He jumped from the bridge, walked over the almost completely capsized hull, saluted his ship, and then jumped into the cold Atlantic. The wreck lies about 10 miles off Fire Island in a little over 100 feet of water. The *San Diego* is facing with her bottom up and her superstructure mostly crushed underneath the weight of the hull.

There were now over a thousand sailors in the water clinging to the few lifeboats afloat, and any floating wreckage they could find. They reportedly sang "the Star Spangled Banner" and "My Country 'Tis of Thee" as their ship slipped beneath the calm seas. Shortly after the ship disappeared, a naval floatplane patrolling from its' base on Long Island sighted the men in the water and immediately landed near the Fire Island radio station to call for help. The radio put out the news and civilian ships began to respond to the call and save the men despite the obvious danger from enemy mines or torpedoes. Multiple men on the *San Diego* performed great acts of bravery during the ordeal. However, the unsung heroes of the event are the ships and crews in the New York area who came to the rescue of a ship and sailors who were protecting their craft and livelihoods from German attack just a short time before.

Christy also sent two of his few rowboats left afloat to shore with news of the sinking, and those men also spread the alarm of what had happened. The story was widely carried in the papers. The *U-156* had already made an impact on the American people and their navy after only a few days on station. Feldt didn't know it at the time, but he and his men had just sunk the largest American warship lost in World War I, and they had done it within a few miles of the Long Island shore near the largest port city in America.[5]

Two days later, the British naval commander in chief for North America, Admiral Grant, based in Washington, D.C., asked his superiors at the Admiralty if more American destroyers could be retained for coastal defense instead of sending them to British waters. The Admiralty strongly rebuked him, and in so doing counteracted what could have been a measure of success for Feldt's mission.[6] He had convinced one influential British Admiral to retain destroyers in the western Atlantic, although unfortunately for the Germans the rest of the Admiralty was not so keen on the idea.[7]

On 20 July, navy minesweepers destroyed six more German mines near where the *San Diego* had met her end.[8] There was no doubt as to what had happened. No torpedo had taken down the mighty warship. In the meantime, Feldt headed north toward his next target. He and his men likely heard the radio transmissions about the *San Diego*'s sinking from rescue ships and the U.S. Navy's shore stations at this time. We know Feldt and his crew were aware of their success due to decoded radio intercepts and the accounts of the *U-156*'s prisoners later on when the German crew bragged about the score to them, but exactly how they found out must remain an educated guess.

In 1962 a salvage company bought the rights to salvage the *San Diego* wreck for $14,000. The company wanted to blow up the *San Diego* and harvest her scrap metal to make a profit. Various groups opposed the operation and after a very public battle they were able to force the salvage company to give up the rights. The *San Diego* is now a registered U.S. National Historic Site.[9]

The same day the *San Diego* sank, Nauen sent a message to Feldt about land targets in the United States he could bombard with his 5.9-inch guns. The specific nature of the targets suggests Nauen had a source of information with current knowledge of military activities related to the east coast. It is likely we will never fully know how Nauen obtained this information as German intelligence destroyed much of their confidential records at the end of the war in 1918 and 1919. This was an intelligent decision at the time that was likely meant to protect their most covert sources. Historians will always lament this type of practice due to the loss of valuable information much further down the road.

However, we can still make more than an educated guess about the nature of continued German intelligence operations in the United States after war was declared between the two nations in April 1917. That month and before, most German agents fled or were kicked out of the country. All known German sabotage activities with a few possible exceptions ceased since sabotage could now be punished by steep penalties due to the recently passed Espionage Act.

However, Germany likely still had intelligence gathering assets in the United States who communicated with home through neutral ships, or the still open German embassies and consulates in neutral Mexico and other countries in South America where a few of the former U.S. based agents fled. The Mexicans had several wireless towers that could definitely receive and possibly communicate with Nauen in Germany on their own, or through other radio towers in neutral territories.[10] The Germans were involved in the funding and construction of some of these radio sites. The Germans also had couriers who took neutral ships to get messages to Germany. This was a very laborious, lengthy, and expensive process which meant the information would be somewhat dated by the time it reached the Reich. However, it did the job and allowed the agents in the Americas to get important messages and intelligence to the Fatherland.[11]

Also Paul Hilken of Baltimore, a known German agent, had not been arrested nor had he fled once war was declared even though he was deeply involved in sabotage and intelligence gathering activities. After the war started with the U.S., Hilken continued to act as paymaster for German agents in South America and Japan. He also communicated with agents in Mexico and reportedly used Swedish seamen as couriers to Germany after the U.S. entered the war. He also had a company in New York, which was run by another known German agent. These men or others unknown could have utilized sources at the docks and navy facilities up and down the coast to report back to Germany.[12]

There is precedent for this happening in Europe at this late date in the war. In a 22 May 1918 transmission, Nauen told all U-boats that a Spanish officer had reported a minefield south of Brescon, and lively transport traffic along the coast at Nice in France. Clearly, Nauen was in the habit of transmitting information directly from spies on the ground.[13] Even Mata Hari, the most famous German spy of World War I, was betrayed by radio transmissions intercepted and decoded by the Allies. The Germans, as usual, gave a little too much detail in some of their messages.[14]

Also, Nauen appears to have been using intercepted Allied radio traffic to report on ship movements. On 9 July, Nauen informed *U-156* of a convoy leaving New York and Allied "transports" waiting for orders in the Azores Islands based on "enemy reports."[15] Indeed, the Germans had their own codebreakers too, but they were not as organized and integrated as the British. Despite this it seems unlikely Nauen could glean the type of information it transmitted to Feldt from American radio intercepts about the east coast of the U.S. all the way in Europe.

Another possibility were pro–German neutrals traveling on neutral ships, rather than actual German born agents, who clearly provided background intelligence when transiting through North American ports, but this information would be somewhat dated by the time a U-boat could be put on station.[16] The Secretary of the U.S. Navy had forbidden all reporting about shipping traffic in American waters by making an appeal to the newspapers to omit that information in their stories, but it is unclear that all papers followed his directive to the letter.[17]

In this case, Nauen stated Feldt could attack munitions with thirty large cranes south of Revere, Massachusetts, a dock and munitions depot with a large electric crane near Portland, Maine, and a shipyard at Newport on Narragansett Bay with two battleships under construction.[18] Nauen also suggested more targets in New Jersey including a shipyard at Beach Haven, North Tucker Beach, a railway near Barnegat, a dock in Atlantic City, and oil tanks on Cape Henlopen.[19] Nauen also stated the Cape May lighthouse was not in use, and that several factory chimneys were located there.[20] Feldt never attacked these land targets. He may not even have received the transmission due to his sometimes faulty radio, or the targets had to do with Holtzendorff's earlier mentioned plan to institute a full blockade of the U.S. coast.[21] As stated earlier, the *U-156* was to be the first U-boat on station when Holtzendorff schemed to announce the blockade of the U.S. in late June.[22] However, the announcement never came and the planned unrestricted war in the western Atlantic never materialized.[23]

Although American and Canadian hysteria about German spies around every corner was overblown, the brutal truth was that the Germans had obtained information about American naval activities on the coast, which was likely provided by a few still active spies.

13

The Battle Off Nauset Beach

The morning of 21 July 1918 began as a normal hot and humid Sunday summer morning in the small Massachusetts' beach town of Orleans. A scenario that is common to this day in the town at the eastern edge of America. The people in Orleans were concerned with small matters like attendance at church and the war seemed very far away. Despite the raging conflict across the ocean, locals and tourists alike were enjoying the beaches, the summer cottages, and the peace and quiet on the elbow of Cape Cod away from the hubbub of cities like Boston. The same elbow that offered those delights to the tourists and locals also made for an extremely exposed position. The Cape Cod land mass juts out into the Atlantic Ocean surrounded by water on all sides save one part in the south to connect the sandy oasis to the continent.

Shortly before 10:30 a.m., the 452-ton steel hulled tugboat *Perth Amboy* and the tug's tow of four sailing barges of a few hundred tons each were traveling empty, except for one, which was hauling granite stones. A crewman on board the *Perth Amboy* was alerted to something amiss in the calm waters three miles off Nauset Beach when he witnessed three objects streaking quickly by his ship.[1]

One of the near misses—or perhaps they were the customary but unnoticed warning shots across the tug's bow—struck a spot on the beach below a bluff and exploded. Although likely unintentional, Feldt had just shelled the mainland of the United States. The few shells launched from Feldt's guns that landed on the beach were the only bombardment of the United States by a foreign power in the First World War, and the first bombardment of U.S. soil by foreign artillery since the Mexican-American War in the 1840s.[2]

The confused crewman on the *Perth Amboy* soon found out what had caused the streaks when a shell struck the pilothouse on the *Perth*

Amboy and set her aflame.[3] The shell or pieces of the damaged pilothouse had also almost severed the arm of the tug's helmsman, John Bogovich, who had been steering the ship moments earlier. John Zitz, another Perth Amboy crewman, was also wounded in his hand. The captain of the *Perth Amboy* woke up from a Sunday morning slumber, and witnessed the massive profile of the *U-156* sending shell after shell toward his boat. The *U-156* disabled the *Perth Amboy* and sent its' sailors rowing to shore with their wounded comrades. The hardy *Perth Amboy* itself did not sink, and would ply the seas for almost another 30 years.

Next in line was the 830-ton sail barge *Lansford*, crewed by the Ansleigh family. The family also called the *Lansford* home. The youngest son, Jack, grabbed an American flag and .22 rifle before heading to the lifeboat. His older brother, Charles, wanted to use the .22 to fire back at the Germans before their shrapnel wounded father convinced him the gun would do little damage to the massive submarine and its' crew. Jack hoisted the American flag on the lifeboat as a less threatening sign of defiance. The *Lansford*, *Barge 766*, *Barge 703*, and *Barge 740* all ended up on the bottom.

In the meantime, the *Rose*, a fishing schooner that had seen the *U-156* emerge from the depths of the waters off Cape Cod had been watching the attack commence. The *U-156* suddenly started to pay attention to her and sent several rounds to chase her off while simultaneously spraying the *Rose* with machine gun fire. The *Rose* and her crew went toward shore where they hit the beach and safety in their dory.[4]

Coast Guard Station number 40, located on Nauset Beach, was also full of activity during the assault. They sent their surfboat into the water to advance unarmed into the flying shells of the *U-156* to rescue the survivors of the attack. They also succeeded in treating the badly wounded Bogovich and Zitz, as well as helping land the survivors quickly and without further injury or any loss of life. However, one of the most important jobs the lifesavers performed on that day was also the easiest. They telephoned the Chatham Naval Air Station a few miles away with the following urgent message "Submarine sighted. Tug and three barges being fired on, and one is sinking three miles off Coast Guard Station 40." They had the number of barges wrong but it didn't really matter. The Coast Guard lifesaving station men and a few others were the true American heroes of the *U-156*'s raid that day.

In the meantime, the temporary officer in charge of the Chatham Naval Air Station heard the distinct sound of the *U-156*'s guns 10 miles away off Nauset Beach, and he didn't feel the need to wait for a telephone call from the Coast Guard station to confirm an enemy attack. He scrambled to find a pilot he could send to investigate the sounds of warfare right off the American shore. Unfortunately for the officer, his commander and most of the other pilots were off flying in the station's planes looking for one of their patrol blimps which had gone missing two days earlier. The first HS-1L flying boat they were able to outfit with a bomb and send off toward Nauset Beach had engine problems and had to return immediately.

Finally, an HS-1L piloted by Ensign Eric Lingard and Ensign Edward Shields, and with Chief Special Mechanic Edward Howard in the bomber seat took off from the station and headed toward the action. They would participate in the first and only naval-air action to occur in the American theater of World War I in the western Atlantic. The SM *U-117* would also be attacked by a seaplane later in the campaign. However, that U-boat did not get a chance to fire back. The HS-1L carried only one Mark IV bomb, which meant there was no room for error in this era of inaccurate bombsights. If the bomb came near the submarine and exploded there was no doubt the sub would at least be severely damaged, if not completely destroyed.

By the time Lingard and his crew arrived over the scene, the *U-156* had been bombarding the boats offshore for about a half an hour. In that time, the beach had become crowded with hundreds if not thousands of beachgoers who had come out of their summer cottages to witness the

An American HS-1L floatplane from the Chatham Naval Air Station attacked the U-156 off Nauset Beach on 21 July 1918 (*National Naval Aviation Museum's Photograph Collection*).

German Navy use a tug and a few barges as target practice just two to three miles from land. These same witnesses were also about to view the fight between the American airmen and Feldt's powerful U-Kreuzer. The crew of the HS-1L saw what they described as a submarine "the size of a destroyer or small cruiser" about 500 yards away from the line of barges. Howard stated the *U-156*'s crew was wearing white caps and about 30 were on deck manning the guns.

According to Shields, the *U-156*'s crew did not see the HS-1L until it was too late. After they sighted the plane, the deck was a commotion of running men. On the first run at 800 feet, the bomb's release failed to work and the bomb did not drop. Lingard made a second pass at 400 feet over the sub, and once again the bomb failed to hurtle toward the massive target. Frustrated, a third pass was made and Howard jumped out of the plane onto the lower wing, held a strut to keep his balance, and released the bomb with his hand. The missile dropped and landed only a few feet from the submarine.[5]

An American R-9 seaplane from the Chatham Naval Air Station attacked the U-156 off Nauset Beach on 21 July 1918 (*National Naval Aviation Museum's Photograph Collection*).

Unfortunately for the Americans, the bomb failed to explode and the *U-156* had escaped yet another brush with certain death due to a faulty enemy explosive.[6] It was like the waters off the Canaries all over again when the British submarine's torpedo had proved defective. According to the flying boat's crew, the *U-156* then fired at least three rounds in the air at them from the deck guns, which could also double as pretty good anti-aircraft weapons if needed. Lingard continued to circle the U-boat, but climbed higher to get out of range of the enemy's fire.[7]

In the meantime, Captain Phillip Eaton, commander of the Chatham Naval Air Station had finally landed after a fruitless five-hour aerial search for the downed blimp. Once he heard about the submarine attack only a few miles away, he immediately prepped his R-9 seaplane for an assault on the marauder. He lifted off solo at 11:15 a.m. with one Mark IV bomb strapped to his plane about 45 minutes after the *U-156* commenced her attack on the barges. Eaton claimed the *U-156* fired at least four anti-aircraft rounds from the deck guns at him before he had made his bomb run.

Eaton's bomb release worked perfectly and he made his attack from 500 feet. The recommended height to drop a Mark IV without blowing your own plane out of the sky was 1,000 feet. The bomb splashed about 100 feet from the U-boat and once again did not explode. Eaton did see the Germans running for the hatch as he made his run, and the *U-156* started to get underway.

Feldt must have realized he was drawing too much attention, and that the next bomb might actually explode. He apparently ordered his boat to dive around 11:25 a.m. The battle off Nauset Beach was over. The media had been aware of the attack at the exact same time it was happening, and in what must be one of the first live reports from the scene of a newsworthy event, Dr. Danforth Taylor of Orleans called the Boston Globe from his seaside home and gave a blow by blow account of the battle as it unfolded. The media all over the country picked up the story, and many papers ran with the raid on their front pages.[8]

Soon, baseless accusations and suspicions ran rampant about alleged German spies who had aided the German submarine directly during the incident, false U-boat sightings, and derogatory remarks about the U.S. Navy and its fliers. Feldt's attack was a clear success if seen in this light, and his actions pushed the American people ever closer to demanding more protection for their own coast. The story of the battle was even covered in German newspapers.[9] However, despite some slight delays caused by the search for the missing blimp, the fliers from Chatham had performed well. They would certainly have damaged or destroyed the *U-156* had their bombs worked, and they likely hastened Feldt's exit from the scene.

On the American side, the raid provided a needed kick in the pants to redesign the Mark IV bomb, which had a reported problem with detonation upon impact long before the *U-156* appeared off Orleans.[10] Unfortunately for the navy, there would be only one more chance to attack a U-boat on the coast from the air before the war ended. As a direct result of the *U-156*'s attack, the government took over the Cape Cod Canal, and made the passage toll free so ships would no longer have to traverse the outside of the cape so dangerously exposed. High tolls to use the canal had kept ships like the *Perth Amboy* and her barges from using its' shorter and safer route. Chatham shortly received ten new flying boats equipped with Davis guns that could fire a six pound shell. Unfortunately, it was all too late to be of any use since history had already passed Chatham Naval Air Station by.[11]

Another side effect of the action was a 24 July order by the commander of the First Naval District based in Boston, Admiral Wood, to issue a warning to all ship and dock workers in the port of Boston to avoid any discussion or public demonstration when a troop transport was ready to leave since that could theoretically be reported to a U-boat by German spies.[12]

Feldt and his crew had made a big splash at Orleans, except for the opinions on his crew's gunnery. Multiple victims and witnesses to the assault on the barges commented on the use of about 150 rounds of 5.9-inch ammunition to sink such small vessels, and the repeated misses noticed by the multitude of spectators. This can likely be attributed to the general inability of the ex-merchant U-Kreuzers to handle the recoil of their heavy guns. It was well known by U-Kreuzer crews that the guns would shake the boat so badly that sometimes they would loosen the supports holding the massive artillery to the deck. It is a good thing the U-Kreuzers had so much ammunition since they needed it to make up for what had to be many missed shots.[13]

Later in the cruise Feldt sent a signal to Germany wherein he reported he had cut a communications cable. The exact text sent to Germany was "P5 cut cable." This transmission along with his aforementioned operations orders confirms Feldt had a cable cutter attached to the *U-156*, and that he was likely fishing for the communications cable that went from Orleans to Europe when the *Perth Amboy* and her barges stumbled into his operation as he was finishing up. His orders specifically indicated he should cut cables near Canso, but Feldt likely had some leeway to decide what he could target. The locations of cables were generally known and maps of them existed at the time.

13. The Battle Off Nauset Beach

After dragging for the Orleans cable, Feldt probably decided to sink the little ships he saw just offshore as part of his general mission to sink ships off the American coast, but also as a demonstration to those on shore of how close the war had come to their homeland. Feldt had to have known that part of his purpose was to stir up the American public so they would force their politicians to bring back part of the U.S. Navy to protect the coast.[14]

Feldt probably spent two days or less fishing for the transatlantic telegraph cable which went direct from Orleans to Brest, France after he mined the approaches to New York harbor. The cable was a strategic level military target, and was used to communicate with the American forces in France.[15] A break in this direct cable or the secondary one that went from Orleans to New York City and then on to Washington, D.C., could cause communications delays between the leadership in the U.S. capital and their troops in France.[16]

However, it would not have caused a complete break as the U.S. had control of two wireless radio transmitters, which could reach Europe from New Jersey.[17] The stations had been taken over from their German owners in 1917.[18] Still, the target was just too important not to be attacked by the Germans. Why else would Feldt go to this relatively heavily defended stretch of coast to sink a few empty barges?

This part of Cape Cod was protected by a U.S. Navy seaplane base, which was connected to the Orleans U.S. Coast Guard station by telephone as we saw in the previous battle account. The lifesaving station did not have weapons, but they could relay intelligence on enemy attacks to the air station in what was lightning speed in 1918. Also, nearby Provincetown naval base had dozens of sub chasers at its command, which were theoretically primed to respond to any attack off Cape Cod. In this case they never showed, since the commander in Provincetown did not act quickly enough, and was trying to organize his small under-armed boats into a little flotilla so they could marshal their firepower against the massive U-Kreuzer.

Feldt likely thought he had already cut the Orleans cable, and only decided to reveal himself when the targets of opportunity appeared while he was still in the area. The fact remains the cable was not cut that day. However, one of the barges sunk by Feldt did fall on one of the Orleans' cables. A repair team found the sunken ship on top of the communications link when they were fixing a damaged cable some years after the battle.[19] After his partial success and near destruction at Orleans, Feldt and his crew headed north for more daring operations.

14

Low Hanging Fruit

In early August 1918, Feldt's *U-156* opened up a campaign against the North American fishing industry in a possible last attempt to create the uproar the Germans wanted. The small fishing craft also served as easier targets for the slow moving U-Kreuzers, since they were some of the few vessels with a top speed less than the unwieldy German craft, and never traveled in convoy like the more important shipping. Also, they were very unlikely to be armed, and most had no radio to communicate with the U.S. and Canadian coastal defense forces. In short, they were helpless victims when confronted by the might of a German submarine.

The precedent for the Germans targeting such vessels in European waters was well established. At the start of the war U-boats had begun to sink British fishing vessels. By August 1918, the German submarine arm had sunk 660 British fishing boats in European waters and killed 434 fishermen. The average size of the victims was 103 tons. The hitherto safe fishermen in the western Atlantic were in the crosshairs for the first time. Feldt would sink many small fishing vessels from early to late August when the *U-156* began her return voyage to Germany.[1]

After Feldt's grand show off Orleans he headed north and stopped the 112-ton fishing schooner, *Robert and Richard* of Gloucester, Massachusetts on 22 July. The ship was returning to port after a big catch on the Grand Banks. The captain of the fishing vessel thought the *U-156* was a friendly naval patrol boat until a shot splashed across his bow. As the *U-156* approached the *Robert and Richard*, the captain noted who he thought was the commander of the U-boat, the first officer, and a seaman climb onto the deck of the U-Kreuzer. The fishing captain rowed the ship's boat over to the *U-156* after one of the officers ordered him to approach.

The men then boarded his boat and he had them rowed over to his schooner. The fishing captain boarded his vessel with the Germans. His appraisal of the officers he interacted with is likely false, since it is clear

Feldt would not have boarded such a small prize himself, and past history showed a U-Kreuzer's captain would rarely if ever board a captured vessel. The fishing captain was likely dealing with the prize officer, the ever-present Knöckel, and another officer. The boat captain remarked both officers spoke English well.

One went down to the cabin for the ship's papers and came back with the captain's American flag. The *U-156*'s crew also collected flags and souvenirs from most of their other captured prizes during this time. The officer and sailor wore what he described as rough looking working clothes like a regular seaman. The underdressed officer told the captain he had a summer home in Maine and had lived in America. This was probably a lie. However, some took this story as evidence of how the *U-156* could know the hazardous waters just off the North American coast so well when the real explanation was the crew's stated history on German trade and passenger ships prior to the war.

The Germans had picked some sailors with knowledge of the American coast for the *U-Deutschland* voyages, and it stands to reason they would continue the practice for their North American war patrols.[2] Before the captain of the *Robert and Richard* and his crew set off in five dories for shore, he noted the only person wearing a uniform was the person he misidentified as the captain, and could have been Knöckel. The Germans told the crew to tell the authorities that they were out to sink ships only, and not kill the seamen on them.[3]

After this meager catch, Feldt did not sink another ship for almost ten days. He could have been attempting to cut cables again as his orders did specify he would cut cables off Canso. On 22 July he had received a message from Nauen, which stated if he could not carry out an operation in the Gulf of Maine due to foggy weather, he should operate off Delaware Bay.[4] Later in the cruise, Feldt radioed home that the Gulf of Maine had no shipping traffic.[5] In addition, sailors of the *U-156* told the sailors of later victims that they had waited three miles off Portland, Maine for shipping that never materialized.[6] As many U-boat commanders could attest, sometimes the hunting just wasn't great in areas where they thought it would be. During this time the SM *U-140*, also off the American coast, called the *U-156* twice and could not reach her.[7]

Feldt then entered Canadian waters. To face Feldt's boat the Canadians had a grab bag of armed converted trawlers, drifters, yachts, aged torpedo boats, a few older cruisers, and six American submarine chasers with American crews under the aegis of the Royal Canadian Navy's East Coast Patrol Force. All told the Canadians had about 100 of the above types of vessels available for convoy and patrol duties in the western Atlantic.[8] All of them were outgunned, and some would be outpaced by the *U-156* even with the U-Kreuzer's notoriously slow speed.[9]

The Canadians, like the Americans, made the convoys their top concern, and the number of boats on patrol would be significantly lessened when a convoy was outgoing to Europe. The United States Navy also agreed to set up Naval Air Stations at Sydney and Halifax with American crews under American officers. The commander of the Halifax station was Lieutenant Richard E. Byrd who would later become famous as a daring aviator and polar explorer after the war. The stations didn't open until late August 1918, and their duties consisted of patrols and escorting convoys from the air about 50 to 80 miles out. The activities of the *U-156* would speed the plans to build the air stations since Feldt showed the Canadian coast was no safer than the American.[10]

The French also had a naval presence in Canadian waters since they still owned the islands of St. Pierre and Miquelon off the coast near the entrance to the Gulf of St. Lawrence a little south of Newfoundland.[11] The contribution of the French ally to Canada's coastal defense was several armed schooners equipped with radios and stationed on the fishing banks to warn the fishermen about U-boat activities, and patrol for the enemy.[12]

On 2 August, after his fruitless attempts at hunting off the coast of Maine had failed, the *U-156* fired two shots across the bow of the four-masted 766-ton motor schooner *Dornfontein*, which was carrying a fairly large load of lumber to South Africa. The *Dornfontein* had been stopped a mere seven miles from the shore of Grand Manan Island in New Brunswick, Canada.

This was the *Dornfontein*'s maiden voyage and all eyes in the port of St. John, New Brunswick, were upon the schooner since she was their newest ship, and had been built with special funds from the Canadian government to stimulate the local shipping industry. The ship had all the comforts a crew would want in 1918 including electric lights, a modern bath, and of course the two brand new engines.[13]

Captain Charles Dagwell and his nine-man crew were kept prisoner aboard the U-boat for four and a half hours while Feldt's men ransacked their boat for provisions.[14] The crew of the *Dornfontein* were given a meal of canned beef and rice while their boat was lit on fire and set adrift. The *Dornfontein*'s crew described the *U-156* as painted black on the top half and grey on the bottom. This corroborates other descriptions of the U-boat on this cruise. They also stated the German captain was about 5'7" and could speak little English while the second lieutenant, likely Knöckel, could speak English. They added almost all the crew could speak at least some English.¹⁵

The Germans also told them some lies which included that the *U-156* could go 18 knots on the surface, 12 knots submerged, had 36 torpedoes, and would be on the coast for 10 months with six other submarines. In reality there were only three submarines on the coast in August, and that would be the high water mark for German submarines in American waters during the whole of the Great War. The other two U-boats were the *U-140* and the *U-117*. The tall tales were likely meant to frighten the North American public when the sailors went into town after rescue and told their story.¹⁶

Of course, the crew also bragged about sinking the *San Diego*, a repeated theme during their conversations with their victims. A Swedish seaman from the *Dornfontein* spent a few hours on board the *U-156* while the Germans poured oil on his boat in preparation to light her on fire. The prisoner noted that four officers paced the deck while smoking cigarettes, and another four were constantly on the lookout with binoculars scanning in all four directions. The Germans then ordered him below.

The Swede could speak German and started a conversation with Heinrich Kamps who worked in the engine room.¹⁷ The German sailors asked the Swede if he had seen any warplanes or American warships around. Perhaps the *U-156*'s encounter with American planes off Cape Cod had made an impression. He replied in the negative.

Kamps stated he was from Hamburg and gave the Swede a picture postcard of himself with another *U-156* crewman. The postcard had his mother's address on the back and Kamps instructed his prisoner to deliver the card to his mother if he heard the *U-156* had been lost. The picture ended up in the hands of a *St. John Standard* newspaper reporter who printed it in the 7 August paper. Kamps and the other *U-156* sailors then had a good chuckle at the Swede's expense when he jumped at every shadow on the boat and expressed his unfounded worry that the German officers would throw him overboard. The Germans explained to him that they were not interested in hurting sailors, and would only use unprovoked force if they were attacking an armed vessel.¹⁸

The ever courteous Germans wished the crew good luck and released them to the *Dornfontein*'s lifeboat to make for the shore close by.¹⁹ The Swedish prisoner stated that many of the crew appeared on deck to wish them well and gave them an enthusiastic goodbye.

As the *Dornfontein*'s crew rowed away they saw their ship fully

The German prize crew of *U-157* sports their menacingly large naval revolvers after taking over a steamer during their cruise to the waters around the Canaries and Azores Islands (*Lowell Thomas Papers, James A. Cannavino Library, Archives & Special Collections, Marist College, USA*).

engulfed by flames. Three hours later the crew reached a lifeboat station and spread the alarm. The *Dornfontein* was badly burned to the waterline. However, the hulk was still afloat and the *Dornfontein* was salvaged and repaired to serve another day.

Captain Dagwell was not as lucky and bore the brunt of unfair punishments and accusations since he had almost lost the ship that had carried so much promise for the port of St. John. Local Canadian government officials suspended his license on a trumped up charge of letting his ship's papers fall into enemy hands, which was a ridiculous argument given that correct conduct and law mandated a ship present her papers to a warship for inspection.

In response to the capture and near sinking of the *Dornfontein*, the port of St. John ordered all lights in the city put out.[20] The attack on the *Dornfontein* also initiated the first operational wartime experience in the history of the Royal Canadian Navy. The Canadians finally had an actual enemy warship in their waters, and it remained to be seen what they would do under the stress of real battle.²¹ The reappearance of the *U-156* also caused an alert to go out to the Canadian and U.S. Navy with the U.S. sending the destroyer USS *Jouett* and her group of small subchasers north from Cape Cod to see if they could seek and destroy Feldt. They arrived in the Bay of Fundy on 4 August.

The *Jouett* and her hunting pack were to be frustrated for the first of many times. As alluded to above, most of the *U-156*'s victims in this period were small fishing vessels with no radios. By the time they made shore, the elusive U-boat had moved on from the area and the naval defense forces were left with little to go on for clues to where the Germans may strike next. In the event, Feldt headed north and on 3 August started a string of attacks off the coast of Nova Scotia. The first prize he sank was the 120-ton *Muriel* out of Boston after a short chase. The *Muriel* was eventually stopped by two warning shots. The survivors were ordered to the boats, the Germans looted their ship, and placed a bomb onboard. The *Muriel* sank in two minutes after the bomb detonated.²²

The sinkings in this period were similar, and started with a few shots across the bow of the doomed fishing vessel. The Germans then boarded the stopped ship, confiscated some provisions, took the ship's pennant or life ring as a souvenir, and then a time bomb was placed. A short time after the *Muriel* was sunk, the *U-156* sank the American flagged *Sydney B. Atwood*, a fishing vessel of 100 tons in the same manner.

An hour and a half later, the *U-156* fired a warning shot when three miles away from the American fishing schooner *Annie Perry* in calm weather. The crew set off in their boats. Afterwards, they were ordered to the side of the U-boat where they were told not to worry since the Germans were after their ship and not them. They also bragged yet again about the *San Diego* and asked for newspapers.²³ The 116-ton schooner was sunk by a bomb.

Three hours later the *U-156* stopped the 112-ton American fishing vessel *Rob Roy*. The *Rob Roy* was also sunk by a bomb, and the Germans talked about the other schooners they had sunk that day with the captive crew. They must have been tired of mentioning the *San Diego* finally.²⁴ On 4 August, the *U-156* sank the Canadian flagged *Nelson A.* of 72 tons southeast of Shelburne, Canada. The *Nelson A.* had a catch of 17,000 pounds of fish when she was sent to the bottom by a bomb.²⁵

The *U-156* then bore down on another schooner named the *McLaughlin*. However, the *McLaughlin* was able to escape when the *U-156* spotted a large steamer in the distance. The U-boat gave chase, lost the juicier target, and lost the *McLaughlin* too.

As we have seen, there were now three U-Kreuzers in operation off the American coast or on the way over. It was the height of U-boat activity in the western Atlantic, and the U.S. Navy decreed that at least one new United States Navy destroyer would escort every troop convoy the whole way across the Atlantic. This measure and others would make an attack on a troop convoy a much more difficult venture for the U-Kreuzers in August 1918. Smaller ships or those few still traveling alone remained the best targets.[26]

On 5 August, the *U-156* sank the Canadian flagged vessel *Agnes G. Holland* of 100 tons. She also damaged the Canadian *Gladys M. Hollett* of 203 tons southeast of the Lahave banks. The *Agnes G. Holland* was sunk by a bomb, but the *Gladys M. Hollett* survived the scuttling charges and was eventually towed into Halifax and repaired. The crew of the *U-156* had ransacked the *Hollett* before they attempted to sink her. They had taken clothing, the watch and nautical instruments of her captain, and other items.[27]

In the meantime, news of the attacks spread through the Canadian government. A member of the Canadian parliament for Yarmouth, E.K. Spinney, sent a telegram and letter to the Royal Canadian Navy on 5 August, which informed them the recent German assault had resulted in the stoppage of all coastal steamer traffic from Yarmouth. He went on to state his view that the coast was clearly not defended and the Germans could apparently operate with impunity. He was told the Royal Canadian Navy and the United States Navy were doing all that was possible to counter the *U-156*.[28]

A little later in August 1918, the Americans wrote an intelligence report about the known activities of the U-Kreuzers off the coast. In the section on *U-156* they give Feldt the highest praise by misidentifying him as the most successful U-boat commander of both world wars. It was perhaps in a forgivable case of ego that the Americans thought the U-boat captain who was thumbing his nose at them was none other than the redoubtable Lothar von Arnauld de la Perière. Perière was the most famous U-boat officer of World War I, and his record for Allied shipping sent to the bottom remained unbroken in either world war. He sank over 500,000 tons and was a holder of Germany's highest honor, the Pour le Mérite.[29]

15

Halifax, Gateway to the East

The port of Halifax in Nova Scotia was one of the most important in North America since it was a natural port of embarkation for convoys carrying supplies and men to Europe. Halifax has an excellent harbor, which is also one of the deepest in the world to remain ice free most of the year. Since 1914, Halifax had been used to ferry Canadian soldiers to their eventual destination in Flanders, holding the trench lines against the German army.

Halifax was defended by artillery batteries, retractable anti-submarine nets, a garrison, and a few Royal Canadian Navy patrol boats. The artillery was needed in case a German submarine attempted to enter the harbor since the Canadians knew their ships would be outgunned and possibly need to retreat behind the protection of the big guns.[1]

All convoys were escorted by Royal Canadian Navy or Royal Navy ships. Halifax handled the medium Home from Canada "HC" convoys from North America, and continued to have a busy war after the entry of the U.S. despite the use of New York for some of the faster convoy traffic, which was designated "HX." By 1917, the population of the small city had grown to 60,000 persons due to jobs related to the war industry in town. Halifax was experiencing the same economic boom effect from the war that had taken hold in the United States.

The city was the recipient of a lot of infrastructure, communications, and transportation improvement due to the port's importance to the Allied war effort. Brand new railway lines were near completion as the war rolled into 1917. Canada was at war but no German submarine had operated against the shipping coming out of Halifax until the *U-156* arrived. Halifax was free of the ill effects of war until a dark day in the winter of 1917.

On 6 December 1917, while Gansser was attempting to win glory in the Canaries, the SS *Imo*, a Norwegian steamer charged with taking relief supplies to Belgium was finally able to leave after taking on coal once the submarine nets in Halifax harbor were lowered. At the same time, the French cargo ship, the SS *Mont-Blanc* was traveling into the harbor. The Mont-Blanc was carrying a load of TNT, high-octane fuel, and guncotton for the war.

The two ships collided and a short time later the Mont-Blanc caught fire and her cargo exploded with a hitherto unimaginable blast. The massive explosion killed 1,900 people and wounded 9,000 more. The parts of Halifax unlucky enough to be within a few miles of the explosion were severely damaged or completely leveled altogether. The people of Boston heard of the emergency on the same day and sent a trainload of supplies and medical staff to help the beleaguered people of Halifax.

As the recovery dragged on the people of Massachusetts continued to give supplies, help, and newly built housing to those in need to the north of their border. The people of Nova Scotia never forgot the generosity of the people of Boston, and to this day the Christmas tree on Boston Common is a gift from that province of Canada to Massachusetts in remembrance of their help in Halifax's hour of need.[2] The disaster, which was a complete accident, had taken a great toll on the premier Allied port in Canada. However, Halifax recovered its usefulness quickly and by the time July 1918 rolled around the port was humming with activity again, and Feldt would have found the shipping in its approaches an irresistible target.

On 4 August 1918 Convoy HC-12 exited Halifax and headed east into the vast expanse of the Atlantic Ocean with 18 ships ferrying 21,000 Canadian and American troops. The force of eight Royal Canadian Navy trawlers and drifters along with three American sub chasers were fully engaged in escorting the convoy out from the coast where the danger from U-boat attack was greatest. The convoy was on a zigzag course, and was escorted safely out until the patrol left it on 5 August.[3]

The approaches to Halifax were very lightly guarded due to the preponderance of the meager forces in the area being detailed to convoy duty. In a signal home decoded by the British at the end of Feldt's cruise he noted the shipping traffic from New York to Halifax was heavy but protected. He also noted that "large troop transports" proceeded "out and back alone by the shortest route," and that convoys went by no regular routes. Feldt evidently spent some time off Halifax and New York simply observing how the shipping moved and was protected for intelligence gathering purposes.

It may be a sign of Feldt's timidity, or of his knowledge about the potential weaknesses of his own boat that he never attacked a convoy despite the fact that at least some of the convoys in the area at the time had no ships capable of outgunning him in a surface engagement. The little convoy escort ships were weak, but their scarecrow effect on a U-boat commander could be decisive in preventing an attack.[4]

At the same time Feldt was cruising near Halifax, the 4,868-ton Canadian tanker *Luz Blanca* was in the Canadian port ready to go down to Tampico, Mexico, in ballast. The *Luz Blanca*'s captain did not wait for the escorts to return, and was released by the port authorities who cautioned him to leave after dark and travel a zigzag course to avoid torpedoes.

Captain J. Thomas ignored both of these very smart suggestions and headed out alone in the daylight of 5 August in hazy conditions. Feldt had missed, or chose not to engage, the large convoy HC-12 only a day before, but five hours into the *Luz Blanca*'s voyage Feldt spotted her, fired one torpedo at the tanker, and watched as Thomas, who thought he had hit a mine, turned his ship around and headed back to Halifax.[5]

Thomas and his crew then saw the *U-156* surface about four miles away and the U-Kreuzer started to fire her big guns at the damaged ship.

This photograph shows *U-157*'s large artillery rangefinder positioned on the conning tower, specialized equipment needed for the long range gun battles engaged in by the U-Kreuzers in 1917 and 1918 (*Lowell Thomas Papers, James A. Cannavino Library, Archives & Special Collections, Marist College, USA*).

Thomas attempted to run for his ship's life at full speed while his men manned the little 3-inch gun on deck. Thomas had no radio since it had been knocked out by the torpedo explosion. He could not call for help, but maybe he could escape given the slow speed of the big U-boats.[6]

For an hour and a half, Thomas and his crew valiantly drove their damaged ship as fast as they could while firing shots from their inadequate piece of naval artillery, which was manned by two Royal Navy reservists. The *U-156* was able to stay out of range while her own 5.9-inch guns scored one direct hit on the ship's propeller, and a second which killed two of the *Luz Blanca*'s crew, the chief cook and the chief steward.[7]

Thomas gave the order to abandon ship, and his three ship's boats pulled away as the Germans continued to bombard the doomed and burning tanker until she sank.[8] An American ship witnessed part of the battle and broadcast the danger to Halifax while escaping the area in case the U-boat's attentions should come her way. The obsolete Canadian escort force that had been with convoy HC-12 had released their ships at the designated point in the Atlantic, and were on their way back. However,

Two typical U.S. Navy sub chasers docked next to each other in port. The sub chasers participated in the hunt for *U-156*, and saved some of the U-Kreuzer's victims while they were in their lifeboats adrift on the ocean (*U.S. Naval History and Heritage Command*).

they were still too far away to help the wrecked ship or attack the *U-156*. The U.S. destroyer *Jouett* and her hunting pack of small sub chasers were ordered north to the site, and one American sub chaser was able to rescue two of the boats from the *Luz Blanca*. A third lifeboat made landfall a short time later.

The *U-156* then headed south again and the hunting group had no luck with their elusive quarry. Feldt likely didn't know it but his sinking of a fairly large ship for its' time in the approaches to Halifax had scared the Canadian and American governments to the point that they closed Halifax to fast transatlantic convoy traffic, and directed all fast convoys to assemble and debark from the more protected inland waters of Québec City and Montreal in the St. Lawrence River.[9] Slow convoys from Sydney and fast convoys from New York would continue to use those ports.[10] Although the British Vice-Admiral Grant in Washington, D.C., immediately ordered the Royal Navy port officer in New York to temporarily detain all ships in harbor until further notice, which caused a small delay there.[11]

The sinking also caused U-boat hysteria in the Royal Canadian and U.S. navies, and many false sightings and attacks on suspected U-boats were reported later in August.[12] A declassified American memorandum marked "Very Secret" detailed that authorities were also worried about mines being placed in the approaches to Halifax, and that the move to the Straits of Belle Isle was considered more favorable due to the depth of the water and the strong current, which would mitigate some of the danger from enemy mines.[13] The fears of the authorities were proven correct when another U-Kreuzer placed mines in the approaches to Halifax soon after Feldt and his crew began their return to Germany.

On 10 August some convoy ships coming from New York to Canada for transatlantic passage were given destroyer escorts whereas previously they had sailed independently. Coastal convoys and individual ships still continued to use Halifax, but the city's days as a major transatlantic port during World War I were over. A few German shells and one torpedo had finally convinced the Allied naval leaders that Halifax was too exposed, and Feldt had closed the door on the port with a move that had a small strategic impact, and moderately lengthened the journey of convoys across the Atlantic by pushing them into the St. Lawrence River.[14]

The meager resources of the RCN and the slow or nonexistent support coming from the U.S. and Britain during this time in August made the Canadian coast a very vulnerable place to be for a ship that summer. This was also the first operation carried out by the Canadian Navy against a real enemy vessel, and there were bound to be problems. The sinking of the *Luz Blanca* hurried along the plan to construct air stations at Sydney and Halifax, and the U.S. also sent an obsolete gunboat named the USS *Yorktown* to reinforce the area. After yet another coup, Feldt returned to what he and his men did best, sink ships and cause some measure of panic in the new world.[15]

On 7 August, the *U-156* captured the *Elizabeth von Belgie*, a Belgian steamer with a special pass issued by the Kaiser's government to bring humanitarian aid to occupied Belgium. Feldt decided to let the ship go as her papers were in excellent order and she was clearly involved in neutral and German approved business.

On 8 August, Feldt captured the Swedish ship *Sydland* after firing two warning shots and ordering the captain to come over with his papers. The captain of the *Sydland* argued that his ship was also working for the Belgian relief effort. The argument impressed Knöckel and he apparently went to discuss the matter with Feldt. However, the *Sydland*'s captain did not have a pass from the German government and after hours of vacillating argument with his own officers Feldt decided to sink the 3,031-ton *Sydland* with bombs brought on board.

The *Sydland* went down south of Cape Sable and east of Cape Cod.[16] The crew rowed off in three boats and were picked up two days later.[17] Captain Alexandre Larsen of the *Sydland* demanded a receipt for his boat from the Germans. They provided one as they did for some of the other ships they had sunk. Basically, the receipt was proof that the boat had been destroyed by a submarine so when the captain rowed to shore his employers couldn't claim he had made up the story to cover up an accident or negligence.[18] The *Sydland*'s receipt was signed by Knöckel and stated "I testify that the steamer SYDLAND was stopped by a German submarine on August 8, 1918." "Because of the charter party, and the complete lack of any German evidence that the ship belonged to the Commission for the Relief of Belgium,[19] the ship was destroyed, since the suspicion of enemy ownership was considered proven."[20] A *U-156* crewmember reportedly told the men of the *Sydland* he had been serving on Hamburg-Amerika line ships prior to the war.

Feldt then moved farther south, back into the approaches to New York harbor, a place he had not visited since the sinking of the *San Diego* in July. As the U-Kreuzer headed towards the waters off the big apple, an 18 ship convoy escorted by an American armored cruiser left for the other side of the Atlantic. Feldt would not damage the convoy proper. However, there was a straggler, and the German spider was about to catch another British fly.

On the morning of 11 August, the 4,139-ton British merchant ship *Penistone* could not make pace with the 9 knot convoy ahead, and had been left a few miles behind the protective guns of the escort cruiser. Feldt conducted an underwater attack and torpedoed the *Penistone* without warning. The explosion damaged the engine room, killed one engineer and one fireman, and severely burned four other members of the crew.[21] The radio was still operable and Captain David Evans had his operator transmit an urgent call for help. The call went unheeded for the immediate future, and the convoy escort would not turn back since her duty was to protect the bulk of the convoy and leave any unfortunate stragglers behind.

The captain and crew left the sinking ship in their boats. However, Evans returned to board the ship when he saw she was not sinking quickly in order to dispose of his confidential papers, which he was afraid would fall into the hands of the enemy. As he was engaged in this duty, the Germans sent a boarding party over to finish the job with timed explosives.

A *Penistone* crewman described the bombs used by the boarders as narrow with fuses three or four yards long. The crewman accompanying Evans and the boarders was also forced to fetch the captain's bedding for what became an extended stay on the *U-156*. The lead officer of the German boarding party took pictures of the captive crew and the sinking of the British merchant ship. Apparently, the Germans wanted a record of the raid for propaganda purposes back home. The boarders took Evans prisoner and he became a guest of the *U-156* for a week. It is thanks to his observations that we have some of the information about the crew and officers of the *U-156* already recounted in prior pages.

Evans also confirmed the *U-156* did not submerge often, and stayed on the surface most of the time while he was a "guest."[22] The Germans even allowed him to walk on the deck until they spotted a ship on the horizon. The American Navy sent the destroyer USS *Walke* to investigate the scene of the sinking but she found nothing.[23]

On 9 August, the *U-156* fired on the American merchant ship *Herman Winter*, but she got away. On 10 August, she attacked the 4,125-ton British merchant vessel *Lackawanna* with artillery and torpedoes east southeast of Cape Cod, which also escaped after it put on steam and fired back with a defensive gun.[24]

The prisoner, Captain Evans, stated the *U-156*'s gun attacks against these vessels showed him how overpowered the guns were for the size of the boat, and that the whole submarine would shake when they were fired. Speed and well-aimed firepower were the two things Feldt and his U-Kreuzer could rarely overcome in their merchant ship enemies. The *Lack-*

awanna incident in particular showed how intent the *U-156* was to engage a vessel of this size, but also how Feldt was foiled by the Allies' effective countermeasures. According to the crew of *Lackawanna*, the Germans fired two torpedoes at the ship which both missed. The *U-156* then surfaced but failed to stop the ship with her 5.9-inch guns. The *Lackawanna* replied with enough fire to ward off their German foe.[25]

In the meantime, on 12 August in Washington, D.C., a U.S. Congressman from Kansas introduced proposed legislation into Congress to request the Navy provide information about the U-boat attacks off Cape Cod. Clearly, the congressman had heard of the *U-156*'s exploits and was responding to his constituents' pressure for more information about what was being done to combat the threat far outside of their own state. The proposed law went to the Naval Affairs committee and disappeared from history, apparently killed by members who knew what was actually going on, and understood the reason for the secrecy surrounding the wartime operations off the coast.[26] The Canadians were also feeling the pressure. On 14 August, they received a request to convoy fishing vessels to their grounds. The request was denied due to a lack of forces for such a time consuming job.[27]

Feldt continued to move north, finding no success until the next morning on 17 August. On that day, Feldt captured the Norwegian steamship *San Jose* of 1,586 tons, which was empty on its way to New York to pick up foodstuffs for neutral Norway. Feldt's officers discussed the matter of the ship's neutrality with him, and there appears to have been some hesitation on the part of the Kapitänleutnant, which as it turned out was an occasional negative feature of his leadership. However, Feldt was not in a giving mood, despite the vehement protestations of neutrality by the Norwegian Captain Hans Thorbyonson. Feldt decided the ship would be sunk some distance south southeast of Cape Sable. Thorbyonson was given a receipt by Knöckel, told to take the prisoner Captain Evans of the *Penistone* with him on his lifeboats, and ordered to push off toward the Nova Scotia coast after his crew was given a half hour to gather their personal belongings and whatever they needed to survive the pull to shore.[28]

Of note is that Feldt gave them so much time when most of the *U-156*'s victims were given ten minutes or less at most if any time at all. Norwegians traded with the enemy but they were also not at war with Germany, and thus likely had an easier time when faced with destruction by a German crew. A passing ship heard the sound of the bombs exploding in the *San Jose* and picked up the survivors a few hours later. In the meantime, Feldt headed back for another rendezvous with Britain's staunchest ally, Canada.

The *U-156* disappeared from 17 to 20 August and may have been sitting in the approaches to Halifax as it headed northeast. However, Feldt would have found no merchant shipping in the area since the sinking of the *Luz Blanca*. All of the shipping lanes had been cleared, and the only unprotected targets were now the fishing fleets.[29]

16

Seiner Majestät Schiff Triumph

On 20 August, around noon, the *U-156* approached a 122-foot Canadian steam driven fishing boat slowly cruising with her nets out. The 239-ton *Triumph*, built in 1907, was known on the Grand Banks by all the local fishermen. She was unassuming, and her captain known as a friendly sort. The *U-156* was about to turn her into the most feared and hunted vessel on the east coast.

After her capture Feldt heard about the 10-day supply of coal in the *Triumph*'s bunkers and decided to make the green steam trawler an auxiliary raider, and attack the fishing industry of America and Canada with one of their own.[1] It was the perfect ruse, would surprise the fishermen, would cause alarm up and down the coast by its audacity, and give Feldt yet another first.[2] He and his men were the only enemy to successfully utilize a surface raider off the east coast of Canada and the United States during wartime since the Civil War, a feat which would not be repeated by the Germans during their copious attacks on the North American coast in World War II. Much like the name of the boat itself, the operation was a triumph if seen in the light of a publicity stunt, even though the shipping sunk was fairly insignificant.

At this time the Germans still had three submarines in North American waters from Canada all the way down to Cape Hatteras in addition to the little surface raider. American intelligence thought the Germans were attempting to spread thin the American defenses in a last ditch effort to get the destroyers in European waters recalled. In August they reported that 20 percent of the world tonnage sunk by U-boats had been destroyed in American waters, which was more than the tonnage sunk in the war torn Mediterranean Sea that month. The Germans were making an impact, but they wouldn't be able to keep up the pressure due to the relatively few U-boats on station, and the lack of will and resources to send more from their leaders back home.[3]

16. Seiner Majestät Schiff Triumph

The episode began when the captain and crew of the *Triumph* saw the *U-156*'s conning tower rise out of the water about 2 miles away, and five minutes later a shot was fired across their bow. They stopped their engines, hopped in their lifeboats, and rushed away from the ship with a box of biscuits in each dory. After the crew had abandoned ship the *U-156* came up to within 150 feet of the *Triumph* and the captain of the doomed ship rowed over to the sub in his dory with his papers. Two of the dories' crews, including the captain's, were ordered aboard the submarine and Feldt took the ship's documents.[4]

The Germans had all the equipment to turn the fishing trawler into a weapon of war, and it is clear that arming a raider was part of the German plan from the start given their preparations and the *U-156*'s earlier mentioned orders.[5] The 20 man prize crew, led by the experienced Knöckel, installed two 2-inch light artillery pieces on board, a small extra wireless transmitter the Germans brought along to communicate with the *U-156*,[6] and a German flag flying from the *Triumph*'s masthead.[7] Some information also suggests the Germans flew a Canadian flag as a ruse until they were close to their prey and then raised the German battle ensign.[8] They also

The Canadian steam fishing trawler *Triumph* was turned into a surface raider by the crew of *U-156* when they assaulted the North American fishing fleets in August 1918. This rare photograph of the trawler prior to her capture is one of the few known to exist. The *Triumph* was the only enemy surface raider to prowl the east coast of North America for victims during the 20th century (*photograph from the* Halifax Herald, *August 23, 1918; reproduction courtesy of Library and Archives Canada*).

brought about 25 bombs with a time fuse visible, two boxes of shells for the guns, and a large sea bag with unknown contents. This was all witnessed by the captured crew.

A U-Kreuzer had never used a captured prize as a weapon before. Captured U-Kreuzer prizes had been utilized as re-supply ships for provisions and fuel as the *U-155* and *U-157* had done earlier off West Africa, but Feldt had upped the game.[9,10] The news of the new raider traveled quickly, and was even reported on in a Berlin newspaper which claimed the *U-156* had captured an auxiliary cruiser.[11] The Germans treated their prisoners well and plied them with brandy and cigars.

By 1:15 p.m., about an hour after stopping the *Triumph*, the prisoners were released to their boats and the Germans started the new raider's engines. The Germans explicitly told the *Triumph*'s crew that their boat would be used to sink fishing vessels. This move was apparently for the benefit of Canadian officials and the public in order to ramp up the feeling of fear they knew must already exist on shore. *U-156* and *Triumph* continued east northeast for about an hour and a half before they spotted an American fishing schooner by the name of *A. Piatt Andrew*.

Triumph could approach the vessel south southeast of Cape Canso without suspicion while the *U-156* lingered about three miles off. The *Triumph* was well known in these waters and no one suspected the worst until it was too late. The 141-ton schooner didn't know anything was amiss until a few warning shots splashed near her. The schooner's captain was ordered to bring his papers to the *Triumph* and three Germans went over with bombs to sink his vessel.[12]

Later that same day, the 117-ton American fishing schooner *Francis J. O'Hara* was sailing along the Grand Banks about 60 miles southwest of Canso in Nova Scotia.[13] Captain Joseph Mesquita of the *O'Hara* saw two fishing vessels very close to each other. He decided to go over and talk to them about how much they had caught. He saw the first boat was the *A. Piatt Andrew* and the second was the *Triumph* out of Halifax. Mesquita knew both boats and knew the captain of the *Triumph* personally as he had fished with him on the last trip out. About 450 feet away from the *Triumph*, someone on the boat ordered him to stop through a megaphone. Mesquita thought it was a joke and kept on. He stopped laughing and stopped his boat when four shots were fired across his bow from the *Triumph*.

The *Triumph* came alongside of Mesquita's boat, and he saw the German crew and the German battle ensign flying from the masthead unfurl. Knöckel ordered Mesquita to come aboard with his papers and chastised him for not stopping his vessel sooner. Knöckel also ordered three of the raider's crew to get in the dory with Mesquita with a bomb. The *O'Hara* went to the bottom after the crew was set adrift and the German bomb exploded. The *A. Piatt Andrew* succumbed in the same fashion.[14]

The *Triumph* then sank the Canadian schooners *Lucille M. Schnare* of 121 tons and the *Pasadena* of 119 tons on the same day using the same tactics. The *Triumph* would sink six schooners during her short career with the *U-156* supporting her smaller sister from a short distance away at every sinking.

During this time, the *U-156* also sank the 125-ton Canadian fishing schooner *Uda A. Saunders* without *Triumph*'s help. The U-boat came up on the bow alongside the small vessel with her decks awash while the captain was alone on the ship. The rest of the crew was out in their fishing dories hauling in the catch about a half-mile to a mile away. The Germans ordered a dory alongside and three of them went to the captured ship. A German officer told the crew "Don't be afraid, we are going to sink your vessel, I will give you 10 minutes to gather up food and water enough to last you until you get ashore."

One German went down into the hold, placed a bomb, and the crew heard a muffled explosion. The two masts immediately broke off, the ship collapsed in the center, and sank quickly. The Germans took the ship's papers and her flag. The crew was on shore and telling their story about 18 hours later.

After this sinking, the *U-156* and *Triumph* headed to the northeast through the night. This was probably to distance themselves from the patrols they knew would be roaming the area of their prolific sinkings on the 20th. *Triumph* and the *U-156* arrived at the Banquereau fishing bank east southeast of Scatari Island on the very early morning of 21 August. The Germans snuck up on the 145-ton French schooner *Notre Dame de la Garde* from one of *Triumph*'s dories and succeeded in boarding her with three men before the Frenchmen knew what was happening. The schooner was carrying a load of 640,000 pounds of fish.[15]

The crew was ordered into their boats at revolver point, and their schooner was sunk by a bomb, which sent their catch back to the bottom. According to Captain Royer Raoul, the Germans took one life buoy from the doomed schooner, probably as a souvenir from the prize. *Triumph* and the *U-156* were both in sight during the attack.[16]

Three hours later the *Triumph* came up alongside the 136-ton American schooner *Sylvania* out of Boston right before dawn, fired a shot across her bow, ordered her crew to send a boat over, and then a uniformed

Knöckel asked for the "skipper." Knöckel told the crew they had 10 minutes to leave the ship. One petty officer and two men jumped in the dory and returned to the schooner with the crew and some bombs. The Germans took the ship's papers and flags. The survivors of the *Notre Dame de la Garde* looked on too as the *Sylvania* sank. Afterwards, they saw the *U-156* and her raider leave slowly to the east. After the sinking of the *Sylvania* the *Triumph* was never seen again and the *U-156*'s whereabouts remained unknown for three days.[17]

The supply of coal for *Triumph* may have exhausted itself and Feldt probably ordered the guns and radio removed before the ship was scuttled.[18] Feldt had to have realized the raider had become a liability due to its likely infamy on shore, and he didn't need it unnecessarily revealing his position to the avenging defense forces he knew would be close on his heels. The Kaiser's smallest raider likely had a career spanning less than a day.[19] The company that owned the *Triumph* successfully petitioned the government to replace her with a yet to be built naval trawler by citing the grievous damage submarine warfare had inflicted on the supply of fish to the North American market.[20]

The *Triumph*, even after its service ended, caused quite a sensation with the American and Canadian Navy who sent reinforcements to the area to destroy the unexpected threat. The U.S. Navy and government were worried about the effect the raider and the U-Kreuzer would have on the fishing business and the supply of fish to the U.S. market. They knew the *U-156* couldn't sink enough schooners to cripple the industry, but they were worried about fishermen staying home instead of doing the vital work of continuing to haul in the catch.[21]

The navy sought to reassure the fishing community they were doing all they could to help catch the raider. The Maine Committee of Public Safety even sent out a message for their members to keep a watch for German spies.[22] At least one Canadian officer found the public's efforts at spy hunting around this time less than helpful "It is felt that some curb should be put upon Miss Meister and Miss MacGuire. Their unbridled tongues may cause a great deal of mischief if they are allowed to run as wildly as do their pens."[23] More effective than amateur spy hunts, the destroyers USS *Jouett* and USS *Bell* along with their hunting packs searched the area for days.[24] Their efforts were supplemented by five of the Royal Canadian Navy's ragtag bag of patrol ships returned from convoy duty who were also told to help locate and destroy the raider. The *Triumph* was the number one target for both navies on the coast for those few days in late August.

The Canadian Navy also sent ships to warn the fishing banks of the impending danger. Commander Ferlicot, head of the French armed schooners from the French territories of Saint-Pierre and Miquelon also warned fishing vessels about the *Triumph*.[25] Unfortunately for the crews of those ships they were hunting for a vessel that was already on the bottom, and Feldt had already moved farther north again.

Feldt had succeeded in diverting some minor naval assets from their primary duties of convoy protection with his surface raider stunt, and had given the media a story to run with about the audacity of the Germans. He had also stirred a contentious debate in the U.S. Senate where several Senators questioned why the navy had not captured or destroyed both the *Triumph* and the submarine. Those who supported the navy found themselves stating once again why it would be folly to bring back forces from Europe to deal with the comparatively small threat posed by the German U-boats off the American coast.[26]

On the morning of 25 August 1918, Feldt was close to Saint-Pierre and Miquelon. He had run north after the *Triumph* was scuttled and succeeded in avoiding his pursuers once again. The small British steamship *Erik* was in the *U-156*'s sights on that foggy but moonlit morning at 1:30 a.m. The *Erik* was under charter to the Newfoundland government en route from St. John to Sydney to pick up a load of coal.

The USS *Jouett* chased *U-156* up and down the North American east coast for weeks. This photograph depicts the *Jouett* in 1918 when she was the head of a naval hunt squadron ordered to destroy U-boats off the coast (*U.S. Naval History and Heritage Command*).

Feldt made his second artillery attack without warning of the cruise on the small ship, which was running without lights west-northwest of Saint-Pierre. The Germans had mistaken her for a larger vessel in the dark, and when they saw what their accurate five shot bombardment of 5.9-inch fire did to the tiny 583-ton ship they were very apologetic to say the least. Five of the crew were wounded including the captain, a mate, and engineer. Minutes later the submarine was next to the *Erik* and someone hailed the boat to ask if anyone had been killed. The crew replied in the negative and the German stated he was glad as he was "after ships and not lives."[27]

The *Erik*'s wireless operator, John Ryan, later recalled his radio set was thrown to the ground and destroyed during the bombardment. Ryan was a wounded veteran of Gallipoli and Ypres and immediately knew they were under enemy attack. Knöckel, described as the "boarding officer" asked Ryan "did you send out any SOS?" Ryan responded in the negative and told him of the set's destruction. As Ryan and the others attempted to patch up the damaged lifeboat, Knöckel grew impatient due to fears about enemy patrols, and ordered the *Erik*'s crew to the submarine.

As only one lifeboat remained undamaged, the 18-man crew was taken on board the U-boat while the *Erik* was sunk by bombs. The prisoners were given coffee, brandy, and cigarettes.[28] The prisoners noted the interior of the U-Kreuzer was adorned with a few life buoys bearing the name *Triumph*.[29]

The *U-156*'s thirty-year old Doctor Martin Schlemm treated the wounded, and Feldt stopped the small schooner *Willie G.* a few hours later, and ordered her to take the *Erik*'s crew on board.[30] The *Willie G.* escaped destruction due to her utility as a makeshift lifeboat for the *Erik*'s crew, and the Germans' mistake of bombarding a helpless target. Feldt had wanted to destroy the *Willie G.* too, but her available lifeboats could not carry both crews. The lucky *Willie G.* landed with her oversized complement at Saint-Pierre.[31] Ryan summed up the episode years later by saying "It was a different war, you know," "They were different men. They weren't the same Germans that fought with Hitler. I mean, there was a little more humanity," "He was after the ships, not the men."[32]

The *U-156* then turned south southwest and plowed right into a group of four fishing schooners at anchor less than a mile apart from each other. The schooners were the Canadian flagged *E.B. Walters*, *C.M. Walters*, and *Verna D. Adams* whose crews were all aboard their vessels since it was customary for Canadian fishermen to be off on Sundays. The last and largest boat was the 162-ton American flagged *J.J. Flaherty*. The *U-156* approached the *E.B. Walters* first but the crew was not concerned as they thought it was a friendly patrol boat until they saw the German flag. The Germans ordered Captain Cyrus Walters over to the U-boat. Four Germans jumped in his dory, boarded his vessel, and completely ransacked it. The Germans must have been low on supplies after months at sea since they tore into the personal chests of the crew and confiscated a huge quantity of canned food.

The *Walters'* crew quickly gathered their personal belongings and then shoved off in a few dories. About 10 minutes later they heard a bomb go off in their ship and in 5 minutes the *E.B. Walters* was gone. The *U-156* then towed the same four Germans in the dory to the *C.M. Walters* a half mile away. The *C.M Walters* was sent to the bottom a half hour after she was boarded. The Germans then turned their attention to the *Verna D. Adams*, which had already been abandoned by the crew after they saw what had happened to the other two schooners. The Germans stayed on the *Adams* the longest, since Captain Mosher had large stores of canned food and other supplies aboard. The *Adams* was sunk by a bomb as well. Next came the *J.J. Flaherty* which was sent to the seafloor by a bomb along with her catch of 200,000 pounds of fish.[33]

At 1:45 p.m. on 25 August, while the Germans were ransacking the *Verna Adams*, a Royal Canadian Navy patrol happened by the scene. The first chance to engage an enemy by a Canadian force since the birth of their navy was about to occur. The *U-156* already had the distinction of being the first enemy threat to penetrate Canadian waters since the genesis of the Royal Canadian Navy, and now there was the potential for something even more significant.

As with the Canadian Navy in general at this time, the patrol consisted of four improvised craft which included a former survey ship now styled His Majesty's Canadian Ship (HMCS) *Cartier*, the converted yacht HMCS *Hochelaga*, and two armed trawlers named HMCS *TR 22* and HMCS *TR 32*. During the patrol, *Hochelaga* and *TR 32* went to investigate two stopped schooners to warn them about the *U-156* and *Triumph*. *Cartier* and *TR 22* were a few miles away under the patrol's commander, Lieutenant H.F. McGuirk. At 2:00 p.m., when about four miles away, Lieutenant Robert Legate, in command of *Hochelaga* witnessed the *Verna D. Adams* sink beneath the waves to dramatically reveal the profile of the *U-156* behind her.

Legate had the first chance since the attack off Nauset Beach to engage Feldt and his behemoth U-boat. Legate sounded action stations. However,

Legate did not go in guns a blazing. Instead, he likely realized his own boat was slower, had only a 3-inch gun compared to Feldt's two massive cannons, and the *Hochelaga* had no depth charges for a submerged attack should Feldt run rather than fight. Legate decided to turn back and call for help from his patrol.

Hochelaga and *Cartier* had radios so Legate messaged *Cartier* with "allo port beam," which meant submarine sighted. *TR 32* followed Legate's lead. Legate's message was picked up by Royal Canadian Navy command at Sydney and Halifax who forwarded the exciting message to Ottawa where it was eventually passed to the acting Prime Minister of Canada.

Cartier gathered the patrol and all went to attack the *U-156* at full speed. This order was given about 10 minutes after Legate's initial sighting of the U-Kreuzer. Legate challenged *Cartier's* order when he radioed that they should wait for reinforcements he saw astern. McGuirk's reply was quick and to the point, "negative." By the time the patrol reached the site of the attack all they found was a capsized schooner with a few empty dories bobbing in the water. Unfortunately for the Canadians, the

The commander of HMCS *Hochelaga* famously hesitated to engage *U-156* in an August 1918 confrontation (*Library and Archives Canada, Royal Canadian Navy negative number CN-3400*).

schooners were all sunk, and the *U-156* was nowhere to be found. The schooner crews stated the *U-156* had leisurely left the scene on the surface and headed southeast.[34]

The patrol rescued the survivors, headed towards land, and alerted the Canadian Navy to the presence of the *U-156*. The reinforcements Legate had referred to were in actuality a small five ship coastal convoy being escorted by two armed trawlers. Feldt must have seen the escorted convoy, possibly heard Legate's radio message, and then saw the patrol heading towards him, and obviously he had no desire to engage as he disappeared.[35]

The Royal Canadian Navy brass court-martialed and arrested Legate. He was eventually ejected from the navy since he had not immediately attacked the U-boat. Legate was fully aware of the standing order for any patrol boat to attack the enemy no matter how outgunned after the *Luz Blanca* was sunk, which in the Canadian Navy's case was every time since their ships did not possess armament to equal the Germans. The *U-156* had claimed her second to last victim, Lt. Legate's career.

On 26 August, the *U-156* sank the Canadian fishing schooner *Gloaming* of 130 tons by bombing her southwest of Miquelon Island. As was usual for this cruise, Feldt's men helped themselves to the *Gloaming*'s provisions and her flag.[36] The *U-156* had made her last kill, and she ended her cruise off the North American coast with a whimper rather than a bang.

Around the same time the Canadians planned to use their two obsolete submarines CC1 and CC2 in an ingenious and concerted decoy attack against the *U-156* or any of the other German raiders in their waters. The tactic was reminiscent of the one used by Commander Taylor during his successful sinking of *U-40* in 1915. They would lie in wait next to a schooner as bait and then torpedo the U-Kreuzer as it approached. The long shot plan was scrapped a few months later when the war ended.[37] The *U-40* sinking had happened in the submarine infested waters near Scotland in the North Sea. In 1918, the chance of sighting and springing a trap on a U-Kreuzer due to their small numbers in American waters was almost nil.

On 31 August the *U-156* encountered the USS *Westhaven*, a 5,699-ton American Naval Overseas Transportation ship some distance southeast of Cape Race.[38] The *U-156* started to bombard the worthy target with her deck guns. The *Westhaven* replied eagerly and a 20 minute engagement ensued before the *U-156* broke off the attack.[39]

In the early morning hours of 3 September, the *U-156* shelled the

British merchant ship *Alcinous* before it got away. This was the last attack undertaken by the *U-156* during her noteworthy career.

An American intelligence report written by the navy's historical section on 14 April 1921 summarized the *U-156*'s performance in glowing terms almost three years after her raid had ended. The report begins with "The *U-156* was perhaps the most effective of all the submarines sent to these shores" and "Its depredations upon the American and Canadian cod-fishermen on the Nova Scotian banks were conducted with skill and served the purpose of badly crippling the industry for the period of the raid." The historical section continued "there is no question that it was a daring commander who ran into the shoal water off Cape Cod," "laid in wait and torpedoed a steamer three miles behind its convoy," "and who negotiated the shallow waters in the Gulf of Maine as though familiar with it."[40]

17

U-Kreuzerkrieg Amerika

As Feldt left the scene of his last sinking the other U-boats on the North American coast had a big job ahead of them. They were still expected to attack convoys if possible, cause public outcry to get the American destroyers recalled, and sink as much of the war winning American shipping to the Allies as they could. Germany was still not officially blockading the coast, so the limited number of U-boats were still only raiders off a faraway shore to the Kaiser and his government.

It is clear that in future years, planned in detail from 1919 to 1921, the Germans were going to increase the number of U-Kreuzers to the point where they would have enough to blockade the North American coast, and alleviate the Kaiser's fears of becoming a laughingstock for declaring the zone with only a few U-boats on hand. The war would end before the Germans could build the necessary U-boats, and the western Atlantic blockade remained an unfulfilled dream until the Second World War. However, Germany's U-boats on station during and after the *U-156* did their best to continue the mayhem despite recurring technical difficulties with the old ex-merchant boats, the newer mine laying U-Kreuzer, and the faster warship style U-boats.

The *U-140* was one of the last type, built for war from the very beginning unlike her ex-merchant U-Kreuzer cousins. She sailed for North America on 2 July. The *U-140* was an over 300 foot long monster with six torpedo tubes, two 5.9-inch deck guns, and two 3.5-inch guns near the conning tower. The *U-140*'s class was faster than the ex-merchant boats, but suffered from some of the same shoddy construction and design flaws, which severely crippled their performance and slowed their speed. The formidable weaponry they possessed meant they could be a dangerous tool in the hands of an aggressive and experienced commander, unless the technical faults outweighed their deadly potential.[1]

U-Kreuzer Command was not messing around with their new U-boats, and wanted the best to take them into battle against the Americans. Korvettenkapitän Waldemar Kophamel, the skipper of *U-151* in the Canary campaign, was chosen to lead the new vanguard of German U-boats into the last stages of World War I at sea. He was as experienced as one could be in submarines since he had been in the crew of U-1, and commanded U-2. He served in a U-boat during the whole of the war.

Kophamel was ordered to attack shipping near the Nantucket Lightship and off New York Harbor. Once *U-117* began her return home he could widen his operations area south to Cape Hatteras if he so desired. Kophamel had taken the *U-140* on her trials and was not impressed with the submarine due to the leaks, instability, periscope problems, and engine failures he witnessed. Kophamel blamed the problems on cheap workmanship by the Germania yard.

On 15 July Kophamel reported to Nauen that he had seen a convoy of large liners fourteen miles away heading towards France at 20 knots. They were the troop transports *Mauretania, George Washington, Kronprinzessin Cecelie*, and the *Kaiser Wilhelm II*. Three of the ships had been seized by the Americans from the Germans. It was the most valuable of all convoys but *U-140* could never hope to catch it. The sighting was a fleeting chance to score a big success. However, even the new U-Kreuzers couldn't catch such a valuable and fast target.[2]

On 26 July, Kophamel attacked the huge 13,967-ton British flagged *Melita* and lost her. He then fought a ferocious gun duel with the armed British merchant ship *British Major*. The *British Major* outpaced the *U-140* and escaped in a scenario that would be very familiar to any of the ex-merchant U-Kreuzer captains. On 27 July, Kophamel captured and sank the Portuguese sailing vessel *Porto* with explosives after confiscating food supplies from the ship's hold.[3] *U-140* also attempted to contact the *U-156* but got no answer after Kophamel allegedly heard the steamer *Osterley* report an attack by Feldt's boat. Kophamel imitated American calls to try to get *Osterley* to report her position, and received no reply from the vessel.[4]

On 30 July, the *U-140* fired her first torpedoes in anger against the armed American merchant steamer *Kermanshah* within a few hundred miles of the U.S. coast. *U-140* had a difficult time aiming her tubes due to the unstable nature of the U-boat. She fired two torpedoes at the big ship while *Kermanshah* dodged both and increased her speed to get away. Kophamel had attempted to surface and engage. However, the steamer was just too fast.

On 2 August, after a short interlude with no activity, Kophamel sank the 7,029-ton Japanese steamer *Tokuyama Maru* with a torpedo about 200 miles from New York with a cargo of chalk from Great Britain.[5] No lives were lost during this attack without warning on a pretty large ship for 1918.

An even larger catch was in the *U-140*'s sights on 4 August when she attacked the 10,289-ton oil tanker *O.B. Jennings* returning from an oil delivery trip to Great Britain back to Newport News, Virginia. The *Jennings* was in convoy until she peeled off in the Atlantic to make for her port alone. The *Jennings* had a 4-inch artillery piece manned by a British naval crew and was about 100 miles from her destination when the captain saw a torpedo approaching his ship at about nine in the morning.

The ship dodged the torpedo, ramped up to full speed, and called for help on her radio. Kophamel surfaced and started an artillery duel from eight miles away. Over two hours later one of the 5.9-inch shells finally scored a direct hit on the engine room and stopped the *O.B. Jennings* dead in the water. The crew took to their boats and the *U-140* bombarded the doomed ship with shells and two torpedoes for two more hours before she finally succumbed to her injuries and sank.

The Americans sent the destroyer USS *Hull* and other ships to the scene to assist but they were too late to catch the *U-140*. The next day found Kophamel lingering about 100 miles off Cape Hatteras, North Carolina where he sank a 1,060-ton coal carrying schooner bound for Santo Domingo called the *Stanly L. Seaman* after explosives were placed on the now abandoned boat. The crew had gone to their lifeboats without proper food and water for the voyage, which caused Kophamel to allow them back aboard their vessel before it was sunk so they could survive the ride back to shore.

On 6 August, Kophamel lay in wait while submerged off of the *Diamond Shoals Lightship* close in to the coast. The lightship's lights were not turned off since American authorities thought it was more important to warn coastal shipping about the dangers to navigation in the area than it was to worry about becoming a location beacon for a U-boat. An American merchant ship carrying coal to Chile named the *Merak* came into sight, and *U-140* surfaced to attack the ship with her deck guns. The *Merak* fled and grounded on the very shoals the lightship was there to warn shipping about. The *Merak* radioed for help and the lightship repeated the doomed ship's call. Kophamel attacked the navigational aid with his two smaller 3.5-inch guns and sank the lightship after the crew abandoned the vessel. His men then went over to the *Merak* and ended her career with explosives placed on board.

The *U-140* then attempted to chase two more merchant ships that had stumbled on the scene. However, they were too fast and escaped while broadcasting warnings to shipping in the area. On 10 August, the *U-140* spotted the Brazilian passenger liner *Uberaba*. *U-140* fired a warning shot across the large ship's bow and she stopped. The *Uberaba* signaled a somewhat jumbled message in reply "Who is which me attacks, give your name please." The captain had thought *U-140* was an American patrol boat at first and once he realized his mistake had started fleeing at full speed, zigzagging, and radioing out calls for help. He had endangered the 250 civilian passengers on board with a potential fiery death, but it is hard to blame him for making the attempt to escape. There were also 100 American naval personnel on the ship and they proceeded to help stoke the fires to drive the ship ever faster to escape from the enemy in pursuit.[6]

Kophamel's guns were spraying the deck with shells when the news came that American warships were on the way. The *Uberaba* continued to run as fast as she could. It was then that the American destroyer USS *Stringham* came up at full speed while using the *Uberaba* as a shield for her own approach. The *Stringham* had been on her way from Norfolk to join a convoy near Bermuda when the destroyer heard the call for help and sighted the *Uberaba* about 20 minutes later.

The *U-140* was caught by surprise, barely able to dive on time, and was subjected to an accurate depth charge attack by the destroyer. The *U-140* was already trailing an oil slick before the attack so the *Stringham* knew exactly where to drop the charges. The first of the depth charges had exploded very close to the submarine so Kophamel had taken her down to 245 feet. The boat leaked profusely after the attack and the *U-140* took on 45 tons of water.[7] When she surfaced the destroyer had gone. Kophamel criticized the captain of the destroyer in his log for not staying around to destroy the *U-140*.

According to a prisoner on the U-boat at the time, the depth charge attack had shaken the crew terribly and the U-boat dived very deep to avoid the explosives. The assault had led to a serious leak in the oil tanks which caused an even larger oil slick to follow the boat wherever it went, and used up vital fuel necessary for the U-Kreuzer's long mission far from home.[8] Kophamel surfaced, checked the damage, and decided to head home. His America cruise was over, and the American coastal defenders finally had a clear victory on their belts.

The Americans had sent one of Germany's most feared captains packing back to the Fatherland after a respectable but still somewhat disappointing 30,594 tons of shipping sunk.[9] Kophamel was stubborn though.

On the way back home during his retreat from American waters he sank the 7,523-ton British troop transport *Diomed* traveling empty back to the United States after transiting in convoy to France. He sank her with his deck guns, and took out the ship's defensive artillery during the first salvoes.[10] Once *U-140* returned U-Kreuzer command questioned the naval staff as to why she had been deemed safe enough to cross the Atlantic when *U-140* was clearly an unstable boat, and hard to maintain without listing while surfaced or submerged.

On 11 July, U-Kreuzer command sent a new long range mine laying U-boat to the North American coast. The new submarine was technically not a U-Kreuzer, but a mine laying U-boat, although the vessel's guns allowed it to engage targets in the time honored cruiser warfare fashion much like the *U-156* and her sisters had done. The *U-117* was 267 feet long, displaced 1,164 tons on the surface, carried 42 mines launched from stern chutes, four bow torpedo tubes, one 5.9-inch deck gun, and a smaller 3.5-inch gun. Kapitänleutnant Otto Dröscher commanded her on her first voyage.

Dröscher was a U-boat mine laying expert with extensive experience in smaller minelaying U-boat classes under his belt.[11] The trip over was not easy. Dröscher found that his U-boat had just as many technical failings as Germany's other large undersea vessels. He had to carry out an overhaul of both his engines at sea, the fresh water evaporator and dive planes worked imperfectly, and there was a leak in a fuel tank which caused an oil slick showing the trail of the *U-117* to any potential pursuers.

The *U-117* started her attack on 10 August when she sunk nine small fishing schooners at or below the 50-ton mark on the Georges Banks near the coast of New England. As with the other U-boats on the coast, *U-117*'s crew ransacked the small boats of all of their food supplies.[12]

Dröscher now focused on his main mission, which was to lay mine fields from the New York area to Chesapeake Bay and sink merchant ships with her guns and torpedoes in the U-Kreuzer war. On 12 August, *U-117* spotted the 3,875-ton Norwegian steamship *Sommerstadt* near Long Island. The *U-117* attacked from underwater with a torpedo. The weapon did not run true and missed the Norwegian ship. However, in a scene reminiscent of the *U-156*'s experiences in Naos Bay, the torpedo circled and dove under the unlucky Norwegian vessel. Then the torpedo circled again and detonated against the ship. The crew escaped and the ship sank.

The *U-117* headed south after this victory and laid a minefield perpendicular to the New Jersey coast off Barnegat to catch coastal shipping.

This was a change in tactic from prior U-boats who had mined the approaches to major harbors and bays.

On 13 August, Dröscher torpedoed the 7,127-ton oil tanker *Frederick R. Kellogg* off the New Jersey coast near the *Ambrose Channel Lightship*. The tanker was carrying 7,500 barrels of valuable oil from Tampico, Mexico. Seven men died in the initial explosion and later when the ship sank. The ship's bow remained above the surface as this was shallow water so the *Frederick R. Kellogg* was salvaged to serve another day. However, the oil was lost to wartime America and plagued the local beaches in what was a small ecological disaster for the New Jersey coast.

On 14 August, *U-117* stopped the 2,088-ton sailing ship *Dorothy B. Bartlett* close to the mouth of the Delaware River. Dröscher sank the schooner with his guns. The sound of the artillery brought the U.S. minesweeper *Kingfisher* to the scene. The *Kingfisher* had two three inch guns that were hardly a defense against the much larger U-boat. The minesweeper picked up the crew of the *Bartlett* and then watched the U-boat. During the tense standoff, the American oil tanker *William Green* came into view and the *Kingfisher* positioned herself between the valuable target and the U-boat. The *Kingfisher* was ready to make the sacrifice the *Hochelaga* had run from in the presence of the *U-156*.

The *Kingfisher* radioed for help, and a nearby lightship re-transmitted the message. The *U-117* started to move toward the lightship when the radio crackled with the sounds of submarine chasers telling the threatened vessels they were on the way. At the same time a U.S. Navy seaplane cruised overhead. The *U-117*'s log often mentions diving before U.S. Navy patrol planes could spot her. The entries are more evidence that the Americans were tightening their coastal defenses.[13]

Dröscher knew the full weight of American defenses in the area were about to come down on him so he dived his boat. The seaplane and the subchaser *SC-71* dropped nine depth charges on the *U-117*'s obvious oil slick from the still leaking tank, and shook Dröscher and his men up a bit. No further damage resulted to the *U-117*, but the defenders had managed to stop him from sinking any more ships in the area. He was forced to remain submerged until nightfall. Later on 14 August, Dröscher laid a minefield of seven mines near the Fenwick Island lighthouse off Delaware. He also laid a third minefield near the *Winter Quarter Lightship*.

On 15 August he sank the 1,613-ton schooner *Madrugada* with a cargo of cement. The bow remained above water since the cement had shifted. The Coast Guard exploded the wreck since she was a navigation hazard.

Dröscher laid his last minefield of nine mines off of Cape Hatteras.

The *U-117* was engaged in this task when the 6,978-ton British tanker *Mirlo* stumbled into his operation. The *U-117* fired one torpedo from about 1,200 feet and hit the gasoline loaded ship with a fatal blow. The *Mirlo* was immediately on fire, the abandon ship order was given, and the lifeboats prepared. Ten men died in the water due to capsized lifeboats and the burning oil now crowning the ocean around the dying vessel. The men thought they were going to die in the flames. However, there was a Coast Guard lifeboat station nearby and the brave men inside had seen the *Mirlo* explode and immediately put their powered rescue boat into the surf. They braved the burning sea, risking their own lives, and saved all of the remaining men.

The captain of the *Mirlo* correctly surmised he had been hit by a torpedo. However, the U.S. authorities thought the ship had hit a mine and sent minesweepers to the area to clean out the suspected field. They found and destroyed the *U-117*'s last minefield before it could claim any victims. Dröscher's victory over the *Mirlo* had come at the cost of his southernmost minefield.

On 17 August, *U-117* sank the 2,846-ton Norwegian sailing vessel *Nordhav*. On 24 August she attempted to sink a small 408-ton schooner, which ended up not sinking after the explosives were placed due to the cargo of tobacco sealing the holes in the hull. The ship was repaired to serve another day. On 26 August, Dröscher captured an oil burning trawler which he used to replenish some of his lost fuel from the still leaking *U-117* before he sank the ship. Dröscher's next big kill was the 2,550-ton Norwegian steamer *Bergsdalen,* which he sunk without warning after a submerged torpedo attack. One of the crew died during the attack when many of the men had to jump directly into the water before their ship sank. The neutral Norwegians were not having an easy time off the North American coast.[14]

On 30 August, the *U-117* made her last attacks with the sinking of two fishing schooners off Canada. Both were commanded by German immigrants who were threatened with a forced trip back to the Fatherland before they were released to their dories. Later, the *U-117* was ordered to meet up with the returning *U-140* to transfer some much needed fuel to the wounded U-Kreuzer. *U-140* was on her last legs and ran out of fuel a few hundred miles west of Scotland. The *U-117* passed the wounded giant extra fuel in tin cans. Both boats ran out of fuel before they reached port and had to be towed home by German destroyers.[15]

On 29 September, the *U-117*'s minefield near the Delaware River almost broke the *U-156*'s record for sinking the largest U.S. warship in

World War I. The huge 16,000-ton battleship USS *Minnesota* hit one of the mines, and barely managed to get up to Philadelphia for repairs that would keep her in dock until the war ended.[16] In October and November, Dröscher's minefields claimed a Cuban sugar ship, a steamer, and a small U.S. army transport vessel. The *U-117* had sunk or damaged 35,020 tons and disabled the 16,000-ton USS *Minnesota* for the duration of the war.[17] She had experienced some success but both her and the *U-140* had encountered formidable Allied defenses in the North American theater, and were forced to limp back home damaged and out of fuel.[18] The new U-Kreuzers had failed to live up to the expectation that they would outperform the ex-merchant U-boats.

The first and second time the *Deutschland* came to North America she had been on a peaceful trade mission to Baltimore, Maryland, and New London, Connecticut. On 11 August 1918 she left Germany prepared to attack the very trade network that she had so recently been a part of. Korvettenkapitän Ferdinand Studt commanded her on her voyage to Canadian waters. Studt's initial focus on Canadian waters was the only new part of an old mission given to the previous U-Kreuzers, which included minelaying, attacks on shipping, and cable cutting. The cruise started out badly with the *U-155* traveling through a large storm from 18 to 30 August. During this time it was difficult for Studt to make any attacks.

On 27 August, the *U-155* ran into a miniature American convoy consisting of the armed ships *Montoso* and *Ticonderoga* along with the unarmed *Rondo*. The *Ticonderoga* was also the escort for the three vessels as she was a well armed naval cargo ship, which meant she was manned by sailors from the U.S. Navy trained in gunnery. The *Ticonderoga* had been a German ship until war was declared and she was seized by the American government.

The *U-155* first attempted a torpedo attack against the *Montoso* while submerged. The attack failed because the *U-155*'s equipment was characteristically faulty, and a malfunctioning diving plane motor caused the U-boat to surface uncontrollably. The conning tower rose out of the water about 6,000 feet from the targets and they ran off at full speed. The two armed vessels also started to fire at *U-155*. There was a long range gun duel between the ex-merchant U-Kreuzer and the convoy until nightfall when Studt finally accepted defeat. The Allies were aware of the attack shortly after it started since the victims had radios and reported to base about their experience.

On 31 August, the *U-155* had her first victory of sorts for this cruise. She stopped and sank the 305-ton Portuguese sailing ship *Gamo* with bombs placed on board. The next day, the *U-155* spotted the well armed U.S. Naval tanker *Frank H. Buck*. The *Buck* had one 3-inch gun along with a 6-inch gun for defense against U-boats. In the morning, the *U-155* opened the action against the *Buck* with artillery fire from almost 8 miles away. The *U-155*'s shots were falling so close that shrapnel was hitting the deck. However, the *Buck*'s gunners were also getting close to the hull of the U-Kreuzer. The *U-155* broke off the action after she apparently realized the U.S. Navy ship had the same range as her guns. The *Buck* had hit the *U-155* twice but had caused only minor damage prior to the end of the engagement. The next day the unfortunate 1,560-ton Norwegian steamer *Shortind* was torpedoed and sunk by the *U-155*. After this attack, the *U-155* finally moved out of the mid–Atlantic and toward the shores of North America.[19]

On 7 September, she sank another small Portuguese sailing vessel. The *U-155* then attempted another long range battle with a British steamship. The ship got away due to the same old story. The ex-merchant U-Kreuzer was slow, and some of their intended victims were not. On 12 September, Studt torpedoed and sank the 3,245-ton Portuguese steamer *Leixoes*. Studt questioned the crew in their lifeboats, but did not give them a course for land or any provisions. Two died in the open boats before they reached shore four days later. Studt, unlike Feldt and von Nostitz, was not in a merciful mood.

On 13 September still far out from Nova Scotia, the *U-155* had an intense artillery fight with the British steamer *Newby Hall*. Studt's boat was too slow yet again and the *Hall* escaped. The *Hall* had landed several shots near the U-Kreuzer and made a few small holes in the hull. The *U-155* could not submerge until repairs were made.

Unlike when the *U-156* had penetrated this area earlier, there were now coordinated and formidable defenses in place against the U-boats. The North American defenses had not been bolstered by ships and aircraft slated for Europe as the Germans would have liked, but were reinforced and better organized with materials and men already committed to coastal defense and just now coming into the battle. The Germans had not convinced the Allies to shift their primary focus on what was still a naval backwater for them. This fact was well shown when *U-155*'s battle with the *Hall*, as well as radio intelligence from Room 40, alerted the Canadians and Americans to the *U-155*'s approach, and they reacted with an organized response and more force deployed to the appropriate area.

The Canadians sent every patrol boat they had, while the Americans stepped up their air patrols from Halifax, and all ships were provided with naval escort. The minesweepers were also sent out to sweep the sea lanes since the *U-155* was expected to lay mines off Halifax or St. Johns per radio intercepts.

The *U-155* dodged many patrol ships during this time frame and found the sea lanes empty of unescorted ships. She laid her mines in three fields around Halifax from 17 to 18 September but none sank any tonnage.[20] The minesweepers did their work well, as did the currents off of Nova Scotia which knocked the mines off of their moorings toward the beaches. Studt attempted to cut communications cables off of Sable Island for a few days. This was also a wasted effort since the cable cutter broke down several times, and he failed to cut the targeted cables from Canada to Great Britain. Utterly defeated in Canadian waters by the Canadian and American defensive forces, the *U-155* headed south into U.S. waters where Studt hoped the pickings would be easier.

On 20 September, the *U-155* stumbled into the American steam fishing trawler *Kingfisher* close to the Grand Banks.[21] This was not the American minesweeper of the same name that had tangled with the *U-117*. Studt ordered the crew to abandon ship and sunk her with bombs. Over the next few days the *U-155* attacked two fast steamers which both got away. On 3 October, the *U-155* torpedoed the 3,838-ton Italian ship *Albert Treves* hundreds of miles east of Chesapeake Bay. The crew got in three lifeboats, two of which were lost forever, 21 men out of a crew of 34 died. The *U-155* sank a small sailing vessel after sinking the Italian ship, and then headed down to the waters off Cape Hatteras where she had no luck for more than a week.[22]

From 6 to 8 October 1918 the *U-155* encountered very stormy weather, and Studt took the time to write about the horrible air circulation system in an ex-merchant U-Kreuzer. "The air-conditioning system was built for a crew of twenty-nine but is unable to cope with a seventy-two man crew." The boat was saturated with the smell of body odor and diesel mixed with stuffy and humid air.[23]

On 12 October, the *U-155* attacked the *Amphion*, a huge steamship employed by the U.S. Transport Service and manned by a U.S. Navy gun crew. Studt fired over 200 shells at the fleeing boat. He landed multiple hits and wounded some of the crew but could not stop the strong and fast ship from getting away. Studt turned away from the American coast after this last defeat and headed back to Germany. On 17 October, Studt ran into the steamers *Lucia* and *Hawaiian* traveling in company with a cruiser about 1,000 miles from the U.S. coast carrying supplies for the American Expeditionary Forces in France. The *Lucia* had been fitted with a special system of air tight boxes, which were an experimental flotation system to defeat holes in the hull created by torpedoes and mines. The *U-155* torpedoed the *Lucia*, the crew manned the guns, and the U-boat never surfaced.

The *Hawaiian* got away at full speed although the escorting cruiser stayed in the area. The *U-155* did not attack again since the armed ship was still in the vicinity. The *Lucia*'s special flotation system kept her above the surface for a few hours but eventually she slowly slid beneath the waves.

Studt had tried his best to sink multiple larger cargo carrying vessels, and had been effectively thwarted by armed merchant ships, patrols, convoys, radio decrypts, minesweepers, aerial assets, and his own mechanical failures. The North American defenses were hardening without weakening the main Allied naval effort in the eastern Atlantic and Studt went home with a paltry 17,525 gross registered tons to his credit.[24]

On 5 September, the ex-merchant U-Kreuzer *U-152* left Germany bound for North American shores.[25] Kapitänleutnant Adolph Franz and his men were supposed to lay mines off Atlantic City and Currituck Beach. *U-152* was also supposed to hunt for shipping off the New Jersey coast. On 14 September the British Admiralty notified the Americans of the German plans. The Americans increased navy patrols off New Jersey due to the intelligence warning. The U.S. Navy's preparations worried Admiral Sims who was perpetually stressed about the secret of decryption being revealed to the Germans by any actions taken in advance of U-boat attacks.[26]

On 24 September Franz attacked the British *Alban*, but she got away after one of her defensive guns scored a hit on *U-152*. The U-boat lost a significant amount of oil due to the damage. On 29 September, the *U-152* had a long gun battle with the American naval transport *George G. Henry*. The intended victim also had a 6-inch gun, and although the *U-152*'s rounds started a fire on the ship, and wounded 17 of the crew, the damaged *Henry* kept up her speed. The *U-152* had blown up the *Henry*'s magazine and sprayed the ship with a mostly near miss bombardment. In the end the ship was just too fast for the *U-152*.[27]

On 30 September, the *U-152* spotted the 5,130-ton American naval transport *Ticonderoga*. The *Ticonderoga* had engaged in an artillery exchange with the *U-155* earlier in the campaign. The transport was headed back to war torn France with 115 soldiers, 124 navy officers and enlisted men, and a hold full of railroad ties. The *Ticonderoga* was in a convoy protected by a U.S. Navy cruiser but she was lagging behind the other ships by a few miles.

In the very early morning of that late September day, Franz crept ever closer to his target and initiated a surface attack from the ridiculously close range of 600 feet before the lookouts on the naval ship spotted the assailant. The *Ticonderoga*'s captain ordered the ship to ram the U-boat. The *U-152* was able to dodge the attempt and started to savage the battle tested ship with both 5.9-inch guns. The bridge was smashed, the captain severely wounded, and the helmsman was killed. The forward gun was put out of action and the crew neutralized by Franz's accurate fire.

The U-boat dove before she finished the job. The American cruiser protecting the far away convoy heard the artillery and went to investigate. However, she mistook the ship for a different one traveling alone in the same area. The *Ticonderoga*'s radio was out so she couldn't communicate with the cruiser that could have saved their lives and their vessel. After making contact with the ship she thought she was looking at, and confirming that boat had not been attacked, the cruiser heartbreakingly left the scene of what would become a tragedy.

The Germans waited until the big combat ship left and then surfaced. While the Germans hid from the cruiser the men on the *Ticonderoga* were busy. They prepared their still operating six inch gun, the captain's wounds were stabilized and he was placed on deck to command the ship, and the fires were put out. The *U-152* opened her second attack from two miles away and rained shot on the deck of the *Ticonderoga*. The six inch gun on *Ticonderoga* fought bravely for a while but the crew took several hits and eventually the gun was knocked out.

The ship was on fire again and the Germans were basically using the *Ticonderoga* for target practice. The captain was unconscious so his second in command decided to surrender by putting a sheet up where the Germans could see it. The Germans either ignored this gesture or didn't see the white sheet since they continued to pound the ship into oblivion. The crew attempted to signal surrender again by waving a pillow case around and finally the shelling stopped. Most of the men on the ship were now dead, and the evacuation was a complete mess since most of the lifeboats were destroyed or damaged. Only one lifeboat made it off the ship with fourteen men inside, another raft with about the same number of men, and a few unlucky men still in the water.

As the crew and military passengers evacuated the ship the Germans callously fired a torpedo into the side of the naval transport, and it sank quickly to the bottom. The Germans fired two shots across the bow of the lifeboat and irately asked the survivors where the captain and head gunner were. The captain was in the lifeboat, still seriously wounded.

Franz noted several of the U.S. survivors were from Germany and had immigrated to America before the war. Franz was angry about these men who he viewed as traitors fighting against their Fatherland. He was also convinced that the *Ticonderoga*'s gun had fired after the white sheet was run up. The Germans took two Lieutenants as prisoners and then left the rest to their fate in the middle of the Atlantic. The two prisoners were treated very well and once the *U-152* returned to Germany in November they witnessed the chaos in the country as the old government faded away and the new republic was established. They were taken to England on the *U-152* for her last voyage to surrender to the Allies.[28]

In the meantime, the *Ticonderoga*'s raft drifted away from the lifeboat and the men on it were never seen again. The now packed lifeboat, with 22 men aboard after some on the raft swam over before they were separated, headed east toward Spain. Three days later they were picked up by a British ship. The captain of the *Ticonderoga* was awarded the Medal of Honor for the action, which ended up being the highest loss of life on any ship attacked during the U-Kreuzer raids. 213 lives were lost as a result of the furious battle between the merciless Franz and his American enemy.[29]

On 11 October Franz was summarily ordered to the Azores operating area. He did not know it at the time but the Kaiser himself and the foreign office were involved in the redirection of his patrol as we can see here from a quote dated 10 October 1918.

> Grünau telephoned me that official quarters are very touched by (Woodrow) Wilson's note. The foreign office has recalled our U-boat cruisers (two ancient vessels) from the American coast to spare the feelings of the American nation. Grünau wants to know how the Chief of the Naval Staff stands in this matter. I told him to contact Scheer at Spa. This afternoon I learned that the Kaiser has accepted the Foreign Office view.

One day later Franz was sent packing. The Germans had finally come around to the fact that the U.S. may be the only merciful negotiator at the peace table once the war had finally ended. The fury of Franz was never felt on the American coast itself.[30] The other submarine recalled in the same message was *U-155*.

On 13 October, Franz captured and sank the 1,746-ton Norwegian sailing ship *Stifinder* in the middle of the Atlantic. The *Stifinder* was taking an insignificant load of turpentine from New York to Australia. Franz did let the neutral crew stock provisions, navigation equipment, and charts with them but they were over 1,000 miles from land with only lifeboats to sustain them. It is hard to see the utility of this attack as most soldiers and sailors realized the war would be over soon. After three terrible weeks, the crew of the *Stifinder* made landfall at different points up and down the North American east coast. Franz made one more attempt to catch a convoy straggler but was thwarted by the escorting forces. Shortly thereafter the German naval command announced the end of the commerce war and recalled all U-boats to base. Franz's cruise was a dismal failure with 7,975 gross registered tons sunk.[31]

The last U-Kreuzer whose eventual destination was supposed to be North American waters was German hero Kapitänleutnant Lothar von Arnauld de la Perière's *U-139*, which left Germany on 11 September. The *U-139* was of the same specifications as the *U-140*, and was built for war from her birth. The submarine was faster and more maneuverable than her merchant submarine cousins. De la Perière handled the new U-Kreuzer well but still complained about her maneuverability despite the improvements over the ex-merchant design.

> In a surface fight they could hold their own with anything short of really big guns, but submerged it was difficult to maneuver for a torpedo shot. They were clumsy and did not swing around quickly, as is necessary for a craft that aims its shot by aiming itself.

De la Perière headed south towards the Azores Islands in a roundabout route to North America, which would threaten the U-Kreuzer hunting grounds off West Africa as well as attack the principal German foe on the other side of the Atlantic. Once he arrived off North American shores he was supposed to attack shipping off Cape Hatteras and then head north to Halifax while sinking ships along the whole of the coast.[32]

On 1 October the U-boat ace and his crew spotted a thirty ship convoy off the coast of Spain with protection consisting of the British armed boarding steamer *Perth* of 2,502 tons with three 4.7-inch guns and one other escort. Perière was no timid commander and moved to attack the irresistible target. Perière's first salvo consisted of a torpedo, which missed the convoy altogether. After the attempt at underwater attack failed he surfaced and began shelling the merchant ships. He was forced to dive twice due to the heavy fire from the escorts and the armed merchant ships.

However, the experienced and daring Kapitänleutnant managed to stop two merchantmen. One of them was already sinking but the other was so close that after he torpedoed her he had to crash dive. The deafening roar of the explosion over the U-boat when the torpedo ripped into its' victim was a shock to the men on *U-139*. This was followed by a crash into the U-boat itself. The lights on the U-boat went out and water started to leak into the submarine.

Perière immediately noted that they had gone under their last victim, and she was sinking on top of them. It was literally dragging them down to a watery grave. The experienced commander ordered all tanks blown so the *U-139* would pop to the surface. The *U-139* got out from beneath the sinking ship and surfaced only to be attacked by the escorts with artillery and depth charges. The *U-139* dived again and escaped. Her conning tower and deck were severely damaged but she lived to fight another day.[33]

Perière sank one more ship before he was recalled to Germany on 21 October prior to even obtaining a chance to head west toward the North American shore. He attacked a large Portuguese liner on 14 October and was challenged by a small Portuguese gunboat who bravely but hopelessly fought the massive U-Kreuzer. Perière destroyed the little defensive ship and killed 14 of the 40 man crew. However, he had mercy within him still, unlike Franz and Studt, and picked up the survivors in order to hand them off to the next small ship he met. The liner the small boat was defending escaped with her valuable cargo of alleged American generals.[34] Perière had sunk only 6,223 gross registered tons.[35]

He ended his final cruise with a bittersweet return to Germany on 14 November when he found the High Seas Fleet in mutiny and his country embroiled in a revolution. In addition, SM *U-141*, also a newer U-Kreuzer, didn't even get the chance to sink a single ship before the end of the war.

Perière's cruise was exciting, but it was the final reminder of the futility of Germany's war overall, and of her naval and U-Kreuzer war in particular which had failed to stop American supplies from crossing the Atlantic to Europe, and did not obtain the recall of the U.S. Navy to its own coast. Perière had only sunk three ships during a time when Germany was clearly losing.[36] It is fitting to give the Kaiser the last word on the U-Kreuzer campaign's utility in the wider war. On 19 September in Mainz, Germany he let his subordinate know his true feelings on the matter with the blunt force typical of the German sovereign.

> I spoke to him of last night's announcement that our U-boats had sunk 80,000 tons, our first new U-boat cruiser, which has been active since July 2 having sunk only 30,000 tons. The Kaiser stated "Not a very good announcement. Unless one of these U-boat cruisers returns home having sunk 100,000 tons the U-boat war serves no useful purpose."[37]

18

Indecision, Loss and a Mystery Solved

On 6 September, Feldt radioed Nauen that he had sunk 41,000 tons, including the American armored cruiser USS *San Diego*, gave his current position, and stated he had cut a communications cable. On 7 September, U-Kreuzer command sent orders to Feldt regarding his route through the increasingly dangerous northern mine barrage. The Americans and British were busy while Feldt was causing havoc on the eastern seaboard, and had significantly extended the barrage over areas earlier deemed safe by U-boats. As a result, Feldt could not be sure routes traveled even recently by U-boats were as clear as they had been only a few weeks or months before.

The Northern barrage was a massive undertaking augmented routinely by more American and British mines from March 1918 on. The Americans laid over 56,000 mines in the barrage by war's end while the British laid about 13,000.[1] However, the barrage was by no means perfect, and had many large gaps in its coverage which could allow a U-boat to slip through, and most did. The mining operation was also riddled with problems, which included premature mine explosions that could detonate dozens of mines at the same time. Despite corrective measures the unplanned detonations continued as the operation dragged on.

The U-boats also soon figured out that the presence of floating glass balls indicated a deep minefield was in the area. The balls were still hard to detect as it wasn't the easiest item to spot on the surface of a roiling sea. Before war's end, six submarines were likely destroyed in the mines of the barrage. Despite the increased danger, U-boats continued to use the north-about route often until the end of the war.[2]

U-Kreuzer command's message told Feldt to head to the western end of the barrier and avoid the eastern side of the barrage in Norwegian territorial waters since they believed them to be mined. Shortly thereafter,

18. Indecision, Loss and a Mystery Solved   163

Nauen sent signals to *U-152* about transiting the barrage one way, and then changed the instructions a short time later. Nauen advised the *U-152* to go another way based on a recent successful crossing of the field by SM *UB-94*. Feldt may have heard both these signals, and been further confused about the current makeup of the mine fields.

At this moment, Feldt's limited experience in U-boats and in command of his own vessel may have started working against his better judgment. The daring moves he made during his attack off Orleans, his ravaging of the fishing fleets, the mining operation off New York, and the capture and arming of the *Triumph* were all in the past, replaced by uncertainty and indecisiveness.

On 18 September, *U-139*, commanded by de la Perière reached out to *U-156* via radio. On 20 September, Feldt replied to *U-139* with his own position and asked for a safe route through the northern barrage. Feldt then radioed Germany and reported on what he had observed off the North American coast. He specifically commented on sighting shipping traffic with "protection" in the waters between Halifax and New York. Feldt was apparently attempting to warn his superiors about the increasingly formidable defenses off North America.

Perière and Feldt finally rendezvoused in person after *U-156* overcame yet another problem with her faulty radio. Perière likely advised Feldt his route east of the Shetlands was a workable one. Feldt was obviously not convinced of the continued feasibility of Perière's route since on 22 September he asked SM *U-161* how she had passed through the barrage after hearing a radio signal announcing the boat's successful transit of the barrier.

U-161 replied in a new code cipher which *U-156* apparently could not read. *U-161* then asked Feldt to "come within reach of visual signal." *U-156* again asked for a report by radio due to "lack of time" despite the obvious dangers of British interception as experienced firsthand by the crew of the *U-156* in Naos Bay.

Although Feldt was not on the *U-156* at the time of the ambush by the British submarine he had to have known about the incident due to Gansser's very detailed notes in the *U-156*'s war diary, and the stories doubtless told to him by one of his own officers who was there, Knöckel.

U-161 gave a cautious answer, which did not reveal her route to Feldt. In fact, *U-161* had been lucky in her crossing since she had encountered both mines and destroyers near the barrage, which she was barely able to avoid. On 23 September, U-Kreuzer command received a report from *U-139* that she had met with Feldt three days before. U-Kreuzer command radioed *U-156* and asked her to report her current position and expected arrival in friendlier waters. On 24 September, Feldt's 36th birthday, he replied he was in between the Faroe Islands and the Shetland Islands and was rounding Scotland. He also stated the *U-156* would likely be near Skagen, Denmark on the night of 27 September at the soonest.[3]

Feldt then made a transmission that would prove decisive for the fate of him and his crew, and answered questions U-Kreuzer command had not asked. He reported to them that he would pass through the middle of the barrage on 25 September and then supplied exact coordinates for his proposed route. Feldt had chosen to utilize the route used by *UB-94* on 27 August and suggested for *U-152*'s use on 10 September. U-Kreuzer command replied that Feldt should only use the proposed route during the daytime in calm weather. They also warned him to keep a sharp lookout for the infamous glass balls floating on the surface since they indicated the presence of mines. They then asked him to report when through the barrage, and advise Nauen of his expected arrival at Skagen.

Feldt should have known better, but he had just given the British code breaking team in Room 40 his exact position and time of arrival on the northern edge of the barrage. The British must have been following *U-156*'s signals closely since they were decoding Feldt's messages in almost real time, and acted quickly and decisively when presented with Feldt's ridiculously specific radio messages.

The British immediately sent the information to the northern submarine patrol for action. The Admiralty advised the patrol to send HMS *L8* to the area of expected contact with *U-156* in order to wait in ambush for the U-Kreuzer. *L8* was commissioned in 1916 and was faster and more maneuverable than the *U-156*. She had more torpedo tubes than the big German boat, and was more suited for a submerged attack than an engagement on the surface since she had only one 4-inch gun to face off against the formidable firepower available to the *U-156*. The L class submarines were very new and not many saw action before the war ended.[4]

On the morning of 25 September, *L8* was on the surface when her lookouts spotted a "vessel nature indistinguishable" and the British quickly dived beneath the choppy seas. The sighted "vessel" also dived. *L8* popped to the surface an hour later and searched for the *U-156*. The commander of the *L8* stated the vessel must have been a submarine since it had dived and had no masts or funnels in sight. He also expressed his opinion that the submarine must have seen them too and dived to escape.[5]

Feldt must have finally realized his mistake in including so many details in his radio transmissions. He likely now knew the British were

18. Indecision, Loss and a Mystery Solved 165

reading his radio messages and understood they could have set up another trap for him on the other side of the barrage. He probably continued on the same route he had proposed in his plan on his birthday, although he would now make the transit underwater.

This was highly dangerous and the atmosphere on board the submarine would have been unbelievably tense. Feldt was about to ignore his superiors' advice to make his trip on the surface in calm weather only. Ominously, the seas were becoming rougher during this time frame and Feldt would be blind to the presence of any "glass balls" while making his run.[6]

Nothing more is heard in the historical record from Feldt, his 76 men, or their huge U-boat. Feldt's boat likely struck an American laid mine planted on 30 July a few hours after her encounter with *L8* and sank with all hands. After so much luck, a faulty torpedo warhead in Naos Bay, two faulty aerial bombs off Nauset Beach, a patrol boat commander who ran for help rather than engage the sub, and finally an eagle eyed lookout on *U-156* who spotted *L8* before she could fire her torpedoes. The American mine was not faulty like some of the other weapons deployed against the *U-156*, and there was no looking out underwater. All we can hope is that the end was swift and merciful for the crew.

U-Kreuzer command asked *U-156* for her anticipated arrival time on 26 and 27 September. Feldt did not answer. The British intercepted these calls and were able to inform the Americans that the submarine that had so recently terrorized their coast did not arrive at Skagen on schedule.[7] On 7 October, U-Kreuzer command admitted *U-156* had likely been sunk, and four days later ordered that there would be no published death notice for Feldt in order to deny the British the knowledge of *U-156*'s apparent destruction. The attempted veil of secrecy around Feldt's death was another sign of how little the Germans realized the nature of the compromise of their communications network despite plenty of circumstantial evidence.

Fast forward 80 years later and Carl-Henrik Ankarberg of Sweden took an interest in the fate of the *U-156*. He utilized maps of the Northern barrage from 1918, compared them to Feldt's reported position by radio on the 25th, and overlaid this information with modern shipwreck charts, and found what is likely the *U-156* marked on a modern chart as an "unknown non-dangerous wreck" at a depth of over 300 feet. Ankarberg also had reports about Norwegian fishing boats fouling their nets on an obstruction in this area.[8]

The alleged wreck lies right underneath the northernmost American mine line in the barrage as it existed on 25 September 1918. This area was covered with American Mark VI mines, which were spherical devices with about 300 pounds of TNT anchored to the ocean floor by a mooring cable. One can imagine that even today, after almost 100 years entombed on the ocean floor, the damage from the hundreds of pounds of TNT is probably still evident. The final resting place of the *U-156* is likely at Latitude 594415 North and Longitude 015600 East.

No one has ever confirmed if the wreck is the *U-156* or not, and no divers who have tried to locate the wreck have succeeded. Even with the coordinates from Ankarberg's research the North Sea is a very big place and the discovery of the *U-156* may take a dive team with a lot of technical equipment, time, good funding, and some luck. The wreck of the *U-156* is very unique since the only ex-merchant U-Kreuzers sunk in wartime are the *U-156* and *U-154*, and these machines of war are extremely rare examples of a type of U-boat which accomplished so much despite some of their poor seagoing qualities. The *U-154* was almost completely blown apart according to multiple eyewitnesses so the wreck of the *U-156* may be the only complete ex-merchant U-Kreuzer wreck sunk in combat.

The *U-156* and her exploits were forgotten fairly quickly. World War II eclipsed the Great War in the popular imagination of many Americans and others. Also, the U-boat's Kriegstagebuch (war diary), which would have provided so much information about the actions of the *U-156* and possibly ensured her immortality, still rests on the bottom with Feldt. As a result, her full story was unknown until now.

Back in 1918, a little over a month after Feldt and his men dived for the last time, Kommodore Michelsen, still the head of the U-boat arm, ordered all German submarines back to base. If the *U-156* had survived she still would have never been on another combat cruise due to the time taken for repairs and refits after such a long voyage.

Heinrich Kamps, who gave a picture postcard of himself to the Swedish sailor on the *Dornfontein* to mail in case the *U-156* didn't make it home, was lost to his beloved mother forever. She sat in Hamburg and never received his final message to her. The card ended up in the hands of a Canadian newspaper. In an oddly balanced comment about the postcard in the midst of such a terrible war the *St. John Standard* editorialized.

> The incident only goes to show, that no matter whether the soldier or sailor be enemy or otherwise they have among their first thoughts that of the dear old mother they have left at home.[9]

18. Indecision, Loss and a Mystery Solved

The as yet unconfirmed wreck of the *U-156* would have great meaning for those of us who still honor the memory of those who fought the Great War, and I know somewhere on the bottom of the dark and murky North Sea the same guns that shelled Funchal and Nauset Beach are waiting to

Heinrich Kamps, standing on the right, gave this picture of himself and an unidentified *U-156* crewman to a Swedish sailor on one of the ships they sank off Nova Scotia. Kamps instructed the Swede to mail the card to his mother if *U-156* should be destroyed (*photograph originally from the* Saint John Standard, *August 7, 1918. Reproduction courtesy of the Provincial Archives of New Brunswick*).

be discovered by divers who understand the *U-156* is a protected war grave for 77 men.

For Americans, the *U-156* represents one of the few times when the U.S. itself was attacked by a far away enemy who did damage right off of our shores. The fact that the *U-156* was able to pull off the attack near Orleans, the sinking of the USS *San Diego*, and the arming of a surface raider is rightfully astonishing given our isolation from world affairs in those days. Americans can be proud of their fliers over Orleans in particular that showed such bravery in the face of the *U-156*'s awesome weaponry. The fact remains the Cape Cod defenses had worked except for the bombs themselves. The *U-156* may have met its end off Nauset Beach if the bombs had detonated. They didn't, but that is not the failure of the Navy fliers who risked their lives that day.

America would learn some of the lessons needed for survival against the later Nazi German threat off their shores in this first 1918 U-boat battle, but would unfortunately forget much of the knowledge they had gained regarding coastal convoys and the importance of naval air stations and patrols. Even if the U.S. Navy had learned all of the lessons from the German U-boat raids of 1918 and utilized them in the early days of World War II they may not have been able to do much to combat the new generation of Germans because of the even greater threat posed by the huge Japanese Navy against the west coast after Pearl Harbor. In addition, the irony is not lost on many commentators that the *U-156* was likely the victim of an American laid and manufactured mine, which was a part of the very defenses in European waters that the *U-156* was attempting to have recalled to the North American coast.

For Canada, the *U-156* represents the first time their navy was operationally tested. Although the Royal Canadian Navy did not successfully engage the *U-156* the lessons learned would help them organize their defenses for the much worse challenge they would face from the German U-boat threat in World War II. The *U-156* had boldly attacked ships in Canadian waters using her torpedoes, deck gun, bombs, and her surface raider. She had attained a strategic goal with the closure of Halifax as a transatlantic convoy assembly point. One U-boat had affected Canada and her navy in a way that would not be topped until Canada entered the Second World War and was able to successfully implement some of her defensive and offensive ideas from that first war in 1918.

In Britain, the *U-156*'s sinking is yet another success in a long line of naval successes for the island nation. It was their code breakers and the submarine *L8* who had forced *U-156* to make the transit through the mine

18. Indecision, Loss and a Mystery Solved   169

barrage submerged, which likely resulted in the destruction of the boat. The British would have destroyed the *U-156* in spectacular fashion early in 1918 off El Hierro Island if only their torpedo had functioned properly. The British also had the last word when they were able to tell their American allies that the U-boat that had snubbed its' nose at their coastal defenses had not reported home on time.

For Germans, I believe the *U-156* represents a story about some of their most gallant sailors who tried to bring some small measure of humanity to a war that had thrown all of the rules out the window. Feldt and Gansser did not unnecessarily endanger their crews, and were not above attacking without warning. However, whenever they could, they gave mercy to those who did not resist, and whose ships were unarmed. Gansser is tainted by some of his earlier alleged actions in *U-33*, but he did not further sully his reputation while in command of *U-156*.

The *U-156* achieved many notable successes untainted by any behaviors which could be denounced as war crimes despite Allied attempts to classify some of her attacks as such during the war. She crossed the wide Atlantic Ocean twice in different directions, accomplished the mission given her and more despite communications breaches and faulty equipment, and then succumbed to the formidable resources and drive of the Allied navies who laid the northern barrage.

Germany has the most to gain by finding the *U-156* for she would be finding her own lost sons again after so many years. I believe Feldt and his crew deserve that, and that Germany and the crew's surviving family members deserve to know where they may pay homage to sailors they can still be proud of a century after their untimely deaths. Sailors who had shown the possibilities for success in a long range U-boat war with an imperfect but still groundbreaking machine to take them there and almost back.

The *U-156* sunk 25,872 gross registered tons of shipping consisting of thirty-three vessels during her second cruise. She sank the American cruiser USS *San Diego* for a total of 13,680 non-merchant tons. She also severely damaged three ships for a total of 1,421 tons. The sunk and severely damaged vessels are broken down into nine merchant ships, one warship, four barges, one tugboat, and twenty-one fishing schooners. Six of the schooners had been sunk by *Triumph* for a total of 779 tons. The *U-156* sunk or damaged 40,973 total tons including *Triumph*'s kills. If Gansser's total from the *U-156*'s first cruise is added then the U-boat's sunk or severely damaged total comes to 62,457 tons spread out among 45 different ships.

Twenty-two sailors and merchant seamen died during the *U-156*'s assault on North America. They were killed during the few attacks without warning carried out by the U-boat on the British, Canadian, and American ships *Tortuguero*, USS *San Diego*, *Luz Blanca*, and *Penistone*. The loss of these brave Allied merchant and navy sailors during the waning days of an already lost war is yet another entry in the long list of tragedies of the Great War in its final terrible months. Also worthy of mention are the innocent civilians killed during Gansser's bombardment of Funchal, Madeira, and the sole *U-156* sailor who lost his life after he drowned during the attack on *U-156* in Naos Bay, Obermatrose Arthur Reinhold.

The *U-156* had sunk or severely damaged 34 ships with explosives placed on board after capture, torpedoed and sank one ship, torpedoed and bombed another, torpedoed and shelled a third, mined the USS *San Diego*, shelled five vessels off Orleans, shelled and bombed the *Erik*, and burned the *Dornfontein*. As we can see, the prize rules made bombing after capture the most popular method of destruction with shelling and torpedoing in a distant second and third place.

During the whole six months of the German submarine assault against the east coast of North America the Germans had sunk or severely damaged over 175,000 gross registered tons of shipping and almost 30,000 warship tons with six U-boats. The *U-156* had accounted for a little less than one quarter of the tonnage score for the small campaign.

In spite of being only the second U-boat on station in this theater of war the *U-156* still encountered multiple enemy defensive measures including escorted convoys, multiple armed merchant ships, an attack by American coastal defense planes, and a Canadian anti-submarine patrol. The convoys and armed fast merchant ships especially frustrated Feldt's attempts to sink larger vessels. The convoys and armed ships pushed him to attack smaller and slower vessels traveling alone, although he did run across a few larger victims during the cruise. The Americans and Canadians had come up with an effective defense against the small number of U-Kreuzers deployed despite their limited resources and time. Gansser had encountered only the British submarine ambush, armed merchant ships, and the Portuguese coastal artillery at Funchal during his cruise. The North American defenses were definitely more effective as the only attack which could have brought Gansser down was the carefully planned submarine trap laid by the British, which relied exclusively on extraordinary code-breaking information.

However, American and Canadian defenses became even tougher as the submarine raids drifted into the fall of 1918, and subsequent U-boats had less success than the *U-151* and *U-156*.¹⁰ The 77 men aboard the *U-156* did not know about that bleak future yet as they left the North American coast. They were probably ready to take stock of what they had accomplished, receive their laurels in Kiel, and embrace their families. Of course, like many other soldiers in the First World War, they would do none of that.

Despite the less than stellar results of the U-Kreuzer campaign, the Germans continued to plan for their future right up until the end. A German naval memorandum laid out the plan for long-range U-boat operations.

> The use of U-boats and surface cruisers in the blockade of distant countries depends upon the future development of U-boats and on our possessing suitable bases. There is no doubt that the appearance of German submarines around North American harbors, in the approaches to the Panama Canal, at Cape Verde, or in the Indian Ocean would be very effective.

The memorandum then lays out some of the problems of supply which could hamper such a role for U-boats.

> However, with the increase in operational distances, and the duration of journeys, ships to keep U-boats in supplies will be needed and bases will be absolutely essential for all operations in distant waters. The number of U-boats that would be needed to maintain an economic blockade from such bases and the number of U-boats needed to defend these bases depends solely on strategic considerations and local conditions and they are not to be evaluated here. The use then of U-boats in remote parts of the world must remain a question for the future.¹¹

In November 1917, Admiral Scheer attempted to create a central U-boat office to prioritize and control all aspects of U-boat production and training to eliminate unnecessary bureaucracy and order more U-boats so Germany could combat the increasing effectiveness of convoy with greater numbers of attackers.

Scheer got his way in December 1917 and the U-boat office was created. As mentioned before, the U-boat program it ran was called "The Scheer Program." Its mission was to accelerate the delivery of U-boats and make use of newly available shipyards. One of the problems facing the construction delays for German U-boats was the inadequate food given to workers who could not work overtime shifts due to malnutrition. The British blockade was not only affecting German production based on a lack of raw materials, but was now slowing production by slowly starving the workers.

The Germans began to draw up long term and somewhat delusional plans. They envisioned a few new U-Kreuzers operating in the Gulf of

Mexico and off Brazil in 1920. The operations described would come to pass in a future war, but for now they were flights of fancy. The Germans thought they could have six new U-Kreuzers operating in January 1919, 20 in January 1920, and 27 in January 1921. Hindenburg and Ludendorff gave Scheer assurances that the situation on the ground in August 1918 was now so dire that the only hope Germany had of winning was the U-boat war. They promised to do what they could to increase the production of U-boats.

On 16 August 1918, Scheer stated

> It is most essential to limit U-boat construction to a very small number of types; specialization and the desire to work out improvements must be subordinated to the more important aspect of speeding up the construction programme. We must also apply the American building methods of factory, mass-produced ships, of which we are not completely ignorant in Germany.

Scheer went on to explain that the simplification of the designs and the commitment to only a few types of U-boats would make the building process easier by limiting the amount of training needed. As a result, the number of skilled workers required would be reduced. The Germans encountered this problem in both world wars. Rather than stick to one successful design in order to mass produce a weapon, they would often tinker with existing designs and make whole new models, even as the wars turned against them.

The Germans also discussed building 12 new U-Kreuzers a year although as the war dragged on into September and October the focus on U-Kreuzers started to be less and less as the smaller U-boats were more likely to make an impact on Great Britain itself due to the proximity of their bases to their operational areas.[12]

The U-Kreuzer campaigns off of North America and West Africa failed in their objectives despite the audacious moves of commanders like Feldt and Gansser. The U.S. and Canada did not cave into the pressure from their people and politicians, and the convoys and defenses in European home waters were not diluted. In addition, no full troop convoy ships were destroyed on the way to Europe. The Germans simply did not devote enough U-boats to attack shipping in the North American theater of operations, and acted too late to effect the outcome of the naval war. Also, by the time the campaign occurred the land war in Europe was already winding down to the inevitable defeat of the Central Powers as American troops stiffened the Allies and ground the Germans into the mud of northern France.

In spite of this the U-Kreuzers sank or severely damaged close to half a million tons of shipping during their relatively short wartime service of less than a year and a half. The ten U-Kreuzers that saw operational service in the war sank or severely damaged approximately 4 percent of the total U-boat tonnage. This percentage was achieved with only 2.5 percent of the submarine force at their disposal. At over 436,000 gross registered tons sunk or damaged the U-Kreuzers had also eclipsed their eight infamous surface cruiser brethren from the earlier part of the war by over 150,000 tons. The U-Kreuzers also sunk or severely damaged a little over 30,000 warship tons in addition to their merchant shipping score.

The hidden part of these figures is also the most telling, much of the shipping sunk by the U-Kreuzers was relatively unimportant compared to the ships protected by convoys. Despite *U-139*'s dashing attack on a convoy late in the war, most U-Kreuzer captains kept convoys at arm's length, and even if they didn't avoid convoys the protected vessels were often so fast that they outran the U-Kreuzer before she could ever hope to attack. The U-Kreuzers were meant to be a strategic game-changer despite their small numbers. They turned out to be merely an interesting footnote in the wider history of the Great War. It was a footnote that would have much greater import for the next generation of naval fighters.

Imperial Germany may have been better served using the capable seamen from the U-Kreuzers to man U-boats in the main naval theater of the conflict closer to Europe although that campaign was also a failure after the summer of 1917. The U-Kreuzer campaign was a harbinger of things to come, but would largely be forgotten and eclipsed by the much more deadly and effective attacks by German submarines in World War II against Canada and the United States. The Germans used restricted warfare in outlying waters during World War I. In World War II that courtesy would disappear into the abyss of history, like so many Allied ships and the *U-156* herself, since the German Navy in World War II would make far flung unrestricted operations part of their core strategic doctrine.

Epilogue

Deadly Dreams Become Reality

In the Second World War, almost all of the wildest dreams of the Kaiserliche Marine's U-boat arm became reality. The new Kriegsmarine adopted the embryonic wolf pack tactics to combat the Allied convoy system and made a huge dent in that system for a time. U-boats also became more reliable and maneuverable, and could more easily travel the long distances needed to attack shipping off North America, Africa, South America, and the Caribbean.

U-boats even transited half the globe to reach special naval bases they shared with their Japanese allies late in the war. The German effort in the Pacific and Indian Oceans was small and ineffective but fulfilled the Germans' World War I obsession with obtaining bases to operate in far flung waters where they imagined Allied defenses were weaker. The joint effort resulted in one of the few times the Japanese and Germans coordinated their military efforts during World War II.

However, despite the small diplomatic success between the two Axis partners, the Kriegsmarine was wrong about the state of the Allied defenses in the Indian and Pacific Oceans, and the Germans met nothing but problems and danger in Asia with few successes to make it worthwhile.[1] The only reason Admiral Karl Dönitz, head of the German Navy, had consented to war in this area was as part of a strategy that is very familiar to a student of the Great War's U-Kreuzers: he wanted to splinter the enemy's defenses in the Atlantic by forcing them to transfer warships to the Indian and Pacific Oceans. The strategy failed due to the Allies overwhelming aerial and naval defensive forces, their targeted attacks guided by information from code breaking, and the lack of German supplies in the Far East.

The German U-boats could not use the meager and technically incompatible naval repair resources of the Japanese Empire to fix their own U-boats. German U-boats still managed to sink approximately

687,500 tons of shipping in the Indian Ocean while the Japanese submarine force sank only 596,840 tons in the same ocean. Japanese efforts had always been focused on warship attacks rather than serious attempts to curtail their enemy's merchant tonnage. The Germans had shown their skill in attacks on merchant ships in a far off theater and even beaten the Japanese tonnage score in their own backyard. However, Allied defensive efficiency in stopping the U-boats and meager Japanese assistance with the mission made the German foray to the east a sideshow after Dönitz had already lost the all important Battle of the Atlantic.[2]

The U-Kreuzer war off North America in 1918 lasted for about six months. The German campaign against North America that kicked off in January 1942 had its greatest successes in that same amount of time. The German strategy was simple, they surmised the American defenses were weaker than those they faced in European waters. The Kriegsmarine hoped this would allow them to make more of an impact on Allied trade and supplies near the beginning of the ships' journeys rather than at the end near Britain or in the northern Russian ports. The new generation of German U-boat commanders in 1942 were not as worried about recalling Allied defenses to the North American coast, or other concerns the Germans had in 1918 and later in 1944 and 1945. They wanted as many ships sunk as they could manage, and they would eventually commit more U-boats to the theater than von Holtzendorff could ever have dreamed of.[3]

In a more ominous repeat of the show witnessed by the residents of Orleans in July 1918, beachgoers enjoying the Virginia Beach sun on 15 June 1942 saw war come incredibly close to their shores. A short time before, *U-701* had dropped mines at the entrance to Chesapeake Bay and the effort was about to garner fruit. As the beachgoers looked on, a 12 ship convoy arranged itself to head into the bay after a long and dangerous voyage. The sailors on the ships may have breathed a sigh of relief when they saw the friendly and peaceful shore.

After 5:00 p.m., one of the oil tankers was subjected to a large explosion and started to sink. The shock wave, sound, and sight of the explosion could be felt, heard, and seen by the vacationers on the beach. Fifteen minutes later U.S. Navy aircraft and a blimp started to patrol the area over the convoy and even dropped depth charges on what they thought could be the location of the now long gone U-boat. At this time no one was completely sure they had stumbled into a minefield. As the defenders scrambled, a second oil tanker exploded and was disabled. U.S. Navy destroyers arrived and also started to depth charge suspected U-boat locations. As in Orleans 24 years before, the local Coast Guard station sprang into action in their surfboats to save any sailors that may have been in the water or wounded by the explosions. Thousands of people also came down to the beach to witness what they thought was a World War II battle between the U.S. Navy and a U-boat right off Virginia.

A small British anti-submarine trawler was the next victim as it struck a mine and disappeared in a massive explosion with eighteen of her crew.[4] The minefield claimed one more ship before the area was declared mine free again. The Germans had introduced the insulated American public to what a World War looked, sounded, and felt like yet again, and in dramatic fashion. The *U-701* itself didn't have long to celebrate and wasn't even lucky enough to at least attempt the trip home as the *U-156* had done. The Kriegsmarine submarine was sent to the bottom by a U.S. airplane dropped explosive that worked perfectly just three weeks after the Chesapeake Bay mining operation. Unlike *U-156*, there were a few survivors who were rescued, captured, and imprisoned in the United States.[5]

The Germans even penetrated the inland waters of the Gulf and river of St. Lawrence in Canada in 1942 and 1944. The population of Quebec suddenly found themselves with sinking ships in waters that had not been attacked by the enemy in 1918. The *U-156* and other U-Kreuzers had come close to the entrance of the gulf but did not venture inside. The Kriegsmarine sent thirteen submarines into the St. Lawrence with 26 ships sunk or severely damaged in the middle of the Canadian heartland.[6] The Germans also hunted in the waters off West Africa again from the winter of 1942 on in another attempt to chase the ever elusive sweet spot where a U-boat could sink ships and have little in the way of organized defenses to contend with.[7]

The long range U-boat campaign against North America, the Caribbean Sea, and the Gulf of Mexico in World War II from January to June 1942 cost the Allies 226 valuable merchant ships and oil tankers for a total of 1,251,650 gross registered tons. The Germans weren't sinking tiny fishing boats the second time around. The submariners in the navy of the Third Reich were after the biggest and most valuable ships they could find.

The above attacks were all done with U-boats hunting their prey alone as had been done in the First World War. In World War II, due to a substantial increase in the number of U-boats available in 1942 and 1943, Kommodore Bauer's dream of using a central command to coordinate attacks on convoys would come true with terrifying results. Luckily for the Allies, the tactic did not appear regularly on the scene until the second half of 1942 when their defensive capabilities had grown. Prior to and during this period, Nazi Germany had adopted the Milchkuh concept, attempted to have an operational commander on scene within the "wolfpack," and used radio to coordinate the movements of the submarines against the enemy.

Radios had improved so much in the interwar years that the Germans soon found that the on scene commander was unnecessary, and also prone to losing control of the pack since his U-boat would often be forced to deal with convoy defenders and other sudden issues. In effect, Bauer's command and control U-Kreuzer idea was dropped while his supply U-boat idea was embraced. The command boat was replaced by direct control from land with orders being given from headquarters to the U-boats at sea. The instructions in this new war were much more timely and specific than those given by Nauen in 1917 and 1918. The Kriegsmarine had a team to take a look at all of the latest available intelligence centrally, and then feed it back to the submarines so they could assault the convoys in as organized a manner as is possible under sea combat conditions.[8]

From September 1942 to May 1943 Dönitz had his U-boat packs focus on attacks in the North Central Atlantic where there was no Allied air cover. The wolfpack, a quarter of a century after the idea had originated, was finally coming of age. No U-Kreuzer was needed for success. Only a few supply U-boats and dozens of attack submarines were necessary to assault, and the Germans hoped, defeat the Allied convoy system.[9] The unattained goal of the First World War's German U-boat leadership was about to come dangerously close to fruition for this next generation of German naval warriors.[10]

In October 1940 eight U-boats attacked two convoys named SC 7 and HX 79, which sank 31 ships totaling 152,000 tons. No U-boats were lost. The next year also brought successes for the U-boats during convoy operations, but the number of U-boats available continued to limit operations.[11]

In May 1942, Dönitz had a fairly small flotilla of eight U-boats waiting for convoy traffic in the North Atlantic. They intercepted convoy ONS 92 with six escorts comprised of destroyers and corvettes. Five of the patrolling U-boats attacked the convoy and sank seven ships with no loss to themselves.[12]

In June 1942, the worldwide tonnage total reached an appalling 834,196 gross registered tons of Allied and neutral shipping lost. In the same month, convoys ONS 100 and 102 were attacked by a German wolfpack named Hecht. It took twelve U-boats to sink twelve merchant ships and an escort corvette without loss to themselves. The Allies were gravely concerned but seemingly not overwhelmed yet.[13]

In the first three weeks of March 1943 Dönitz's wolfpacks, directed from the Admiral's headquarters, had sunk 141,000 gross registered tons of ships in three valuable convoys. The convoys carried vital war materials like meat, trains, ammunition, and supply barges for amphibious invasions.

The Germans lost only one submarine and a few U-boats damaged by the main actions against the convoys from March 16 to March 19. However, the damaged U-boats were still operational, and were able to continue on patrol or return home. It was a stunning success which had been assisted by the bad weather that had limited the convoy escort's effectiveness, and of course the air gap in the North Central Atlantic, which for the time being was out of the range of Allied escort aircraft.[14]

During another March 1943 battle, the wolfpacks attacked convoy HX 228 of 60 merchant ships with protection from four destroyers, five corvettes, a U.S. anti-submarine aircraft carrier, and two more destroyers to protect the carrier from the U-boats. HMS *Harvester*, one of the destroyers, sought out a radar contact and discovered *U-444* cruising on the surface. The U-boat dived, the *Harvester* attacked with depth charges, and the *U-444* was forced to surface again.

The *Harvester* rammed the submarine but unfortunately the U-boat became stuck underneath the ship's propellers. The submarine eventually extricated itself from this uncomfortable position only to be sunk by ramming after the French escort *Aconit* found her. The damage to the *Harvester*'s propeller shafts was fatal, and while she was stopped helpless in the water another U-boat came along, fired two torpedoes into her, and she sank with heavy loss of life. The *Harvester* was quickly avenged when the *Aconit* discovered the U-boat who had sunk her, depth charged the Germans, and then forced them to surface.[15] The *Aconit* then rammed and gunned the U-boat, which destroyed the enemy vessel.[16]

The story of the merchant ship *Mathew Luckenbach* is a perfect example of the fact that U-boats still preferred the lone unprotected target to battling with a protected convoy even during this time of great convoy fights. The *Luckenbach* had been a part of HX 229 in March 1943 when the convoy was attacked, and the crew and captain decided to leave the convoy and go out alone.

The *Luckenbach* was torpedoed the night after her foolhardy decision by *U-527*. The crew abandoned ship after apparently leaving one of their own in the water despite an opportunity to save the unlucky man. The ship settled but then stopped sinking. *U-527* wanted to come in for the kill and finish the ship but saw a destroyer and aircraft approaching so the U-boat escaped the area. The destroyer and another ship rescued the survivors, although the men they saved did nothing to help themselves, and the operation took much longer due to their apparent lack of active assistance to their saviors.

As the *Luckenbach* appeared to be salvageable it was suggested the crew board their damaged ship so she could be saved. The crew of the *Luckenbach* refused and in so doing capped a terrible night caused by their own bad decisions. They had placed two more ships in danger of destruction by the enemy simply by their need to be rescued. Luckily no harm came to the rescuers. *U-523* later came upon the damaged *Luckenbach* and finished the ship off with a torpedo.[17]

The wolfpacks slated to attack the three convoys in the first part of March 1943 were joined over the course of the battle by 42 separate U-boats. They were never all there at once but came into the battle and left as circumstances dictated. Despite the gloomy casualties sustained in this fight the Allies had actually weathered the worst of the storm in 1943, and indeed had lost much less shipping percentage wise than some other notable convoy battles in earlier years. The battle was a big test of convoy due to the number of U-boats involved, but in hindsight convoy had passed the test even with the grievous losses.[18]

Dönitz noted the decreasing effectiveness of his submarines against convoys after the successes of March. The Allies expanded aerial coverage over the gap, inserted better equipped escorts into the convoys' defenses, and utilized new weapons like better radar and hedgehog mortars to make the U-boats' lives shorter and shorter as the months dragged on. In late May Dönitz recalled his U-boats from the North Atlantic after losing over 30 of them to Allied attack. The new focus of Allied defensive and offensive resources on the vital North Atlantic routes was taking a toll on the Germans, and had sent their tonnage scores plummeting to levels not seen since 1941, when there were far fewer U-boats available.[19]

U-boats still prowled the waters off the Americas until the very end of the war with one of them surrendering to Allied forces on the North American coast, but they would never again have the success they achieved in 1942.[20] The Americans learned their lesson for the second time in 24 years and instituted coastal convoys and stronger aerial and seaborne defenses. In total during World War II the Axis Powers sent 95 U-boats to the waters off of North America, 89 more than those sent by the Kaiser in the first war, and still they were defeated.

Dramatis Personæ
(in order of appearance)

Sims
Admiral William Sims was a rising star in the U.S. Navy when World War I broke out. He was the main liaison officer to the Royal Navy at the start of the war and was then promoted to command all U.S. Naval forces in Europe. He was known as an anglophile before, during, and after the war. Sims was an enthusiastic supporter of naval airpower, the convoy system, and naval intelligence. He retired in 1922 and died in 1936.[1]

Benson
Admiral William Benson was the first Chief of Naval Operations in the history of the United States. His job was to quietly prepare the U.S. Navy for war prior to the opening of actual hostilities with the Central Powers. Benson eventually agreed to focus on anti-submarine vessels once it became apparent large warships would not be as vital in the Great War. Benson became disillusioned by the Versailles peace negotiations, which he believed had been too harsh on the defeated Germans. He died in 1932.[2]

von Tirpitz
Admiral Alfred von Tirpitz was the leading figure in the naval arms race Germany engaged in with Britain prior to the beginning of the First World War. After the war began and he realized Germany's fleet was too small to resist the Royal Navy he became a vociferous proponent of unrestricted submarine warfare. After his resignation in 1916 he became a prominent right wing leader in the new Fatherland political party. The party supported the further prosecution of the war and applauded the efforts of Germany's leadership to obtain conquests in Europe during 1917 and 1918. Tirpitz died in 1930 after serving as a deputy in the Reichstag for a few years.[3]

von Ingenohl

Admiral Friedrich von Ingenohl was the commander of the High Seas Fleet from the beginning of the war into 1915 when he was relieved due to his failure to engage part of the Royal Navy after his ships raided the British town of Scarborough to draw a section of the enemy out. Ingenohl thought he had the whole British fleet bearing down on him and retreated. After he was sacked, the Admiral held a minor command and shortly thereafter retired in August 1915. He died in 1933.[4]

von Bethmann-Hollweg

German Chancellor Theobald von Bethmann-Hollweg attempted to placate both the left and the right in Germany during the war. In the end he pleased no one and was forced to resign after eight years as Chancellor. He died in 1921.[5]

von Holtzendorff

Admiral Henning von Holtzendorff had his start in the navy prior to the formation of the German Empire in 1869. He participated in several conflicts, including the Franco-Prussian war and the Boxer Rebellion. He was commander of the High Seas Fleet prior to the beginning of World War I, and was one of the main proponents of unrestricted submarine warfare and U-Kreuzer warfare. He died in 1919.[6]

von Capelle

Admiral Eduard von Capelle was a close confidant of von Tirpitz and succeeded him as Secretary of State of the Imperial Naval Office in 1916. At first he opposed unrestricted submarine warfare but later changed his mind. He unsuccessfully attempted to stop the spread of socialist ideas in the German fleet late in the war. He died in 1931.[7]

von Hindenburg

Field Marshal Paul von Hindenburg upheld the appearance of a strong, smart, and decisive leader in German military and political affairs for twenty years. In World War I he and Ludendorff made a name for themselves after their defeat of a large invading Russian army in easter Germany at Tannenberg. The duo then became the leaders of the German military after Hindenburg's predecessor as Chief of Staff of the Army was removed from command. Hindenburg relied on Ludendorff's energy and ideas while Ludendorff relied on Hindenburg's calm demeanor and popularity with the German people. Together they ruled Germany as virtual military dictators who outlined the grand war strategy for the Second Reich in 1917 and 1918. Hindenburg and Ludendorff's expansionist aims saw their apex in the acquisition of massive Russian territories in the East, which proved ephemeral. Hindenburg eventually re-entered politics and became the President of the German republic prior to and during the rise of Hitler. He died in 1934 after he reluctantly included Hitler in his own government as Reich Chancellor.[8]

Ludendorff

First Quartermaster General Erich Ludendorff was described as nervous, energetic, and prone to fits of anger. Ludendorff was a lifetime army staff officer and an individual who was never off work during a time of war. He made his name during the invasion of Belgium, at Tannenberg, and in other victories on the Eastern front thanks to his partnership with Hindenburg and the talented General Max Hoffman. After defeating Russia he gambled all of Germany's remaining combat power on a series of offensives on the Western front designed to defeat the Allies and occupy France before the Americans could arrive in force. The offensives failed and Ludendorff resigned his post in late October 1918. Ludendorff took part in two attempts to overthrow the Weimar Republic in the 1920s which both failed. Ludendorff and Hitler led the second attempt at revolution in Munich when the police opened fire on the revolutionaries and Hitler was arrested. Ludendorff also served as a Reichstag deputy for the Nazi party and unsuccessfully ran as their candidate for President. Ludendorff died in 1937, and left a legacy of fostering the anti-Jewish "stab in the back" legend as the reason Germany lost the Great War. In fact Ludendorff's own decisions had led Germany to such a disastrous defeat.[9]

Jellicoe

Admiral John Jellicoe commanded the British Grand Fleet at the Battle of Jutland when the German and British navies finally met in combat. The battle was not a clear victory at the time but heralded the end of any German hopes of defeating the Royal Navy in the North Sea. The Germans stayed in the Baltic for the rest of the war except for small forays here and there. Jellicoe later became First Sea Lord and was against convoys until he was ordered to implement them in 1917. He later became the Governor of New Zealand and was made an Earl before he died in 1935.[10]

Scheer

Admiral Reinhard Scheer joined the Kaiserliche Marine in 1879, served as captain of a battleship in 1907, and was the Chief of Staff of the High Seas Fleet in 1910. Scheer commanded the German High Seas Fleet at the Battle of Jutland. Scheer was the last Admiralty Chief of Staff for the German Empire headed by Kaiser Wilhelm II. He attempted to facilitate a last ditch attack by the German navy at the end of the war. However, the fleet's sailors revolted after they learned of the plan to go down fighting, and the final battle never occurred.[11]

König

Paul König was a merchant captain and worked for Norddeutscher Lloyd before the war, but was recalled to active naval service once the Great War began. After his famous adventures in the *U-Deutschland* he assisted in the selection of the combat officers who commanded the seven ex-merchant U-Kreuzers. He also commanded a number of minesweepers until he went into the reserves as a Kapitänleutnant in 1918. König once again worked for Norddeutscher Lloyd after the war until 1932 when he retired. He traveled to the U.S. often for the company and even did a speaking tour at the end of his career to talk about the voyages of his merchant submarine. The tour was not popular due to revelations about German sabotage while the U.S. was neutral, and the passage of time from the events of the First World War. König died shortly after his retirement in 1933.[12]

Rose

Kapitänleutnant Hans Rose was a famous German U-boat ace, holder of the much sought after Pour le Mérite, and the victor over approximately 220,000 gross registered tons of Allied and neutral shipping during the war. Rose also sank the American destroyer USS *Jacob Jones* in December 1917. He was noted for his mercy after attacks when he provided food and supplies to the crews of sunken ships, and even towed survivors' lifeboats until help arrived. Rose ended the war on the U-boat command staff before he retired in 1918. He died in 1969.[13]

Bauer

Hermann Bauer led the U-boat arm from 1914 to 1917 when he moved on to command a battleship. Bauer remained in the much reduced German navy after the war and attained the rank of Admiral in 1928 when he retired. Bauer declared he was available for service in World War II but was never called back to the colors. He died in 1958.[14]

Michelsen

Andreas Michelsen entered the German navy in 1888 and commanded surface ships during most of the Great War. He assumed command of German destroyers and torpedo boats in July 1915. In June 1917 he took over the command of all U-boats from Hermann Bauer, and received the coveted Pour le Mérite for his efforts during a trying time for the U-boat arm. At the beginning of his leadership tenure the U-boats were at the height of their successes. Unfortunately for Michelsen the success was not a lasting one. He became an Admiral in the post war navy and retired from the service in December of 1920. He died in 1932.[15]

Hall

Admiral William Hall was the British Director of Naval Intelligence, and from 1916 to the end of the war he oversaw Room 40's operations, and some of their greatest successes like the Zimmermann telegram, the operation against the *Erri Berro*, and the uncovering of a German spy network in the U.S. Hall took a great interest in his secret operations and often directed them personally in some capacity. After the war Hall became a member of Parliament and commanded a unit of the Home Guard during World War II. He died in 1943.[16]

Valentiner

Kapitänleutnant Max Valentiner was one of the greatest German U-boat aces of the First World War with over 300,000 tons sunk or damaged from 1915 to 1918. Prior to his command of the *U-157* he led the *U-38*, and earned the Iron Cross First and Second Classes, the Royal House Order of Hohenzollern, and the coveted Pour le Mérite. Valentiner died in 1949 in Denmark.[17]

von Nostitz

Korvettenkapitän Heinrich von Nostitz und Jänckendorff's first and only U-boat command was in the *U-151*. He had a reputation for scrupulously following the prize rules on the American coast when possible although civilians did die in open lifeboats after his attacks, which included the sinking of a passenger ship. Von Nostitz retired from the navy in 1919 and died in 1953. He was decorated with both classes of the Iron Cross and received the Royal House Order of Hohenzollern for his exploits on the North American east coast.[18]

Dönitz

Admiral Karl Dönitz started out as a U-boat officer and commander in World War I after a few years on surface ships, and then moved up the ranks of the navy until he became the head of Hitler's U-boat force. Later, he became the head of the whole Kriegsmarine. After Hitler committed suicide he named Dönitz the new leader of Nazi Germany. The Admiral only held the post for a short time before he negotiated the surrender of his country to the Allies. After spending over 10 years in prison for war crimes, Dönitz lived a fairly quiet life in Germany until he died on Christmas Eve 1980. Dönitz is widely credited for inventing the wolfpack U-boat tactic although as we have seen he was not the first to think of the idea, but in fairness he did use his position to implement it effectively.[19]

Sites of Interest

The USS *San Diego* wreck site off Long Island, New York, is a popular scuba diving location. The French Cable Station Museum in Orleans, Massachusetts, tells the story of the French cables Feldt tried to cut, and is only a few miles away from the Orleans Historical Society Museum, which has a few original artifacts from the *U-156*'s attack off Nauset Beach. Nauset Beach itself is only a short distance away from the society's headquarters. The wrecks of the sunken barges are also dived on off Nauset Beach although they are not as well known as the *San Diego* wreck.

Feldt and the other members of the *U-156*'s crew who died in combat are commemorated on a plaque at the Möltenort U-boat memorial in Germany near Kiel along with thousands of other U-boat crewmen killed during both World Wars.

The Nossa Senhora da Paz (Our Lady of Peace) Sanctuary in Terreiro da Luta, Madeira, was built after World War I in thanks for the end of the war, which had seen Funchal bombarded twice by German U-boats. There is also a small museum in the still extant Fort Santiago in Funchal, which had an artillery duel with the *U-156* back in December 1917.

Tables

Ships Sunk or Damaged by *U-156*

Date Attacked	Name	Tonnage	Type	Sunk/ Damaged	Ordnance Used
12/7/1917	W.C. McKay	147	Fishing	Sunk/Canadian	Bombed
12/12/1917	Joannina	4,191	Merchant	Sunk/Greek	Bombed
12/17/1917	Accoriano	312	Merchant	Sunk/Portuguese	Bombed
12/30/1917	Joaquin Mumbru	2,703	Merchant	Sunk/Spanish	Bombed
1/11/1918	Atlas	1,813	Merchant	Sunk/Dutch	Bombed
2/8/1918	Artesia	2,762	Merchant	Sunk/British	Bombed
2/8/1918	Chariton	3,023	Merchant	Sunk/Greek	Bombed
2/8/1918	Nuzza	1,102	Merchant	Sunk/Italian	Bombed
2/9/1918	Atlantide	5,431	Merchant	Sunk/Italian	Bombed
6/26/1918	Tortuguero	4,175	Merchant	Sunk/British	Torpedoed
7/7/1918	Marosa	1,987	Merchant	Sunk/Norwegian	Bombed
7/8/1918	Manx King	1,729	Merchant	Sunk/Norwegian	Bombed
7/19/1918	USS San Diego	13,680	Warship	Sunk/American	Mined
7/21/1918	Perth Amboy	452	Tugboat	Damaged/American	Shelled
7/21/1918	Lansford	830	Barge	Sunk/American	Shelled
7/21/1918	766	527	Barge	Sunk/American	Shelled
7/21/1918	703	934	Barge	Sunk/American	Shelled
7/21/1918	740	680	Barge	Sunk/American	Shelled
7/22/1918	Robert and Richard	112	Fishing	Sunk/American	Bombed
8/2/1918	Dornfontein	766	Merchant	Damaged/Canadian	Burned
8/3/1918	Muriel	120	Fishing	Sunk/American	Bombed
8/3/1918	Sydney B. Atwood	100	Fishing	Sunk/American	Bombed

Date Attacked	Name	Tonnage	Type	Sunk/ Damaged	Ordnance Used
8/3/1918	Annie Perry	116	Fishing	Sunk/American	Bombed
8/3/1918	Rob Roy	112	Fishing	Sunk/American	Bombed
8/4/1918	Nelson A.	72	Fishing	Sunk/Canadian	Bombed
8/5/1918	Agnes G. Holland	100	Fishing	Sunk/Canadian	Bombed
8/5/1918	Gladys M. Hollett	203	Fishing	Damaged/Canadian	Bombed
8/5/1918	Luz Blanca	4,868	Merchant	Sunk/Canadian	Torpedoed and Shelled
8/8/1918	Sydland	3,031	Merchant	Sunk/Swedish	Bombed
8/11/1918	Penistone	4,139	Merchant	Sunk/British	Torpedoed and Bombs
8/17/1918	San Jose	1,586	Merchant	Sunk/Norwegian	Bombed
8/20/1918	A. Piatt Andrew	141	Fishing	Sunk/American	Bombed
8/20/1918	Francis J. O'Hara	117	Fishing	Sunk/American	Bombed
8/20/1918	Lucille M. Schnare	121	Fishing	Sunk/Canadian	Bombed
8/20/1918	Pasadena	119	Fishing	Sunk/Canadian	Bombed
8/20/1918	Uda A. Saunders	125	Fishing	Sunk/Canadian	Bombed
8/21/1918	Notre Dame de la Garde	145	Fishing	Sunk/French	Bombed
8/21/1918	Sylvania	136	Fishing	Sunk/American	Bombed
8/21/1918	Triumph	239	Fishing	Sunk/Canadian	Bombed
8/25/1918	Erik	583	Merchant	Sunk/British	Shelled and Bombed
8/25/1918	E.B. Walters	126	Fishing	Sunk/Canadian	Bombed
8/25/1918	C.M. Walters	107	Fishing	Sunk/Canadian	Bombed
8/25/1918	Verna D. Adams	132	Fishing	Sunk/Canadian	Bombed
8/25/1918	J.J. Flaherty	162	Fishing	Sunk/American	Bombed
8/26/1918	Gloaming	130	Fishing	Sunk/Canadian	Bombed

Specifications of *U-156*
(during her second cruise)

Measurements	213 ft. (length)
	29 ft. (beam)
	30 ft. (height)
	17 ft. (draught)
Displacement (tons)	1,512 (s)
	1,875 (u)
Max Depth	150 ft.
Engines/propulsion	Two Diesel = 800 hp
	Two Electric = 800 hp
	2 propellers
Speed	12.4 knots (s)
	5.2 knots (u)
Range	25,000 miles (s)
	75 miles (u)
Armament	2 bow tubes
	18 torpedoes
	2 deck guns
	7 + mines
Crew	57 with 20 prize crew

(s) = surfaced and (u) = submerged

The Lost Officers of *U-156*'s Second Cruise

Rank	Name	Date of Death
Kapitänleutnant, Kommandant	Richard Feldt	9/25/1918
Kapitänleutnant, 1 Wachoffizier, Kommandant Schüler	Arnold Vorkampff-Laue	9/25/1918
Oberleutnant zur See der Reserve, U-Offiziere, Prisenoffizier	Paul Richard Knöckel	9/25/1918
Leutnant zur See der Reserve, Wachoffizier	Kurt Bugel	9/25/1918
Leutnant zur See der Reserve, Wachoffizier	Albert Lutzner	9/25/1918
Head Engineer	Ernst Niemann	9/25/1918
Doctor/Surgeon	Martin Schlemm	9/25/1918

U-Kreuzer Tonnage Scores Worldwide
(sunk and significantly damaged)*

U-boat	Cruises	Gross Registered Tons	Warship Tonnage
U-151	2	100,722	0
U-152	2	38,555	0
U-153	1	12,742	0
U-154	1	26,352	0
U-155	3	121,467	0
U-156	3 (1 aborted)	48,777	13,680
U-157	2	15,905	0
U-117	1	35,020	16,000 damaged
U-140	1	30,594	0
U-139	1	6,233	485
Totals	17	436,367	30,165

*Significantly damaged indicates a ship had to be brought into dock for extensive repairs and the vessel was not safe to operate until fixed. Note that SM *U-141* did not go out on any patrols and sank no ships before the end of the war.

U-Kreuzer Tonnage Scores for the North American Raids/Campaign
(Exclusively attacks by U-boats who made it to the mid–Atlantic in transit to the American coast)

U-boat	# of ships sunk/damaged	Gross Registered Tons	Warship Tonnage
U-151	23	58,028	0
U-152	3	7,975	0
U-155	8	17,525	0
U-156	36	27,293	13,680
U-117	23	35,020	16,000 damaged
U-140	7	30,594	0
Totals	102	176,435	29,680

Chapter Notes

Prologue

1. *World Atlas*, "Canary Islands," http://www.worldatlas.com/webimage/countrys/europe/canary.htm.
2. Arno Spindler, *Der Krieg zur See 1914–1918: Handelskrieg mit U-Booten Volume 5* (Frankfurt: E.S. Mittler & Sohn, 1966), 241–242.
3. National Archives Microfilm Publications: *Microcopy No. T-1022 Guides to the Microfilmed Records of the German Navy, 1850–1945: No. 1. U-Boats and T-Boats 1914–1918, Kriegstagebuch U-156*. Washington 1984, can be found under *U-156*, Konrad Ganßer, or Richard Feldt at the U.S. National Archives Microfilm Room College Park, MD.

Chapter 1

1. Paul C. Vincent, *The Politics of Hunger: The Allied Blockade of Germany, 1915–1919* (Athens: Ohio University Press, 1985), 10–24.
2. The Declarations of Paris (1856) and London (1909) were maritime agreements meant to govern the conduct of blockades, including what was considered contraband. World War I saw contraband and blockade rules thrown out the window. Total War killed the combatants and their naïve pre-war agreements with equal ruthlessness. (*Laws of War*, Yale.edu)
3. Vincent, *The Politics of Hunger*, 1985, 27–34.
4. *Ibid.*, 36.
5. *Ibid.*, 38.
6. *Ibid.*, 37–41.
7. *Ibid.*, 45.
8. Steve Dunn, *Blockade: Cruiser Warfare and the Starvation of Germany in World War One* (Barnsley: Seaforth Publishing, 2016), 128–130.
9. Vincent, *The Politics of Hunger*, 1985, 49.
10. *Ibid.*, 1985, 103.
11. Edward Hurley, *The Bridge to France* (Philadelphia: J.B. Lippincott, 1927), 274–276.

Chapter 2

1. Carlos Lozada, 2004, "The Economics of World War I, "National Bureau of Economic Research," http://www.nber.org/digest/jan05/w10580.html.
2. Benjamin Fordham, 2007, "Revisionism Reconsidered: Exports and American Intervention in the First World War," Binghamton University, http://dev.wcfia.harvard.edu/sites/default/files/FordhamND.pdf
3. Holger Herwig, *Politics of Frustration: The United States in German Naval Planning, 1889–1941* (Boston: Little, Brown & Co., 1976), 165.
4. The U.S. Shipping Board was originally a pre-war organization given the power to regulate and promote the interests of the American merchant marine. In 1917, when war was declared on Germany by the U.S., the Shipping Board expanded its' mission to include the acquisition of ships for the successful transportation of goods and soldiers to Europe to fight the Central Powers. The Shipping Board's new powers were delegated to the organization by the President of the United States (*U.S. Shipping Board* 8).
5. Hurley, *The Bridge to France*, 1927, 31–41.
6. The 54,282 ton passenger liner *Vaterland* was the largest ship in the world until 1922. At the beginning of her career she traveled to New York in July 1914 and was later interned there for almost three years after the war was declared. It had quickly become abun-

dantly clear that the British control of the seas would never allow the ship to see Germany again. In April 1917 the U.S. declared war on Germany and seized the vessel. The U.S. renamed it the *Leviathan*. The ship was in U.S. service until 1938 when it was scrapped in Scotland (Naval Historical Center "*SS Leviathan*").

7. Hurley, *The Bridge to France*, 1927, 39–41.
8. *Ibid.*, 110–111.
9. *Ibid.*, 209–212.
10. *Ibid.*, 232–233.
11. Herwig, *Politics of Frustration*, 1976, 163.
12. *Ibid.*, 164–165.
13. The Weimar Republic is the name given to the government that existed in Germany after the fall of Kaiser Wilhelm II's Imperial government (Second Reich) in 1918 and before the rise of Hitler's Third Reich in 1933.
14. Hurley, *The Bridge to France*, 1927, 125–135.
15. Herwig, *Politics of Frustration*, 1976, 169.

Chapter 3

1. Nick Hewitt, *The Kaiser's Pirates: Hunting Germany's Raiding Cruisers 1914–1915* (South Yorkshire: Pen & Sword, 2013), 1–205.
2. Edwyn Gray, *The U-Boat War: 1914–1918* (London: Leo Cooper, 1994), 1–266.
3. Hurley, *The Bridge to France*, 1927, 219.
4. Dwight Messimer, *Find and Destroy: Anti-Submarine Warfare in World War I* (Annapolis: Naval Institute Press, 2001), 91–97.
5. Michael Hadley, and Roger Sarty, *Tin Pots and Pirate Ships: Canadian Naval Forces and German Sea Raiders 1880–1918* (Montreal & Kingston: McGill-Queen's University Press, 1991), 225.
6. Uboat.net "Ships Hit During WWI, Losses by Month," http://uboat.net/wwi/ships_hit/losses_year.html.
7. Messimer, *Find and Destroy*, 2001, 147–156.
8. Hadley and Sarty, *Tin Pots and Pirate Ships*, 1991, 232.
9. Dwight Messimer, *The Baltimore Sabotage Cell: German Agents, American Traitors, and the U-Boat Deutschland During World War I* (Annapolis: Naval Institute Press, 2015), 155–156.
10. Herwig, *Politics of Frustration*, 1976, 113–116.
11. John Terraine, *Business In Great Waters: The U-boat Wars 1916–1945* (South Yorkshire: Pen & Sword Military, 2009), 6.
12. William Simpson, *The Second Reich: Germany, 1871–1918* (Cambridge: Cambridge University Press, 1995), 119.
13. Terraine, *Business In Great Waters*, 2009, 8–9.
14. Herwig, *Politics of Frustration*, 1976, 117–119.
15. Terraine, *Business In Great Waters*, 2009, 10.
16. *Ibid.*, 22–23.
17. Gray, *The U-Boat War*, 1994, 136–138.
18. Herwig, *Politics of Frustration*, 1976, 117–119.
19. Simpson, *The Second Reich*, 1995, 119.
20. Richard Compton-Hall, *Submarines at War: 1914–1918* (Cornwall: Periscope Publishing Ltd., 2004), 281.
21. Terraine, *Business In Great Waters*, 2009, 11.
22. Vincent, *The Politics of Hunger*, 1985, 46–48.
23. Terraine, *Business In Great Waters*, 2009, 4.
24. Gray, *The U-Boat War*, 1994, 162–163.
25. Terraine, *Business In Great Waters*, 2009, 12–13.
26. *Ibid.*, 14–15.
27. Herwig, *Politics of Frustration*, 1976, 117–119.
28. *Ibid.*, 121.
29. William Johnston, William Rawling, Richard Gimblett, and John MacFarlane, *The Seabound Coast: The Official History of the Royal Canadian Navy, 1867–1939* (Toronto: Dundurn Press, 2010), 452–453.
30. Gray, *The U-Boat War*, 1994, 171.
31. Vincent, *The Politics of Hunger*, 1985, 121.
32. *Ibid.*, 46–48.
33. Herwig, *Politics of Frustration*, 1976, 124.
34. Terraine, *Business In Great Waters*, 2009, 17.
35. *Ibid.*, 22–23.
36. *Ibid.*, 23.
37. *Ibid.*, 40–46.
38. Herwig, *Politics of Frustration*, 1976, 127.
39. *Ibid.*, 128–129.
40. *Ibid.*, 130–131.
41. Terraine, *Business In Great Waters*, 2009, 48–49.
42. *Ibid.*, 54–56.

43. Ibid., 75–76.
44. Ibid., 79–80
45. Ibid., 80–84.
46. Ibid., 89–90.
47. Ibid., 96–98.
48. Ibid., 132–133.
49. Ibid., 2009, 106.
50. Ibid., 2009, 25.
51. Herwig, *Politics of Frustration*, 1976, 138–141.
52. Terraine, *Business In Great Waters*, 2009, 118–119.
53. Herwig, *Politics of Frustration*, 1976, 142–143.
54. Kaiserliche Marine. *Zum Thronvortrag Berlin*. 28 February 1918 Request for the Kaiser's approval of Holtzendorff's proposed North American blockade zone. Found in the papers of the Michael Hadley collection at the University of Victoria Archives and Special collections 1.13, RG SC 053.
55. Kaiserliche Marine U-Kreuzer Verband, *Document from 19 June 1918* (Proposed North American "Sperrgebiet" blockade zone). Found in the papers of the Michael Hadley collection at the University of Victoria Archives and Special collections 1.13, RG SC 053.
56. Herwig, *Politics of Frustration*, 1976, 142–145.
57. Edited by Walter Görlitz, *The Kaiser and His Court: The Diaries, Note Books and Letters of Admiral Georg Alexander von Muller Chief of the Naval Cabinet 1914–1918* (New York: Harcourt, Brace & World, 1964), 375–376.
58. Edited by Görlitz, *The Kaiser and His Court*, 1964, 376.
59. Herwig, *Politics of Frustration*, 1976, 144.
60. Ibid., 137.
61. Ibid., 145.

Chapter 4

1. Telefunken's radio transmitter at Nauen outside of Berlin was the largest in the world and could transmit farther than any other radio transmitter on the European continent at the time. The transmitter was used extensively to communicate with U-boats and also broadcast news and coded messages from Germany to the Americas and Asia. The station survived World Wars I and II intact until the Soviet Union dismantled the radio equipment after the Second World War. (Tworek, "Wireless Telegraphy").

2. Terraine, *Business In Great Waters*, 2009, 32.
3. Robert Grant, *U-Boat Hunters: Code Breakers, Divers and the Defeat of the U-Boats, 1914-1918* (Cornwall: Periscope Publishing, 2003), 33–41.
4. Patrick Beesly, *Room 40: British Naval Intelligence 1914–1918* (New York: Harcourt Brace Jovanovich Publishers, 1982) 1–33.
5. Grant, *U-Boat Hunters*, 2003, 11–41 & 99–103.
6. Ibid., 41.
7. Ibid., 29–30.
8. Ibid., 41.
9. Ibid., 29–30.
10. Beesly, *Room 40*, 1982, 245–246 & 269.

Chapter 5

1. Messimer, *The Baltimore Sabotage Cell*, 2015, 5.
2. Ibid., 63–75.
3. Ibid., 35, 76.
4. Ibid., 13.
5. Erich Gröner, *Die Deutsche Kriegsschiffe, 1815–1945* (Munich: J.F. Lehmanns Verlag, 1966), 359.
6. Messimer, *The Baltimore Sabotage Cell*, 2015, 19–30 & 41–80.
7. British Admiralty, *Attacks made by U-53*, ADM 137/4131. Found in the papers of the Michael Hadley collection at the University of Victoria Archives and Special collections 1.5, RG SC 053.
8. *The Register-Mail*, "Talbot Fisher: German U-boat fears surface in U.S," October 12, 2016, http://www.galesburg.com/news/2016 1012/talbot-fisher-german-u-boat-fears-surface-in-us.
9. *The Day*, "New London once saw its future in a German U-boat," November 19, 2016, http://www.theday.com/article/20161119/NWS01/161129958.
10. Messimer, *The Baltimore Sabotage Cell*, 2015, 102–107 and 116–139.
11. Eberhard Rössler, *Die Deutschen U-Kreuzer und Transport-U-Boote* (Bonn: Bernard & Graefe Verlag, 2003), 74–77.
12. Eberhard Rössler, *The U-boat: The evolution and technical history of German submarines* (London: Arms and Armour Press, 1981), 67.
13. Messimer, *The Baltimore Sabotage Cell*, 2015, 14–16 & 154.
14. Hewitt, *The Kaiser's Pirates*, 2013, 66–86.

15. Rössler, *Die Deutschen U-Kreuzer*, 2003, 74–77.
16. Messimer, *Find and Destroy*, 2001, 155–156.
17. Bernard Edwards, *Dönitz and the Wolf Packs* (South Yorkshire: Pen & Sword, 2014), 22.
18. Spindler, *Der Krieg Zur See*, 1966, 398.
19. Edited by Hans Joachim Koerver, *German Submarine Warfare in the Eyes of British Intelligence: Selected Sources from the British National Archive* (Berlin: LIS Reinisch, 2012), 234–235.
20. Messimer, *The Baltimore Sabotage Cell*, 2015, 156.
21. *Ibid.*, 180.
22. Koerver, *German Submarine Warfare*, 2012, 632.
23. *Ibid.*, 36, 58.
24. Rössler, *Die Deutschen U-Kreuzer*, 2003, 74–77.
25. Grant, *U-Boat Hunters*, 2003, 15–17.
26. National Archives Microfilm Publications: *Microcopy No. T-1022 Guides to the Microfilmed Records of the German Navy, 1850–1945: No. 1. U-Boats and T-Boats 1914–1918, Kriegstagebuch U-156.* Washington 1984, can be found under U-156, Konrad Gansser, or Richard Feldt at the U.S. National Archives Microfilm Room College Park, MD.
27. Kaiserliche Marine, BA-MA (Bundesarchiv-Militärchiv): RM 5/5962, *Der Kabelkrieg.* 105–108. Found in the papers of the Michael Hadley collection at the University of Victoria Archives and Special collections 1.13, RG SC 053.
28. Office of Naval Intelligence, 1918, *Antisubmarine Information, ONI No. 14: German Submarine Cable Cutter.* Washington: Government Printing Office, http://www.history.navy.mil/library/online/onipubno14.htm.
29. Grant, *U-Boat Hunters*, 2003, 118.
30. Koerver, *German Submarine Warfare*, 2012, 640.
31. Grant, *U-Boat Hunters*, 2003, 112–117.
32. Koerver, *German Submarine Warfare*, 2012, 60.
33. *Ibid.*, 58.
34. Rössler, *Die Deutschen U-Kreuzer*, 2003, 74–77.
35. Spindler, *Der Krieg Zur See*, 1966, 416.
36. Kiel, in northern Germany on the Baltic Sea was and still is a port, shipbuilding centre, and city that played a major role in the development and maintenance of the German navy in both World Wars. In World War I it contained several large shipyards like Germaniawerft and Atlas Werke that churned out the surface ships and U-boats needed by the Kaiserreich. Kiel was also the home port for the U-Kreuzers. Wilhelmshaven, also a northern German port, was used to build naval vessels during the war as well (Encyclopaedia Brittanica, "Kiel, Germany")
37. Koerver, *German Submarine Warfare*, 2012, 21.
38. *Ibid.*, 57.
39. Rössler, *Die Deutschen U-Kreuzer*, 2003, 74–77.
40. Koerver, *German Submarine Warfare*, 2012, 678–679.

Chapter 6

1. Spencer Tucker, *The Great War 1914–18* (Indianapolis, Indiana: Indiana University Press, 1998), 153 & 158, 172–173.
2. *Ibid.*, 184–186.
3. S.L.A. Marshall, *World War I* (Boston: Houghton Mifflin Company, 1987), 305.
4. Tucker, *The Great War*, 1998, 144–147.
5. Marshall, *World War I*, 1987, 322–333.
6. *Ibid.*, 151–158.
7. *Ibid.*, 159–170.
8. Edited by James Hallas, *Doughboy War: The American Expeditionary Force in WWI* (Mechanicsburg, PA: Stackpole Books, 2009), 256–257.

Chapter 7

1. Ancestry.com, *Germany, Select Births and Baptisms, 1558–1898* [database on-line]. Provo, UT: Ancestry.com Operations, Inc., 2014. Original data: *Germany, Births and Baptisms, 1558–1898.* Salt Lake City, Utah: FamilySearch, 2013.
2. Deutsches U-Boot Museum, U-Boot-Archiv. *German Naval Career File on Konrad Gansser.* Stored in Cuxhaven, Germany.
3. *Ibid.*
4. Uboat.net "WWI U-boat Commanders," http://uboat.net/wwi/men/commanders/83.html
5. *The Wartime Memories Project*, "SS Portugal during the Great War," http://www.wartimememoriesproject.com/greatwar/ships/view.php?pid=3092.
6. Edith Cavell was a British nurse who treated wounded soldiers from both sides of the conflict in a Red Cross hospital in Brus-

sels, Belgium. She was also part of a network of Allied sympathizers who smuggled hundreds of Allied troops to Holland so they could escape the occupying Germans and live to fight another day. The Germans soon discovered her activities, put her on trial, convicted her, and executed Ms. Cavell by firing squad on 12 October 1915. The execution shocked Allied and neutral opinion, and was used to the advantage of Allied propaganda to paint the Germans as murderers (*Imperial War Museum* "Who Was Edith Cavell?").

7. Stephen Twigge, 27 July 2016, "Captain Fryatt: forgotten martyr of the First World War," UK National Archives, http://blog.nationalarchives.gov.uk/blog/captain-fryatt-forgotten-martyr-first-world-war/.

8. At the beginning of the war the Germans were nervous about civilian resistance to their rule in occupied Belgium and France. They executed numerous Belgian and French civilians in the name of combating "franc-tireurs" who could simply have been small units of retreating Allied soldiers stuck behind the German advance. The executions quickly turned into a foreign policy nightmare for the Reich. (Firstworldwar.com "Franc-Tireur").

9. Isabel Hull, *A Scrap of Paper: Breaking and Making International Law during the Great War* (Ithaca: Cornell University Press, 2014), 252–255.

10. Gray, *The U-Boat War*, 1994, 212, 214, and 229.

11. The Azores, an autonomous region of Portugal, are nine volcanic islands over 900 miles west of Lisbon in the Atlantic Ocean. Settled in the 15th century by the Portuguese the islands have served as a supply station for transatlantic travel for centuries. The Azores are now a tourist destination famous for fishing and wine (*World Atlas* "Azores").

12. Deutsches U-Boot Museum, U-Boot-Archiv, *Crew List for the U-156*. Stored in Cuxhaven, Germany.

13. Koerver, *German Submarine Warfare*, 2012, 325.

14. Ancestry.com, *Germany, Select Births and Baptisms, 1558–1898* [database on-line]. Provo, UT: Ancestry.com Operations, Inc., 2014. Original data: *Germany, Births and Baptisms, 1558–1898*. Salt Lake City, UT: FamilySearch, 2013.

15. Koerver, *German Submarine Warfare*, 2012, 632–634.

16. Rössler, *The U-boat*, 1981, 64.

17. Javier Ponce, 2014, "Commerce Warfare in the East Central Atlantic during the First World War: German Submarines Around the Canary Islands, 1916–1918," Routledge: Mariner's Mirror 100:3 (August): 335–348.

18. National Archives Microfilm Publications: *Microcopy No. T-1022 Guides to the Microfilmed Records of the German Navy, 1850–1945: No. 1. U-Boats and T-Boats 1914–1918, Kriegstagebuch U-156*. Washington 1984, can be found under *U-156*, Konrad Gansser, or Richard Feldt at the U.S. National Archives Microfilm Room College Park, MD.

19. Rössler, *Die Deutschen U-Kreuzer*, 2003, 93.

20. Grant, *U-Boat Hunters*, 2003, 100.

21. United States Navy, *Daily Memorandum for Force Commander from June 14, 1918*, RG 145, TG Box 557–654 at the United States National Archives, Washington D.C.

22. British Admiralty document, ADM 137 (Operations and Intelligence) / 4155 (U-boat history sheets): *U-156, 1917–1918, 6 pages*, accessed at http://germannavalwarfare.info/02subm/02/U156.html.

23. National Archives Microfilm Publications: *Microcopy No. T-1022 Guides to the Microfilmed Records of the German Navy, 1850–1945: No. 1. U-Boats and T-Boats 1914–1918, Kriegstagebuch U-156*. Washington 1984, can be found under *U-156*, Konrad Gansser, or Richard Feldt at the U.S. National Archives Microfilm Room College Park, MD.

24. Kaiserliche Marine. *Großes Hauptquartier 3 October 1917*, Report on the mission of *U-156* and other U-Kreuzers in the Canaries area for Kaiser Wilhelm II. Found in the papers of the Michael Hadley collection at the University of Victoria Archives and Special collections 1.13, RG SC 053.

Chapter 8

1. Spindler, *Der Krieg Zur See*, 1966, 240.

2. National Archives Microfilm Publications: *Microcopy No. T-1022 Guides to the Microfilmed Records of the German Navy, 1850–1945: No. 1. U-Boats and T-Boats 1914–1918, Kriegstagebuch U-156*. Washington 1984, can be found under *U-156*, Konrad Gansser, or Richard Feldt at the U.S. National Archives Microfilm Room College Park, MD.

3. Madeira is a Portuguese autonomous region which consists of one main island and three smaller islands off of northwest Africa. Funchal is on the main island and stands as the capital of the region. Funchal thrives on

the visits of cruise ships. Madeira is also famous for its wine.

4. Fort Santiago still stands on the edge of Funchal's harbor as it has done for four centuries. The fort was converted from military use in 1992 to a museum (Madeira-web.com "Santiago Fortress").

5. *The Northern Echo*, "Slaughter by the seaside: the shelling of Seaham," July 9, 2016. http://www.thenorthernecho.co.uk/history/14609266.Slaughter_by_the_seaside__the_shelling_of_Seaham/.

6. National Archives Microfilm Publications: *Microcopy No. T-1022 Guides to the Microfilmed Records of the German Navy, 1850–1945: No. 1. U-Boats and T-Boats 1914–1918, Kriegstagebuch U-156*. Washington 1984, can be found under *U-156*, Konrad Gansser, or Richard Feldt at the U.S. National Archives Microfilm Room College Park, MD.

7. National Archives Microfilm Publications: *Microcopy No. T-1022 Guides to the Microfilmed Records of the German Navy, 1850–1945: No. 1. U-Boats and T-Boats 1914–1918, Kriegstagebuch U-156*. Washington 1984, can be found under *U-156*, Konrad Gansser, or Richard Feldt at the U.S. National Archives Microfilm Room College Park, MD.

8. Grant, *U-Boat Hunters*, 2003, 99–103.

9. Beesly, *Room 40*, 1982, 192.

10. Innes McCartney. *British Submarines of World War I* (Oxford: Osprey Publishing, 2008), 11–13.

11. Koerver, *German Submarine Warfare*, 2012, 447–450.

12. National Archives Microfilm Publications: *Microcopy No. T-1022 Guides to the Microfilmed Records of the German Navy, 1850–1945: No. 1. U-Boats and T-Boats 1914–1918, Kriegstagebuch U-156*. Washington 1984, can be found under *U-156*, Konrad Gansser, or Richard Feldt at the U.S. National Archives Microfilm Room College Park, MD.

13. Koerver, *German Submarine Warfare*, 2012, 274–278.

14. British Admiralty document, ADM 137 (Operations and Intelligence) / 4155 (U-boat history sheets): *U-156, 1917–1918, 6 pages*, accessed at http://germannavalwarfare.info/02subm/02/U156.html.

15. Grant, *U-Boat Hunters*, 2003, 99–103.

16. National Archives Microfilm Publications: *Microcopy No. T-1022 Guides to the Microfilmed Records of the German Navy, 1850–1945: No. 1. U-Boats and T-Boats 1914–1918, Kriegstagebuch U-156*. Washington 1984, can be found under *U-156*, Konrad Gansser, or Richard Feldt at the U.S. National Archives Microfilm Room College Park, MD.

17. Spindler, *Der Krieg Zur See*, 1966, 244.

18. Tenerife is the largest island in the Canary chain.

19. Koerver, *German Submarine Warfare*, 2012, 447–450.

20. Spindler, *Der Krieg Zur See*, 1966, 243.

21. Grant, *U-Boat Hunters*, 2003, 102.

22. National Archives Microfilm Publications: *Microcopy No. T-1022 Guides to the Microfilmed Records of the German Navy, 1850–1945: No. 1. U-Boats and T-Boats 1914–1918, Kriegstagebuch U-156*. Washington 1984, can be found under *U-156*, Konrad Gansser, or Richard Feldt at the U.S. National Archives Microfilm Room College Park, MD.

23. Kaiserliche Marine. *Berlin 16 March 1918, Kanzlei schreibe an den chef des marinekabinetts.* Found in the papers of the Michael Hadley collection at the University of Victoria Archives and Special collections 1.13, RG SC 053.

24. Pola was an Austro-Hungarian and German U-boat base in the Adriatic Sea. The base's submarines targeted Allied shipping in the Adriatic and Mediterranean until late in the war when the Allies began to advance rapidly in the Balkans once the Bulgarians, Austrians, and Germans were driven back from their long held front lines in Greece and Albania. Gansser had most of his wartime successes and experiences in this theater of the naval war. (*Uboat.net*, "Deadly Mediterranean").

Chapter 9

1. Uboat.net, "Ships Hit During WWI, *Guahyba*," http://uboat.net/wwi/ships_hit/2637.html.

2. Ibid.

3. Koerver, *German Submarine Warfare*, 2012, 644–646.

4. Ibid., 228–229.

5. Wreck Site, "*SS Johan Mjelde*," http://wrecksite.eu/wreck.aspx?154598.

6. British Admiralty document, ADM 137 (Operations and Intelligence) / 4155 (U-boat history sheets): *U-151, 1917–1918, 6 pages*, accessed at http://germannavalwarfare.info/02subm/02/U151.html.

7. Ibid.

8. Cape Finisterre is a rocky peninsula on Spain's west coast.

9. Spindler, *Der Krieg Zur See*, 1966, 233–235.

10. Edited by Koerver, *German Submarine Warfare*, 2012, 646–647.
11. Spindler, *Der Krieg Zur See*, 1966, 235–237.
12. *U-153* was not a very successful submarine, and had a small tonnage score as compared to the other U-Kreuzers. Her second commander did not even get to take her out on another cruise, and her trip to the Azores was the only time she was operational. *U-153* was surrendered on 24 November 1918 at Harwich and scuttled by the British off the Isle of Wight on 30 June 1921 (Uboat.net, "U-153").
13. British Admiralty document. ADM 137 (Operations and Intelligence) / 4155 (U-boat history sheets): *U-153, 1917–1918, 6 pages*, accessed at http://germannavalwarfare.info/02subm/02/U153.html
14. Spindler, *Der Krieg Zur See*, 1966, 236–238.
15. British Admiralty document. ADM 137 (Operations and Intelligence) / 4155 (U-boat history sheets): *U-154, 1917–1918, 6 pages*, accessed at http://germannavalwarfare.info/02subm/02/U154.html
16. Ibid.
17. Liberia is a nation founded by former American slaves who established an independent republic in West Africa in the mid-19th century. Monrovia is the capital of the country and is situated on the nation's northwestern Atlantic coast (Central Intelligence Agency "Liberia").
18. Koerver, *German Submarine Warfare*, 2012, 230–231.
19. Grant, *U-Boat Hunters*, 2003, 105.
20. British Admiralty document. ADM 137 (Operations and Intelligence) / 4155 (U-boat history sheets): *U-154, 1917–1918, 6 pages*, accessed at http://germannavalwarfare.info/02subm/02/U154.html
21. Cape St. Vincent juts out into the Atlantic Ocean from the southwest coast of Portugal.
22. Grant, *U-Boat Hunters*, 2003, 103–109.
23. Uboat.net, "WWI U-boats, U-154," http://www.uboat.net/wwi/boats/index.html?boat=154.
24. Messimer, *The Baltimore Sabotage Cell*, 2015, 180.
25. Ibid., 170–188.
26. British Admiralty document. ADM 137 (Operations and Intelligence) / 4155 (U-boat history sheets): *U-155, 1917–1918, 6 pages*, accessed at http://germannavalwarfare.info/02subm/02/U155.html
27. Ibid.
28. Koerver, *German Submarine Warfare*, 2012, 228–229.
29. Messimer, *The Baltimore Sabotage Cell*, 2015, 189–199.
30. Spindler, *Der Krieg Zur See*, 1966, 243–245.
31. Ibid., 260–261.

Chapter 10

1. Beesly, *Room 40*, 1982, 260.
2. Deutsches U-Boot Museum, U-Boot-Archiv. *German Naval Career File on Richard Feldt*. Stored in Cuxhaven, Germany.
3. National Archives Microfilm Publications: *Microcopy No. T-1022 Guides to the Microfilmed Records of the German Navy, 1850–1945: No. 1. U-Boats and T-Boats 1914–1918, Kriegstagebuch U-30*. Washington 1984, can be found under *U-30* or Richard Feldt at the U.S. National Archives Microfilm Room College Park, MD.
4. United States Navy, *German Submarine Activities on the Atlantic Coast of the United States and Canada* (Washington, D.C.: Government Printing Office, 1920) 629–632.
5. Rössler, *Die Deutschen U-Kreuzer*, 2003, 74–77.
6. The Imperial German war flag was displayed by the naval vessels of the Second Reich during World War I. The flag consisted of an iron cross and an Imperial Prussian eagle with red, white, and black colors. The flag became a symbol utilized by far right groups, pro-monarchists, and some Nazi supporters after the war during the Weimar Republic to indicate their opposition to the new government. The flag became a symbol to these groups of Germany's allegedly glorious history prior to her defeat in 1918.
7. Koerver, *German Submarine Warfare*, 2012, 56–60.
8. Ibid., 629–632.

Chapter 11

1. Kaiserliche Marine, *Zum Thronvortrag Berlin, 28 February 1918*. Request for the Kaiser's approval of Holtzendorff's proposed North American blockade zone. Found in the papers of the Michael Hadley collection at the University of Victoria Archives and Special collections 1.13, RG SC 053.

2. Herwig, *Politics of Frustration*, 1976, 166.
3. Hadley and Sarty, *Tin Pots and Pirate Ships*, 1991, 225–232.
4. Herwig, *Politics of Frustration*, 1976, 158–159.
5. Hurley, *The Bridge to France*, 1927, 219–224.
6. Ibid., 124.
7. Ibid., 232–245.
8. Herwig, *Politics of Frustration*, 1976, 160–162.
9. Alex Larzelere. *The Coast Guard in World War I: An Untold Story* (Annapolis: Naval Institute Press, 2003), 231–232.
10. Larzelere, *The Coast Guard in World War I*, 2003, 233.
11. Ibid., 180–186.
12. Terrance McGovern, Bolling Smith. *American Coastal Defenses: 1885–1950* (Oxford: Osprey Publishing Limited, 206), 19 & 48 & 57–58.
13. The U.S. Lighthouse Service had a mandate to maintain and operate numerous lighthouses and lightships to aid in the safe navigation of shipping. The service existed as a separate government department until it was folded into the Coast Guard on 7 July 1939 (Truman "Chronology of Aids to Navigation").
14. Larzelere, *The Coast Guard in World War I*, 2003, 74–105 & 133–236.
15. Joseph Buckley, *Wings Over Cape Cod: The Chatham Naval Air Station 1917–1918* (Orleans: Lower Cape Publishing, 2000), 1.
16. The USS *Jouett* was commissioned at Boston in 1912 and afterwards operated off the U.S. east coast with the Atlantic Fleet Torpedo Flotilla until 1914. On 21 April 1914 the *Jouett* participated in the U.S. Marine landing at Veracruz, Mexico in order to deal with yet another crisis in that revolutionary country. The *Jouett* returned to her old station on the east coast and participated in training exercises until the U.S. declared war on Germany in April 1917. The *Jouett* patrolled Delaware Bay from April to August 1917 when she was ordered to be an escort for a five-troopship convoy headed to France. The *Jouett* successfully performed this mission and returned to her patrol duties until January 1918 when she took part in experiments related to antisubmarine equipment in New London, Connecticut. The experiments ended in June 1918 and from then until the end of the war the *Jouett* was the head of her own naval hunt squadron with orders to find and destroy the submarines then attacking the east coast of the U.S. and Canada. The *Jouett* went back to her training exercises after her war service and was decommissioned in November 1919 after entering the Philadelphia Navy Yard. The *Jouett* was loaned to the U.S. Coast Guard in 1924 for use as a cutter until she was returned to the navy in 1931, and was sold for scrap metal to a company out of Brooklyn, NY (Naval History and Heritage Command "Jouett I").

17. Johnston, Rawling, Gimblett, and MacFarlane, *The Seabound Coast*, 2010, 595–600.
18. Hadley and Sarty, *Tin Pots and Pirate Ships*, 1991, 241.
19. British Admiralty document. ADM 137 (Operations and Intelligence) / 4155 (U-boat history sheets): *U-151, 1917–1918*, 6 pages, accessed at http://germannavalwarfare.info/02subm/02/U151.html.
20. Grant, *U-Boat Hunters*, 2003, 110–112.
21. Koerver, *German Submarine Warfare*, 2012, 624–625.
22. Ibid., 2012, 623.
23. *Los Angeles Times*, "A Personal History Beneath the Waves," June 10, 2001, http://articles.latimes.com/2001/jun/10/news/mn-8573.
24. Spindler, *Der Krieg Zur See*, 1966, 251–253.
25. United States Navy, *German Submarine Activities*, 1920, 23–50.
26. Wreck Site, 2010, "SS Dwinsk," http://www.wrecksite.eu/wreck.aspx?132170.
27. German-Argentine relations were strained in 1917 due to the sinking of Argentine ships in April and June. In September the British intercepted and published secret messages by a German diplomat in Buenos Aires through the American Department of State. The diplomat was Count Karl von Luxburg. In his leaked confidential messages, kind of a World War I version of state sanctioned Wikileaks, Luxburg advocated for the sinking of Argentine ships "without a trace" and called the Argentine foreign minister a "notorious ass," Argentina and Germany almost went to war over the gaffes. Neutral Sweden was implicated as a facilitator of German overseas communications during the scandal (Bisher, 151–158).
28. Grant, *U-Boat Hunters*, 2003, 110–112.
29. Koerver, *German Submarine Warfare*, 2012, 231–233.
30. Spindler, *Der Krieg Zur See*, 1966, 251–253.

31. Görlitz, *The Kaiser and His Court*, 1964, 374–375.
32. Johnston, Rawling, Gimblett, and MacFarlane. *The Seabound Coast*, 2010, 600.
33. Koerver, *German Submarine Warfare*, 2012, 645.
34. Grant, *U-Boat Hunters*, 2003, 112.
35. Kaiserliche Marine, *O-Befehl (Operations Orders) fur U-156 10 June 1918* (from the chief of the Admiralstab der Marine). Found in the papers of the Michael Hadley collection at the University of Victoria Archives and Special collections 1.13, RG SC 053.
36. United States Navy, *Daily Memoranda for Force Commander from June 21 and July 4 1918*, RG 145, TG Box 557–654 at the United States National Archives Washington D.C.
37. Grant, *U-Boat Hunters*, 2003, 113.
38. British Admiralty document. ADM 137 (Operations and Intelligence) / 4155 (U-boat history sheets): *U-156, 1917–1918, 6 pages*, accessed at http://germannavalwarfare.info/02subm/02/U156.html.
39. Edited by Koerver, *German Submarine Warfare*, 2012, 649.
40. A.J. Tennent, *British Merchant Ships Sunk by U-Boats in World War One* (Cornwall: Periscope Publishing, 2006), 75.
41. Martin Edwards, 2006, "*Roll of Honour, Lest We Forget. HALE, WADHAM HOUSE SCHOOL WAR MEMORIAL*," http://www.roll-of-honour.com/Cheshire/HaleWadhamHouseSchool.html.
42. United States Navy, *German Submarine Activities*, 1920, 50.
43. Naval Historical Center Website, "USS Lake Bridge (ID # 2990), 1918–1919," http://www.ibiblio.org/hyperwar/OnlineLibrary/photos/sh-usn/usnsh-l/id2990.htm.
44. Johnston, Rawling, Gimblett, and MacFarlane. *The Seabound Coast*, 2010, 610.
45. William Clark, *When the U-Boats Came to America* (Boston: Little, Brown, & Co., 1929), 157–158.
46. Johnston, Rawling, Gimblett, and MacFarlane. *The Seabound Coast*, 2010, 618.
47. United States Navy, *German Submarine Activities*, 1920, 52–53.
48. Ibid., 53–54.
49. Grant, *U-Boat Hunters*, 2003, 112.
50. British Admiralty document, ADM 137 (Operations and Intelligence) / 4155 (U-boat history sheets): *U-156, 1917–1918, 6 pages*, accessed at http://germannavalwarfare.info/02subm/02/U156.html

51. United States Navy, *German Submarine Activities*, 1920, 54.
52. British Admiralty, *War Diary for North America and West Indies, 1 July & 2 July 1918*, PRO ADM 137/903, Pg. 1190. Found in the papers of the Michael Hadley collection at the University of Victoria Archives and Special collections 1.6, RG SC 053.
53. Lowell Thomas, *Raiders of the Deep* (Garden City: Doubleday, Doran, & Co., 1928), 294–295, 302.
54. Thomas, *Raiders of the Deep*, 1928, 270–271.
55. United States Navy, *German Submarine Activities*, 1920, 64.
56. Leo Polaski, Glen Williford, *New York City's Harbor Defenses*. (Charleston: Arcadia Publishing, 2003), 35, 63.

Chapter 12

1. Naval History and Heritage Command, "Today in Naval History: December 14," http://www.history.navy.mil/today-in-history/december-14.html.
2. Naval History and Heritage Command, "California II," www.history.navy.mil/research/histories/ship-histories/danfs/c/california-ii.html.
3. Joey Seymour, "Honorably Representing San Diego: The Story of the USS *San Diego*," www.sandiegohistory.org: The Journal of San Diego History: 122–124.
4. Howard Blum, *Dark Invasion 1915: Germany's Secret War and the Hunt for the First Terrorist Cell in America* (New York: Harper Collins, 2014), 179–184.
5. Clark, *When the U-Boats Came to America*, 1929, 144–155.
6. British Admiralty. *War Diary for North America and West Indies 22 July 1918*. PRO ADM 137/903. Pg. 1191. Found in the papers of the Michael Hadley collection at the University of Victoria Archives and Special collections 1.6, RG SC 053.
7. Johnston, Rawling, Gimblett, and MacFarlane. *The Seabound Coast*, 2010, 618.
8. *New York Times*, "Decide Mine Sank Cruiser San Diego," August 6, 1918.
9. George Albert, 2016, "The USS *San Diego* and the California Naval Militia," California Center for Military History. http://www.militarymuseum.org/USSSanDiego.html.
10. Kaiserliche Marine, *Zum Immediatvortrag 6 June 1917*, Found in the papers of the

Michael Hadley collection at the University of Victoria Archives and Special collections 1.13, RG SC 053.

11. Jamie Bisher, *The Intelligence War in Latin America, 1914–1922* (Jefferson, NC: McFarland & Company, 2016), 217–221.

12. Messimer, *The Baltimore Sabotage Cell*, 2015, 210–214.

13. Koerver, *German Submarine Warfare*, 2012, 554.

14. Grant, *U-Boat Hunters*, 2003, 99.

15. British Admiralty document. ADM 137 (Operations and Intelligence) / 4155 (U-boat history sheets): *U-156, 1917–1918, 6 pages*, accessed at http://germannavalwarfare.info/02subm/02/U156.html

16. Hadley and Sarty, *Tin Pots and Pirate Ships*, 1991, 245.

17. Clark, *When the U-Boats Came to America*, 1929, 132.

18. Grant, *U-Boat Hunters*, 2003, 113.

19. Koerver, *German Submarine Warfare*, 2012, 649.

20. British Admiralty document. ADM 137 (Operations and Intelligence) / 4155 (U-boat history sheets): *U-156, 1917–1918, 6 pages*, accessed at http://germannavalwarfare.info/02subm/02/U156.html

21. Bisher, *The Intelligence War in Latin America*, 2016, 223.

22. Kaiserliche Marine, *Message dated 26 June 1918* (The details for the proposed American blockade zone's initiation with the *U-156* proposed as the first boat to open the blockade). Found in the papers of the Michael Hadley collection at the University of Victoria Archives and Special collections 1.13, RG SC 053.

23. Kaiserliche Marine U-Kreuzer Verband, *Document from 19 June 1918* (Proposed North American "Sperrgebiet" blockade zone). Found in the papers of the Michael Hadley collection at the University of Victoria Archives and Special collections 1.13, RG SC 053.

Chapter 13

1. United States Navy, *German Submarine Activities*, 1920, 54–55.

2. The last time the U.S. had been bombarded by a foreign power prior to the Great War was during the six day siege of Fort Texas on the Rio Grande, which was subjected to artillery fire by Mexican forces in May 1846. The fort consisted of thick earthworks, which withstood the Mexican artillery. The siege was lifted and the fort was renamed Fort Brown, after its fallen commander died of his wounds just prior to the Mexican retreat. The area is now a protected historic site. The next time the continental U.S. was bombed by enemy artillery after World War I occurred when Japanese submarines attacked insignificant targets on the U.S. Pacific coast. (National Park Service "Fort Texas/Fort Brown")

3. United States Navy, *German Submarine Activities*, 1920, 54–55.

4. *Ibid.*, 54–55.

5. On 21 June 1921, American airpower pioneer General William "Billy" Mitchell lined up 47 aircraft arranged in waves to attack and sink the ex-German minelaying U-Kreuzer *U-117* off of Virginia in a test designed to demonstrate the power of aerial bombing against naval targets. The first three planes in the lineup sank the old U-boat in the first 16 minutes of the assault. The test proved airpower could destroy naval craft and cemented the view that the *U-156* would have been damaged at the very least when attacked by the two aircraft from the Chatham Naval Air Station. Chatham's bombs failed, Mitchell's did not (Dubbs 170–172).

6. Jake Klim, *Attack on Orleans: The World War I Submarine Raid on Cape Cod* (Charleston: The History Press, 2014), 41–87.

7. United States Navy, *Daily Memorandum for Force Commander from July 22, 1918*, RG 145, TG Box 557–654 at the United States National Archives, Washington, D.C.

8. Klim, *Attack on Orleans*, 2014, 41–87.

9. Hadley and Sarty, *Tin Pots and Pirate Ships*, 1991, 250.

10. Larzelere, *The Coast Guard in World War I*, 2003, 137.

11. Klim, *Attack on Orleans*, 2014, 105–107.

12. Clark, *When the U-Boats Came to America*, 1929, 171.

13. Messimer, *The Baltimore Sabotage Cell*, 2015, 184–185.

14. Grant, *U-Boat Hunters*, 2003, 113–114.

15. The Orleans cable to France was in operation from 1898 to 1959 and acted as a communications hub and news provider from Europe to the U.S. and back. The station and cable were temporarily shut down in World War II when the Germans occupied France and took control of the other end of the cable. The old cable station is now a museum. (French Cable Station Museum "Museum History").

16. Warren Darling, *The French Cable Sta-

tion Museum: Museum Tour Book. (Orleans: Published by the Museum, Unknown date), 13.

17. United States Navy, *German Submarine Activities*, 1920, 121–122.

18. Hadley and Sarty, *Tin Pots and Pirate Ships*, 1991, 243.

19. Darling, *The French Cable Station Museum*, Unknown date, 13.

Chapter 14

1. Johnston, Rawling, Gimblett, and MacFarlane. *The Seabound Coast*, 2010, 667.

2. Messimer, *The Baltimore Sabotage Cell*, 2015, 31–35.

3. United States Navy, *German Submarine Activities*, 1920, 55–56.

4. The Gulf of Maine is a large gulf off of the Atlantic Ocean which touches on the North American ports of Boston, Portsmouth, Portland, Yarmouth, and Saint John. The shipping off these U.S. and Canadian ports was a special focus of the *U-156* while she was in North American waters.

5. British Admiralty document, ADM 137 (Operations and Intelligence) / 4155 (U-boat history sheets): *U-156, 1917–1918, 6 pages*, accessed at http://germannavalwarfare.info/02subm/02/U156.html

6. Clark, *When the U-Boats Came to America*, 1929, 193.

7. Grant, *U-Boat Hunters*, 2003, 113–114.

8. The Royal Canadian Navy was established in May 1910 only a little over four years before the outbreak of war with the Central Powers. The Royal Canadian Navy had its first small test in World War I, but would have a much more comprehensive threat to deal with in World War II. Canada's still young navy met the challenge and started a proud tradition that continues to this day (Royal Canadian Navy "Commander Royal Canadian Navy").

9. Johnston, Rawling, Gimblett, and MacFarlane. *The Seabound Coast*, 2010, 600–610.

10. *Ibid.*, 626–629.

11. British Admiralty. *Protection of the fishing fleets 1918*. PAC, RG 24, box 4030, 1065-4-3. Found in the papers of the Michael Hadley collection at the University of Victoria Archives and Special collections 1.7, RG SC 053.

12. Johnston, Rawling, Gimblett, and MacFarlane. *The Seabound Coast*, 2010, 668.

13. Clark, *When the U-Boats Came to America*, 1929, 193.

14. Johnston, Rawling, Gimblett, and MacFarlane. *The Seabound Coast*, 2010, 634–635.

15. *Ibid.*, 635.

16. *Ibid.*, 658.

17. Deutsches U-Boot Museum, U-Boot-Archiv. *Crew List for the U-156*. Stored in Cuxhaven, Germany.

18. *The St. John Standard*, "Henrich Kampo, German Sailor on Submarine 56," August 7, 1918.

19. *The St. John Standard*, "Schooner Wrecked by the Germans Towed into Point Along the Atlantic Coast," August 6, 1918.

20. Clark, *When the U-Boats Came to America*, 1929, 194.

21. Johnston, Rawling, Gimblett, and MacFarlane, *The Seabound Coast*, 2010, 653.

22. Clark, *When the U-Boats Came to America*, 1929, 195.

23. United States Navy, *German Submarine Activities*, 1920, 58.

24. Clark, *When the U-Boats Came to America*, 1929, 195.

25. *Ibid.*, 196.

26. Johnston, Rawling, Gimblett, and MacFarlane. *The Seabound Coast*, 2010, 596.

27. Clark, *When the U-Boats Came to America*, 1929, 197.

28. Johnston, Rawling, Gimblett, and MacFarlane. *The Seabound Coast*, 2010, 640.

29. Koerver, *German Submarine Warfare*, 2012, 626–634.

Chapter 15

1. Hadley and Sarty, *Tin Pots and Pirate Ships*, 1991, 238.

2. Maritime Museum of the Atlantic, "Halifax Explosion Infosheet," https://maritimemuseum.novascotia.ca/what-see-do/halifax-explosion/halifax-explosion-infosheet.

3. Johnston, Rawling, Gimblett, and MacFarlane, *The Seabound Coast*, 2010, 641.

4. Grant, *U-Boat Hunters*, 2003, 115.

5. Johnston, Rawling, Gimblett, and MacFarlane. *The Seabound Coast*, 2010, 642.

6. Clark, *When the U-Boats Came to America*, 1929, 197.

7. United States Navy, *German Submarine Activities*, 1920, 59.

8. Johnston, Rawling, Gimblett, and MacFarlane. *The Seabound Coast*, 2010, 643–644.

9. British Admiralty, *War Diary for North America and West Indies, 5 & 6 August 1918*, PRO ADM 137/903, pgs. 1208, 1209. Found in the papers of the Michael Hadley collection

at the University of Victoria Archives and Special collections 1.6, RG SC 053.

10. Johnston, Rawling, Gimblett, and MacFarlane. *The Seabound Coast*, 2010, 651.

11. *Ibid.*, 647–648.

12. *Ibid.*, 663–665.

13. United States Navy. *Daily Memoranda for Force Commander from August 9 1918*, RG 145, TG Box 557–654 at the United States National Archives Washington D.C.

14. Johnston, Rawling, Gimblett, and MacFarlane. *The Seabound Coast*, 2010, 651.

15. *Ibid.*, 649.

16. Cape Sable is an island located at the southern tip of Nova Scotia in Canada.

17. Johnston, Rawling, Gimblett, and MacFarlane. *The Seabound Coast*, 2010, 657.

18. United States Navy, *German Submarine Activities*, 1920, 59–60.

19. The Commission for the Relief of Belgium was started by future American President Herbert Hoover in 1914 and was the first humanitarian relief organization of its kind. Hoover and others organized food deliveries to the millions of starving civilians in occupied Belgium and northern France. Without the Commission many of these people would certainly have died due to the British blockade and food priority in their own country going to the German army and German civilians in the Reich. The Commission made a deal with the Allies and Germans whereby it was agreed the Germans would not take food handled by the Commission and the Allies would not stop food transported by the Commission from entering Rotterdam. After the food made it to Rotterdam it was transported by canal to Belgium and distributed to the millions in need in the western occupied zones. Hoover managed the program with a deft hand and was able to keep it going despite intense pressure from both the German and Allied high commands. As can be seen in the account of the U-Kreuzers, the Commission's ships were greatly respected when they had their papers in order. If they didn't then the Germans sank them, but with the proper paperwork it was a get out of destruction free card (Nash "Herbert Hoover and Belgian Relief").

20. Koerver, *German Submarine Warfare*, 2012, 633.

21. Clark, *When the U-Boats Came to America*, 1929, 200.

22. United States Navy, *German Submarine Activities*, 1920, 61–64.

23. Clark, *When the U-Boats Came to America*, 1929, 201.

24. Johnston, Rawling, Gimblett, and MacFarlane. *The Seabound Coast*, 2010, 657.

25. British Admiralty, *War Diary for North America and West Indies, 17 August 1918*, PRO ADM 137/903, pg. 1222. Found in the papers of the Michael Hadley collection at the University of Victoria Archives and Special collections 1.6, RG SC 053.

26. Clark, *When the U-Boats Came to America*, 1929, 202–204.

27. Royal Canadian Navy. *Fisheries Defense*. PAC, RG 24, box 4030, 1065-4-1. Found in the papers of the Michael Hadley collection at the University of Victoria Archives and Special collections 1.7, RG SC 053.

28. Johnston, Rawling, Gimblett, and MacFarlane. *The Seabound Coast*, 2010, 658.

29. *Ibid.*, 669.

Chapter 16

1. Koerver, *German Submarine Warfare*, 2012, 633–634.

2. Clark, *When the U-Boats Came to America*, 1929, 234.

3. United States Navy, *Section VI: Review of Enemy Submarine Activity On The American Coast, June—October, 1918*, National Archives, Washington, D.C., 49–50.

4. Johnston, Rawling, Gimblett, and MacFarlane, *The Seabound Coast*, 2010, 669–670.

5. Koerver, *German Submarine Warfare*, 2012, 60.

6. *The Ottawa Evening Journal*, "Trawler Triumph Fitted With Two Guns and Manned by the Huns," August 21, 1918.

7. Deutsches U-Boot Museum, U-Boot-Archiv. *List of U-156's Crew Members with Ranks Included*. Stored in Cuxhaven, Germany.

8. WMP Dunne, *Thomas F. McManus and the American Fishing Schooners: An Irish-American Success Story* (Mystic: Mystic Seaport Museum, 1994), 298.

9. Spindler, *Der Krieg Zur See*, 1966, 244.

10. Messimer, *The Baltimore Sabotage Cell*, 2015, 178.

11. Hadley and Sarty, *Tin Pots and Pirate Ships*, 1991, 263.

12. Clark, *When the U-Boats Came to America*, 1929, 234.

13. Johnston, Rawling, Gimblett, and MacFarlane. *The Seabound Coast*, 2010, 670–671.

14. United States Navy, *German Submarine Activities*, 1920, 65–67.

15. Clark, *When the U-Boats Came to America*, 1929, 237.
16. Johnston, Rawling, Gimblett, and MacFarlane. *The Seabound Coast*, 2010, 674–675.
17. United States Navy, *German Submarine Activities*, 1920, 65–68.
18. Johnston, Rawling, Gimblett, and MacFarlane. *The Seabound Coast*, 2010, 670–672 & 675.
19. Clark, *When the U-Boats Came to America*, 1929, 237.
20. British Admiralty. *Naval TR to Replace Triumph, 1918*. PAC, RG-24, Volume 5605, NS 29-16-1v.5. Found in the papers of the Michael Hadley collection at the University of Victoria Archives and Special collections 1.7, RG SC 053.
21. Hadley and Sarty, *Tin Pots and Pirate Ships*, 1991, 264–265.
22. Clark, *When the U-Boats Came to America*, 1929, 238.
23. Canadian Government. *October 7, 1918. Military Intelligence in Ottawa regarding "suspicious lights," Lunenburg, N.S.* Found in the papers of the Michael Hadley collection at the University of Victoria Archives and Special collections 1.7, RG SC 053.
24. United States Government and Canadian Government. *August 22, 1918 from Washington DC to Ottawa*. Box 4040, 1065-4-3. Found in the papers of the Michael Hadley collection at the University of Victoria Archives and Special collections 1.7, RG SC 053.
25. Johnston, Rawling, Gimblett, and MacFarlane. *The Seabound Coast*, 2010, 672–673.
26. Clark, *When the U-Boats Came to America*, 1929, 258–261.
27. United States Navy, *German Submarine Activities*, 1920, 68–69.
28. Hadley and Sarty, *Tin Pots and Pirate Ships*, 1991, 267.
29. British Consulate on Saint-Pierre Miquelon, *"Declaration" of the crew of the Erik*. 520. Found in the papers of the Michael Hadley collection at the University of Victoria Archives and Special collections 1.7, RG SC 053.
30. Ancestry.com. *Germany & Austria, Directories of Military and Marine Officers, 1500–1939* [database on-line]. Provo, UT, USA: Ancestry.com Operations, Inc., 2014. Original data: *Ehrenrangliste der Kaiserliche Deutschen Marine*, Verl: Marine-Offizier-Verband, 1914. Salt Lake City, Utah: FamilySearch, 2013.
31. Johnston, Rawling, Gimblett, and MacFarlane. *The Seabound Coast*, 2010, 678.

32. *CBC News, Newfoundland and Labrador*, "One Last Action: The 1918 U-Boat Sinking of the S.S. Erik," August 29, 2015. http://www.cbc.ca/news/canada/newfoundland-labrador/one-last-action-the-1918-u-boat-sinking-of-the-s-s-erik-1.3205914.
33. Clark, *When the U-Boats Came to America*, 1929, 240.
34. British Consulate on Saint-Pierre Miquelon, *"Declaration" of the crews of the EB Walters, CM Walters, and Verna D. Adams*. 517. Found in the papers of the Michael Hadley collection at the University of Victoria Archives and Special collections 1.7, RG SC 053.
35. Johnston, Rawling, Gimblett, and MacFarlane. *The Seabound Coast*, 2010, 678–684.
36. British Consulate on Saint-Pierre Miquelon, *"Declaration" of the crew of the Gloaming from August 28, 1918*. 518. Found in the papers of the Michael Hadley collection at the University of Victoria Archives and Special collections 1.7, RG SC 053.
37. Johnston, Rawling, Gimblett, and MacFarlane. *The Seabound Coast*, 2010, 694–699.
38. British Admiralty. *War Diary for North America and West Indies, 31 August 1918*. PRO ADM 137/903. Pg. 1241. Found in the papers of the Michael Hadley collection at the University of Victoria Archives and Special collections 1.6, RG SC 053.
39. Clark, *When the U-Boats Came to America*, 1929, 241.
40. U.S. Navy Department Historical Section. *Summary of Results from the Raid of U-156 from April 14 1921*, Received from the U-Boot Archiv at the Deutsches U-Boot Museum in the SM *U-156* file stored in Cuxhaven, Germany.

Chapter 17

1. Rössler, *The U-boat*, 1981, 71–73.
2. Grant, *U-Boat Hunters*, 2003, 119–127.
3. United States Navy, *German Submarine Activities*, 1920, 71.
4. Grant, *U-Boat Hunters*, 2003, 119–127.
5. In World War I the Japanese were on the Allied side from the beginning of the war to the end. Japan eliminated the small German military presence on land in the Pacific in 1914, and provided merchant and warship tonnage to the Allied cause for resupply and patrol purposes across the globe. Japanese ships were repeatedly targeted and sunk by German U-boats as a result. (Tucker, 194–197).

6. United States Navy, *German Submarine Activities*, 1920, 70–82.
7. Grant, *U-Boat Hunters*, 2003, 119–127.
8. Edited by Koerver, *German Submarine Warfare*, 2012, 644.
9. The *U-140* was acquired by the American government in 1919 and was towed across the Atlantic by a surface ship since her engines were missing by the time the Americans had taken ownership of the former German vessel. The *U-140* did not take part in the Victory bond campaign like the *U-117* would do. In a military test of warship artillery's effect on a U-boat, the *U-140* took 19 punishing rounds from an American destroyer. The *U-140* slipped beneath the waves after suffering her numerous wounds in the same waters she had prowled as an enemy U-Kreuzer almost three years before (Dubbs, 88 & 172).
10. Spindler, *Der Krieg Zur See*, 1966, 262–264.
11. Grant, *U-Boat Hunters*, 2003, 120–121.
12. United States Navy, *German Submarine Activities*, 1920, 82–85.
13. Grant, *U-Boat Hunters*, 2003, 120–121.
14. United States Navy, *German Submarine Activities*, 1920, 82–100.
15. Koerver, *German Submarine Warfare*, 2012, 643–644.
16. The battleship USS *Minnesota* was commissioned in 1907 and had her test run off the New England coast. In December 1907 the *Minnesota* and 16 other battleships left Hampton Roads, Virginia on a mission from President Theodore Roosevelt to sail around the world as part of the "Great White Fleet," The stunt was meant to showcase American naval power and impress the world into taking the U.S. seriously as a contender in the world's increasingly dangerous naval power play. After the world tour the *Minnesota* returned to the Atlantic Fleet and patrolled the U.S. east coast. In 1912 the *Minnesota* protected American interests in Cuba. In 1913 she went to Mexico, and in 1914 returned to that country twice for months at a time. In 1915 she was once again patrolling the east coast while also cruising in the Caribbean Sea. In November 1916 the *Minnesota* was named the flagship of the Atlantic Fleet Reserve Force. In April 1917, at the start of World War I, the *Minnesota* rejoined the Battleship Force out of Chesapeake Bay and was given training ship duties. During this mission she struck the *U-117*'s mine and was seriously damaged on her starboard side. No sailors were killed in the massive explosion and the *Minnesota* was taken in for repairs, which lasted five months. In March 1919 the *Minnesota* was back on the waves as a part of the Cruiser and Transport Force returning 3,000 U.S. soldiers to their homes in the U.S. during three trips to Brest, France. After her duty bringing U.S. troops back she was returned to training ship operations until she was decommissioned on 1 December 1921. The USS *Minnesota* was dismantled at the Philadelphia Navy Yard, where she had been repaired after her encounter with a German mine a few years earlier, and in January 1924 was sold for scrap (U.S. Navy "USS Minnesota").
17. Spindler, *Der Krieg Zur See*, 1966, 264–265.
18. On 3 April 1919, after she was surrendered in November 1918, *U-117* along with three other U-boats went to America again, only this time she was crewed by the U.S. Navy. The little flotilla traveled to North America via the Azores and Bermuda for a victory bond drive tour of the U.S. *U-117* did well on the voyage and received permission to sail ahead of the other slower submarines traveling in the group. *U-117* arrived in New York harbor on 26 April 1919 to great fanfare due to the novelty of an ex-German U-boat in the U.S., and the well publicized Victory bond loan campaign. *U-117*'s tour started in New York and then took her to Philadelphia, Wilmington, Delaware, Wilmington, North Carolina, Norfolk, Baltimore, Annapolis, Charleston, and then a final stop in Washington, D.C. (Dubbs, 88–91).
19. Edited by Koerver, *German Submarine Warfare*, 2012, 637–638.
20. *Ibid.*, 647–648.
21. Spindler, *Der Krieg Zur See*, 1966, 257–258.
22. United States Navy, *German Submarine Activities*, 1920, 100–106.
23. Messimer, *The Baltimore Sabotage Cell*, 2015, 194–199.
24. After a long career as the first underwater merchant vessel and an underwater warship, the *U-155* was turned over as a spoil of war to the British on 24 November. After the war ended the *U-155* was put out in public as a display for curious onlookers by the British government in London and other places. In early 1919, a private company bought the *U-155* from the British government in an effort to make money by charging

people to go aboard and sell them souvenirs made from some of the *U-155*'s pieces. The last tour of the U-Kreuzer attracted large crowds but was plagued by scandal when the *U-155*'s owner was accused of fraud and eventually went bankrupt. The old boat was then sold to shipbreakers who dismantled the submarine in 1921. The *U-155* claimed her last victims when five shipbreakers died in an explosion after they apparently lit a cigarette, candle, or match in the hull where hydrogen had escaped from cylinders left by the Germans when they surrendered the boat. The U-boat's weapons had been taken out after the sale of the vessel in 1919, but the cylinders had never been removed (*The Baltimore Sabotage Cell*, 201–205).

25. Spindler, *Der Krieg Zur See*, 1966, 253–257.
26. Grant, *U-Boat Hunters*, 2003, 117–119.
27. Grant, *U-Boat Hunters*, 2003, 118–119.
28. United States Navy, *German Submarine Activities*, 1920, 106–119.
29. Grant Grant, *U-Boat Hunters*, 2003, 117–119.
30. Edited by Görlitz, *The Kaiser and His Court*, 1964, 404.
31. *U-152* was surrendered at Harwich, England on 24 November 1918. She was scuttled by the British government in 1921 near the Isle of Wight (*Uboat.net* "U-152").
32. Grant, *U-Boat Hunters*, 2003, 124–127.
33. Edited by Koerver, *German Submarine Warfare*, 2012, 233–234.
34. Lowell Thomas, *Raiders of the Deep* (New York: Award Books, 1964 (Reprint of 1928 version)), 300.
35. Spindler, *Der Krieg Zur See*, 1966, 261–262.
36. *U-139*'s first and only cruise was the final exciting note struck in not only the U-Kreuzer campaign but in the wider U-boat war. Her captain and the U-boat represented the dash and bravery of the men who manned Germany's submarines. They also perfectly represented the futility of Germany's sea battle against such overwhelming Allied numerical and material superiority. The *U-139* was surrendered at Harwich in November 1918 and became the French submarine Halbronn. The Halbronn served in the French navy until July 1935 when she was scrapped (*Uboat.net*, "U-139").
37. Görlitz, *The Kaiser and His Court*, 1964, 392.

Chapter 18

1. Messimer, *Find and Destroy*, 2001, 187.
2. Terraine, *Business In Great Waters*, 2009, 113–115.
3. Skagen or "the Scaw" was a common word in German naval transmissions in World War I. It was used as a marker for a U-boat returning to what was considered friendly and safe waters controlled by the German navy. Skagen's sighting was usually when a crew could be assured they would reach home port safely. Skagen is the northernmost town in Denmark and sits on a very narrow point of land near to the coast of Sweden, which makes the waterway in between narrow as well.
4. McCartney, *British Submarines of World War I*, 2008, 18.
5. British Admiralty document in the Public Record Office London. ADM 137 (Operations and Intelligence) / 1453: *Report of British Submarine L8 stationed at the Northern Patrol when L8 was sent to ambush the U-156 on September 25, 1918*.
6. Grant, *U-Boat Hunters*, 2003, 114–117.
7. United States Navy. *Daily Memoranda for Force Commander from September 28 1918*, RG 145, TG Box 557–654 at the United States National Archives Washington D.C.
8. Carl-Henrik Ankarberg, 1998, "Search for a Sunken U-Boat," *Shetland Fishing News*: Number 151: (May): 15.
9. *The St. John Standard*, "Henrich Kampo, German Sailor on Submarine 56," August 7, 1918.
10. Grant, *U-Boat Hunters*, 2003, 120–123.
11. Rössler, *The U-boat*, 1981, 64.
12. *Ibid.*, 79–86.

Epilogue

1. Lawrence Paterson, *Hitler's Grey Wolves: U-Boats in the Indian Ocean*. (London: Greenhill Books, 2004), 81–125.
2. Paterson, *Hitler's Grey Wolves*, 2004, 265–267.
3. Homer Hickam. *Torpedo Junction: U-Boat War Off America's East Coast, 1942* (Annapolis: Naval Institute Press, 1989), 7.
4. Ed Offley, *The Burning Shore: How Hitler's U-Boats Brought World War II to America* (New York: Basic Books, 2014), 184–190.
5. Offley, *The Burning Shore*, 2014, 216–234.
6. Roger Sarty, *War in the St. Lawrence:*

The Forgotten U-Boat Battles on Canada's Shores (Toronto: Allen Lane, 2012), 292–293.

7. Bernard Edwards, *Death in the Doldrums: U-Cruiser Actions off West Africa* (South Yorkshire: Pen & Sword, 2005), 10–11.

8. Jürgen Rohwer, *Critical Convoy Battles of WWII: Crisis in the North Atlantic, March 1943* (Mechanicsburg: Stackpole Books, 1977), 3–11.

9. Rohwer, *Critical Convoy Battles of WWII*, 1977, 24.

10. Edwin Hoyt, *The U-boat Wars* (New York: Cooper Square Press, 2002), 162–163.

11. Rohwer, *Critical Convoy Battles of WWII*, 1977, 20.

12. Terraine, *Business In Great Waters*, 2009, 446–448.

13. *Ibid.*, 450–454.

14. Hoyt, *The U-boat Wars*, 2002, 180–186.

15. Rohwer, *Critical Convoy Battles of WWII*, 1977, 63–64.

16. Terraine, *Business In Great Waters*, 2009, 550–553.

17. Rohwer, *Critical Convoy Battles of WWII*, 1977, 197–199.

18. Terraine, *Business In Great Waters*, 2009, 556–573.

19. Hoyt, *The U-boat Wars*, 2002, 191–195.

20. Gary Wray, "Two Submarines Brought WWII to Delaware," Fort Miles Historical Association. http://fortmilesha.org/2015/04/20/two-submarines-brought-wwii-to-delaware/.

Dramatis Personæ

1. Firstworldwar.com, "William Sims," http://www.firstworldwar.com/bio/sims.htm.

2. *Ibid.*

3. Firstworldwar.com, "Alfred von Tirpitz," http://www.firstworldwar.com/bio/tirpitz.htm.

4. Edited by Tucker, Spencer. *World War I Encyclopedia*. Santa Barbara: ABC-CLIO. 578.

5. Firstworldwar.com, "Theobald von Bethmann-Hollweg," http://www.firstworldwar.com/bio/bethmann.htm.

6. Tucker, *World War I Encyclopedia*. 767.

7. *Ibid.*

8. John Lee, *The Warlords: Hindenburg and Ludendorff* (London: Weidenfeld and Nicolson, 2005), 184–195.

9. Lee, *The Warlords*, 2005, 184–195.

10. BBC, "Admiral John Jellicoe (1859–1935)," http://www.bbc.co.uk/history/historic_figures/jellicoe_john_admiral.shtml.

11. Naval Historical Collection, "Admiral Reinhard Scheer," http://www.usnwcarchive.org/items/show/1905.

12. Messimer, *The Baltimore Sabotage Cell*, 2015, 206–207.

13. *Uboat.net*, "WWI U-boat commanders: Hans Rose," http://uboat.net/wwi/men/commanders/273.html.

14. *Uboat.net*, "WWI U-boat commanders: Hermann Bauer," http://www.uboat.net:8080/wwi/men/commanders/603.html.

15. *Uboat.net*, "WWI U-boat commanders: Andreas Michelsen," http://www.uboat.net:8080/wwi/men/commanders/607.html.

16. Beesly, Patrick. 1982. *Room 40: British Naval Intelligence 1914–1918*. New York: Harcourt Brace Jovanovich Publishers. 306 & 312–315.

17. *Uboat.net*, "Max Valentiner," http://uboat.net/wwi/men/commanders/373.html.

18. *Uboat.net*, "Heinrich von Nostitz und Jänckendorff," http://uboat.net/wwi/men/commanders/231.html.

19. *Uboat.net*, "Befehlshaber der Unterseeboote Karl Dönitz," http://uboat.net/men/doenitz.htm.

Bibliography

Primary Sources

Admiralty Document in the Public Record Office London. ADM 137 (Operations and Intelligence) / 1453: *Report of British Submarine L8 stationed at the Northern Patrol when L8 was sent to ambush the U-156 on 25 September 1918.*

Ancestry.com. *Germany and Austria, Directories of Military and Marine Officers, 1500–1939* [database on-line]. Provo, UT, USA: Ancestry.com Operations, Inc., 2014. Original data: *Ehrenrangliste der Kaiserliche Deutschen Marine, Verl: Marine-Offizier-Verband, 1914.* Salt Lake City, Utah: FamilySearch, 2013.

Ancestry.com. *Germany, Select Births and Baptisms, 1558–1898* [database on-line]. Provo, UT, USA: Ancestry.com Operations, Inc., 2014. Original data: *Germany, Births and Baptisms, 1558–1898.* Salt Lake City, Utah: FamilySearch, 2013.

British Admiralty. ADM 137 (Operations and Intelligence) / 4155 (U-boat history sheets): *U-151 to U-157, 1917–1918*, accessed at http://germannavalwarfare.info

British Admiralty. ADM 137 (Operations and Intelligence) / 4155 (U-boat history sheets): *U-151, 1917–1918, 6 pages,* accessed at http://germannavalwarfare.info/02subm/02/U151.html

British Admiralty. ADM 137 (Operations and Intelligence) / 4155 (U-boat history sheets): *U-152, 1917–1918, 6 pages,* accessed at http://germannavalwarfare.info/02subm/02/U152.html

British Admiralty. ADM 137 (Operations and Intelligence) / 4155 (U-boat history sheets): *U-153, 1917–1918, 6 pages,* accessed at http://germannavalwarfare.info/02subm/02/U153.html

British Admiralty. ADM 137 (Operations and Intelligence) / 4155 (U-boat history sheets): *U-154, 1917–1918, 6 pages,* accessed at http://germannavalwarfare.info/02subm/02/U154.html

British Admiralty. ADM 137 (Operations and Intelligence) / 4155 (U-boat history sheets): *U-155, 1917–1918, 6 pages,* accessed at http://germannavalwarfare.info/02subm/02/U155.html

British Admiralty. ADM 137 (Operations and Intelligence) / 4155 (U-boat history sheets): *U-156, 1917–1918, 6 pages,* accessed at http://germannavalwarfare.info/02subm/02/U156.html

British Admiralty. *Attacks made by U-53*, ADM 137/4131. Found in the papers of the Michael Hadley collection at the University of Victoria Archives and Special collections 1.5, RG SC 053.

British Admiralty. *Naval TR to Replace Triumph, 1918.* PAC, RG-24, Volume 5605, NS 29-16-1v.5. Found in the papers of the Michael Hadley collection at the University of Victoria Archives and Special collections 1.7, RG SC 053.

British Admiralty. *Protection of the fishing fleets 1918.* PAC, RG 24, box 4030, 1065-4-3. Found in the papers of the Michael Hadley collection at the University of Victoria Archives and Special collections 1.7, RG SC 053.

British Admiralty. *War Diary for North America and West Indies.* PRO ADM 137/903. Found in the papers of the Michael Hadley collection at the University of Victoria Archives and Special collections 1.6, RG SC 053.

British Consulate on Saint-Pierre Miquelon. *"Declaration" of the crew of the Erik.* 520. Found in the papers of the Michael Hadley collection at the University of Victoria Archives and Special collections 1.7, RG SC 053.

British Consulate on Saint-Pierre Miquelon. *"Declaration" of the crews of the EB Walters, CM Walters, and Verna D. Adams*. 517. Found in the papers of the Michael Hadley collection at the University of Victoria Archives and Special collections 1.7, RG SC 053.

British Consulate on Saint-Pierre Miquelon. *"Declaration" of the crew of the Gloaming from August 28, 1918*. 518. Found in the papers of the Michael Hadley collection at the University of Victoria Archives and Special collections 1.7, RG SC 053.

Canadian Government. *October 7, 1918. Military Intelligence in Ottawa regarding "suspicious lights," Lunenburg, N.S*. Found in the papers of the Michael Hadley collection at the University of Victoria Archives and Special collections 1.7, RG SC 053.

Deutsches U-Boot Museum, U-Boot-Archiv. *Crew List for the U-156*. Stored in Cuxhaven, Germany.

Deutsches U-Boot Museum, U-Boot-Archiv. *German Naval Career File on Konrad Gansser*. Stored in Cuxhaven, Germany.

Deutsches U-Boot Museum, U-Boot-Archiv. *German Naval Career File on Richard Feldt*. Stored in Cuxhaven, Germany.

Görlitz, Walter, ed. *The Kaiser and His Court: The Diaries, Note Books and Letters of Admiral Georg Alexander von Muller Chief of the Naval Cabinet 1914–1918*. New York: Harcourt, Brace & World, Inc., 1964.

Hallas, James, ed. *Doughboy War: The American Expeditionary Force in WWI*. Mechanicsburg, PA: Stackpole Books, 2009.

Kaiserliche Marine U-Kreuzer Verband, *Document from 19 June 1918* (Proposed North American "Sperrgebiet" blockade zone). Found in the papers of the Michael Hadley collection at the University of Victoria Archives and Special collections 1.13, RG SC 053.

Kaiserliche Marine U-Kreuzer Verband, *Document from 19 June 1918* (Proposed North American "Sperrgebiet" blockade zone). Found in the papers of the Michael Hadley collection at the University of Victoria Archives and Special collections 1.13, RG SC 053.

Kaiserliche Marine. BA-MA (Bundesarchiv-Militärarchiv): RM 5/5962, *Der Kabelkrieg*. 105–108. Found in the papers of the Michael Hadley collection at the University of Victoria Archives and Special collections 1.13, RG SC 053.

Kaiserliche Marine. *Berlin 16 March 1918, Kanzlei schreibe an den chef des marinekabinetts*. Found in the papers of the Michael Hadley collection at the University of Victoria Archives and Special collections 1.13, RG SC 053.

Kaiserliche Marine. *Großes Hauptquartier 3 October 1917*, Report on the mission of the *U-156* and other U-Kreuzers in the Canaries area for Kaiser Wilhelm II. Found in the papers of the Michael Hadley collection at the University of Victoria Archives and Special collections 1.13, RG SC 053.

Kaiserliche Marine. Message dated *26 June 1918* (The details for the proposed American blockade zone's initiation with *U-156* proposed as the first boat to open the blockade). Found in the papers of the Michael Hadley collection at the University of Victoria Archives and Special collections 1.13, RG SC 053.

Kaiserliche Marine. *O-Befehl (Operations Orders) fur U-156 10 June 1918* (from the chief of the Admiralstab der Marine). Found in the papers of the Michael Hadley collection at the University of Victoria Archives and Special collections 1.13, RG SC 053.

Kaiserliche Marine. *Zum Immediatvortrag, 6 June 1917*. Found in the papers of the Michael Hadley collection at the University of Victoria Archives and Special collections 1.13, RG SC 053.

Kaiserliche Marine. *Zum Thronvortrag Berlin, 28 February 1918*. Request for the Kaiser's approval of Holtzendorff's proposed North American blockade zone. Found in the papers of the Michael Hadley collection at the University of Victoria Archives and Special collections 1.13, RG SC 053.

Koerver, Hans Joachim, ed. *German Submarine Warfare in the Eyes of British Intelligence: Selected Sources from the British National Archive*. Berlin: LIS Reinisch, 2012.

Laws of War: Declaration of Paris; April 16, 1856. http://avalon.law.yale.edu/19th_century/decparis.asp.

Marist College Archives and Special Collections from the Lowell Thomas papers under "submarines," Boxes 1510 and 1512 for photographs from the cruises of the *U-156* and *U-157*. Available for preview viewing online at URL (Request copies on website): http://library.marist.edu/archives/

LTP/Graphic%20Materials/Photographic Prints2.1.3/submarines2.1.3.1.3.1.xml
National Archives Microfilm Publications: *Microcopy No. T-1022 Guides to the Microfilmed Records of the German Navy, 1850–1945: No. 1. U-Boats and T-Boats 1914–1918, Kriegstagebuch U-156.* Washington 1984, can be found under *U-156,* Konrad Gansser, or Richard Feldt at the U.S. National Archives Microfilm Room College Park, MD.
National Archives Microfilm Publications: *Microcopy No. T-1022 Guides to the Microfilmed Records of the German Navy, 1850–1945: No. 1. U-Boats and T-Boats 1914–1918, Kriegstagebuch U-30.* Washington 1984, can be found under U-30 or Richard Feldt at the US National Archives Microfilm Room College Park, MD.
New York Times. "Decide Mine Sank Cruiser San Diego." August 6, 1918.
Office of Naval Intelligence. 1918. *Antisubmarine Information, ONI No. 14: German Submarine Cable Cutter.* Washington: Government Printing Office. Available online at URL: http://www.history.navy.mil/library/online/onipubno14.htm.
The Ottawa Evening Journal. "Trawler Triumph Fitted With Two Guns and Manned by the Huns." August 21, 1918.
Royal Canadian Navy. *Fisheries Defense.* PAC, RG 24, box 4030, 1065-4-1. Found in the papers of the Michael Hadley collection at the University of Victoria Archives and Special collections 1.7, RG SC 053.
The St. John Standard. "Henrich Kampo, German Sailor on Submarine 56." August 7, 1918.
The St. John Standard. "Schooner Wrecked by the Germans Towed into Point Along the Atlantic Coast" August 6, 1918.
U.S. Government and Canadian Government. *August 22, 1918 from Washington, D.C., to Ottawa.* Box 4040, 1065-4-3. Found in the papers of the Michael Hadley collection at the University of Victoria Archives and Special collections 1.7, RG SC 053.
U.S. Government. 1918. *Second Annual Report of the United States Shipping Board.* Washington, D.C.: Government Printing Office.
U.S. Navy Department Historical Section. *Summary of Results from the Raid of U-156 from April 14 1921,* Received from the Deutsches U-Boot Museum, U-Boot Archiv from the SM U-156 file stored in Cuxhaven, Germany.
U.S. Navy. *Daily Memoranda for Force Commander from August 9 1918,* RG 145, TG Box 557–654 at the United States National Archives Washington, D.C.
U.S. Navy. *Daily Memoranda for Force Commander from June 21 and July 4 1918,* RG 145, TG Box 557–654 at the United States National Archives Washington, D.C.
U.S. Navy. *Daily Memoranda for Force Commander from September 28 1918,* RG 145, TG Box 557–654 at the United States National Archives Washington, D.C.
U.S. Navy. *Daily Memorandum for Force Commander from July 22, 1918,* RG 145, TG Box 557–654 at the United States National Archives Washington, D.C.
U.S. Navy. *Daily Memorandum for Force Commander from June 14, 1918,* RG 145, TG Box 557–654 at the United States National Archives Washington, D.C.
U.S. Navy. *German Submarine Activities on the Atlantic Coast of the United States and Canada.* Washington, D.C.: Government Printing Office, 1920.
U.S. Navy. *Section VI: Review of Enemy Submarine Activity On The American Coast, June—October, 1918.* National Archives Washington, D.C.

Articles and Websites

Albert, George. 2016. "The USS *San Diego* and the California Naval Militia." California Center for Military History. Available online at URL: http://www.militarymuseum.org/USSSanDiego.html.
Ankarberg, Carl-Henrik. 1998. "Search for a Sunken U-Boat." Shetland Fishing News: Number 151: (May): 15.
BBC. "Admiral John Jellicoe (1859–1935)" Available online at URL: http://www.bbc.co.uk/history/historic_figures/jellicoe_john_admiral.shtml.
CBC News, Newfoundland and Labrador. "One Last Action: The 1918 U-Boat Sinking of the S.S. Erik." August 29, 2015. Available online at URL: http://www.cbc.ca/news/canada/newfoundland-labrador/one-last-action-the-1918-u-boat-sinking-of-the-s-s-erik-1.3205914.
Central Intelligence Agency. "The World Factbook: Liberia." Available online at URL: https://www.cia.gov/library/publications/the-world-factbook/geos/li.html.
The Day. "New London once saw its future in a German U-boat." November 19, 2016. Available online at URL: http://www.

theday.com/article/20161119/NWS01/161129958
Edwards, Martin. 2006. "Roll of Honour, Lest We Forget. Hale, Wadham House School War Memorial." Available online at URL: http://www.roll-of-honour.com/Cheshire/HaleWadhamHouseSchool.html.
Encyclopaedia Brittanica. "Kiel, Germany." Available online at URL: https://www.britannica.com/place/Kiel.
Firstworldwar.com. "Alfred von Tirpitz." http://www.firstworldwar.com/bio/tirpitz.htm.
Firstworldwar.com. "Franc-Tireur." Available online at URL: http://www.firstworldwar.com/atoz/franctireur.htm.
Firstworldwar.com. "Theobald von Bethmann-Hollweg." http://www.firstworldwar.com/bio/bethmann.htm
Firstworldwar.com. "William Sims." Available online at URL: http://www.firstworldwar.com/bio/sims.htm.
Fordham, Benjamin. 2007. "Revisionism Reconsidered: Exports and American Intervention in the First World War." Binghamton University. http://dev.wcfia.harvard.edu/sites/default/files/FordhamND.pdf
French Cable Station Museum. "Museum History." Available online at URL: http://www.frenchcablestationmuseum.org/museum-history.htm.
Imperial War Museum. "Who Was Edith Cavell?" Available online at URL: http://www.iwm.org.uk/history/who-was-edith-cavell.
Lettens, Jan. 2010. "Wreck Site: SS Dwinsk." Available online at URL: http://www.wrecksite.eu/wreck.aspx?132170.
Los Angeles Times. "A Personal History Beneath the Waves." June 10, 2001. Available online at URL: http://articles.latimes.com/2001/jun/10/news/mn-8573.
Lozada, Carlos. 2004. "The Economics of World War I. "National Bureau of Economic Research." http://www.nber.org/digest/jan05/w10580.html.
Madeira-web.com. "Santiago Fortress." Available online at URL: http://www.madeira-web.com/PagesUK/funchal-nucleus/santa-maria/santiago-fortress.html.
Maritime Museum of the Atlantic. "Halifax Explosion Infosheet." Available online at URL: https://maritimemuseum.novascotia.ca/what-see-do/halifax-explosion/halifax-explosion-infosheet.
Nash, George. 1989. "Herbert Hoover and Belgian Relief in World War I" National Archives and Records Administration: Prologue Magazine. Volume 21, Number 1 (Spring). Available online at URL: https://www.archives.gov/publications/prologue/1989/spring/hoover-belgium.html.
National Park Service. "Fort Texas/Fort Brown." Available online at URL: https://www.nps.gov/paal/learn/historyculture/siegeoffortexas.htm.
Naval Historical Center Website. "USS Lake Bridge (ID # 2990), 1918–1919." Available online at URL: http://www.ibiblio.org/hyperwar/OnlineLibrary/photos/sh-usn/usnsh-l/id2990.htm
Naval Historical Center. "*SS Leviathan*." https://www.ibiblio.org/hyperwar/OnlineLibrary/photos/sh-civil/civsh-l/leviathn.htm.
Naval Historical Collection. "Admiral Reinhard Scheer." Available online at URL: http://www.usnwcarchive.org/items/show/1905.
Naval History and Heritage Command. "California II." Available online at URL: www.history.navy.mil/research/histories/ship-histories/danfs/c/california-ii.html.
Naval History and Heritage Command. "Jouett I (Destroyer No. 41)." Available online at URL: https://www.history.navy.mil/research/histories/ship-histories/danfs/j/jouett-i.html.
Naval History and Heritage Command. "Today in Naval History: December 14." Available online at URL: http://www.history.navy.mil/today-in-history/december-14.html.
The Northern Echo. "Slaughter by the Seaside: the Shelling of Seaham." July 9, 2016. Available online at URL: http://www.thenorthernecho.co.uk/history/14609266.Slaughter_by_the_seaside__the_shelling_of_Seaham/.
Ponce, Javier. 2014. "Commerce Warfare in the East Central Atlantic During the First World War: German Submarines Around the Canary Islands, 1916–1918." Routledge: Mariner's Mirror 100:3 (August).
The Register-Mail. "Talbot Fisher: German U-boat fears surface in U.S." October 12, 2016. Available online at URL: http://www.galesburg.com/news/20161012/talbot-fisher-german-u-boat-fears-surface-in-us.
Royal Canadian Navy. "Commander Royal Canadian Navy—A Brief History of the Position." Available online at URL: http://www.navy-marine.forces.gc.ca/en/navy-life/history-rcn-commanders.page.
Seymour, Joey. "Honorably Representing San Diego: The Story of the USS San Diego."

Available online at URL: www.sandiego history.org: The Journal of San Diego History.

Strobridge, Truman R. The United States Coast Guard. "Chronology of Aids to Navigation and the United States Lighthouse Service 1716–1939." Available online at URL: https://www.uscg.mil/history/articles/h_USLHSchron.asp.

Twigge, Stephen. 27 July 2016. "Captain Fryatt: forgotten martyr of the First World War." UK National Archives. Available online at URL: http://blog.nationalarchives.gov.uk/blog/captain-fryatt-forgotten-martyr-first-world-war/.

Tworek, Heidi J.S.: Wireless Telegraphy, in: 1914–1918-online. International Encyclopedia of the First World War, ed. by Ute Daniel, Peter Gatrell, Oliver Janz, Heather Jones, Jennifer Keene, Alan Kramer, and Bill Nasson, issued by Freie Universität Berlin, Berlin 2014-10-08. DOI: http://dx.doi.org/10.15463/ie1418.10347.

U.S. Navy. "USS Minnesota (BB 22)." Available at URL: http://www.navy.mil/navydata/nav_legacy.asp?id=97.

Uboat.net. "Befehlshaber der Unterseeboote Karl Dönitz." http://uboat.net/men/doenitz.htm.

Uboat.net. "Deadly Mediterranean." Available online at URL: http://uboat.net/history/wwi/part4.htm.

Uboat.net. "Heinrich von Nostitz und Jänckendorff." Available online at URL: http://uboat.net/wwi/men/commanders/231.html.

Uboat.net. "Max Valentiner." Available online at URL: http://uboat.net/wwi/men/commanders/373.html.

Uboat.net. "Ships Hit During WWI, Acary." Available online at URL: http://uboat.net/wwi/ships_hit/26.html.

Uboat.net. "Ships Hit During WWI, Guahyba." Available online at URL: http://uboat.net/wwi/ships_hit/2637.html.

Uboat.net. "Ships Hit During WWI, Losses by Month." Available online at URL: http://uboat.net/wwi/ships_hit/losses_year.html.

Uboat.net. "U-139." Available online at URL: http://uboat.net:8080/wwi/boats/index.html?boat=139.

Uboat.net. "U-152." Available online at URL: http://www.uboat.net/wwi/boats/index.html?boat=152.

Uboat.net. "U-153." Available online at URL: http://uboat.net/wwi/boats/index.html?boat=153.

Uboat.net. "WWI U-boat commanders: Andreas Michelsen." Available online at URL: http://www.uboat.net:8080/wwi/men/commanders/607.html.

Uboat.net. "WWI U-boat commanders: Hans Rose." Available online at URL: http://uboat.net/wwi/men/commanders/273.html.

Uboat.net. "WWI U-boat commanders: Hermann Bauer." Available online at URL: http://www.uboat.net:8080/wwi/men/commanders/603.html.

Uboat.net. "WWI U-boat Commanders." Available online at URL: http://uboat.net/wwi/men/commanders/83.html

The Wartime Memories Project. "SS Portugal during the Great War." Available online at URL: http://www.wartimememoriesproject.com/greatwar/ships/view.php?pid=3092.

World Atlas. "Azores." Available online at URL: http://www.worldatlas.com/webimage/countrys/europe/azores.htm.

World Atlas. "Canary Islands." http://www.worldatlas.com/webimage/countrys/europe/canary.htm.

Wray, Gary. "Two Submarines Brought WWII to Delaware." Fort Miles Historical Association. http://fortmilesha.org/2015/04/20/two-submarines-brought-wwii-to-delaware/.

Wrecksite.eu. "SS Johan Mjelde." Available online at URL: http://wrecksite.eu/wreck.aspx?154598.

Books

Beesly, Patrick. *Room 40: British Naval Intelligence 1914–1918.* New York: Harcourt Brace Jovanovich Publishers, 1982.

Bisher, Jamie. *The Intelligence War in Latin America, 1914–1922.* Jefferson, NC: McFarland. 2016.

Blum, Howard. *Dark Invasion 1915: Germany's Secret War and the Hunt for the First Terrorist Cell in America.* New York: HarperCollins, 2014.

Buckley, Joseph. *Wings Over Cape Cod: The Chatham Naval Air Station 1917–1918.* Orleans: Lower Cape Publishing, 2000.

Clark, William. *When the U-Boats Came to America.* Boston: Little, Brown, & Co., 1929.

Compton-Hall, Richard. *Submarines at War: 1914–1918.* Cornwall: Periscope Publishing Ltd., 2004.

Darling, Warren. Unknown date. *The French

Cable Station Museum: Museum Tour Book. Orleans: Published by the Museum.

Dubbs, Chris. *America's U-Boats: Terror Trophies of World War I*. Lincoln: University of Nebraska Press, 2014.

Dunn, Steve. *Blockade: Cruiser Warfare and the Starvation of Germany in World War One*. Barnsley: Seaforth Publishing, 2016.

Dunne, WMP. *Thomas F. McManus and the American Fishing Schooners: An Irish-American Success Story*. Mystic: Mystic Seaport Museum, 1994.

Edwards, Bernard. *Death in the Doldrums: U-Cruiser Actions off West Africa*. South Yorkshire: Pen & Sword, 2005.

Edwards, Bernard. *Dönitz and the Wolf Packs*. South Yorkshire: Pen & Sword, 2014.

Grant, Robert. *U-Boat Hunters: Code Breakers, Divers and the Defeat of the U-Boats, 1914–1918*. Cornwall: Periscope Publishing, 2003.

Gray, Edwyn. *The U-Boat War: 1914–1918*. London: Leo Cooper, 1994.

Gröner, Erich. *Die Deutsche Kriegsschiffe, 1815–1945*. Munich: J.F. Lehmanns Verlag, 1966.

Hadley, Michael, and Roger Sarty. *Tin Pots and Pirate Ships: Canadian Naval Forces and German Sea Raiders 1880–1918*. Montreal & Kingston: McGill-Queen's University Press, 1991.

Herwig, Holger. *Politics of Frustration: The United States in German Naval Planning, 1889–1941*. Boston: Little, Brown & Company, 1976.

Hewitt, Nick. *The Kaiser's Pirates: Hunting Germany's Raiding Cruisers 1914–1915*. South Yorkshire: Pen & Sword, 2013.

Hickam, Homer. *Torpedo Junction: U-Boat War Off America's East Coast, 1942*. Annapolis: Naval Institute Press, 1989.

Hull, Isabel. *A Scrap of Paper: Breaking and Making International Law during the Great War*. Ithaca: Cornell University Press, 2014.

Hurley, Edward. *The Bridge to France*. Philadelphia: J.B. Lippincott Company, 1927.

James, Henry. *German Subs in Yankee Waters*. New York: Gotham House, 1940.

Johnston, William, William Rawling, Richard Gimblett, and John MacFarlane. *The Seabound Coast: The Official History of the Royal Canadian Navy, 1867–1939*. Toronto: Dundurn Press, 2010. This massive work is the last word on the history of the Canadian Navy in World War I, and was written as the official Canadian government account of their naval forces during this time period.

Klim, Jake. *Attack on Orleans: The World War I Submarine Raid on Cape Cod*. Charleston: The History Press, 2014.

Larzelere, Alex. *The Coast Guard in World War I: An Untold Story*. Annapolis: Naval Institute Press, 2003.

Lee, John. *The Warlords: Hindenburg and Ludendorff*. London: Weidenfeld & Nicolson, 2005.

Marshall, S.L.A. *World War I*. Boston: Houghton Mifflin, 1987.

McCartney, Innes. *British Submarines of World War I*. Oxford: Osprey Publishing, 2008.

McGovern, Terrance, and Bolling Smith. *American Coastal Defenses: 1885–1950*. Oxford: Osprey Publishing Ltd., 2006.

Messimer, Dwight. *The Baltimore Sabotage Cell: German Agents, American Traitors, And The U-Boat Deutschland During World War I*. Annapolis: Naval Institute Press, 2015.

Messimer, Dwight. *Find and Destroy: Anti-Submarine Warfare in World War I*. Annapolis: Naval Institute Press, 2001.

Offley, Ed. *The Burning Shore: How Hitler's U-Boats Brought World War II to America*. New York: Basic Books, 2014.

Paterson, Lawrence. *Hitler's Grey Wolves: U-Boats in the Indian Ocean*. London: Greenhill Books, 2004.

Polaski, Leo, and Glen Williford. *New York City's Harbor Defenses*. Charleston, SC: Arcadia Publishing, 2003.

Rohwer, Jürgen. *Critical Convoy Battles of WWII: Crisis in the North Atlantic, March 1943*. Mechanicsburg: Stackpole Books, 1977.

Rössler, Eberhard. *Die Deutschen U-Kreuzer und Transport-U-Boote*. Bonn: Bernard & Graefe Verlag, 2003.

Rössler, Eberhard. *The U-boat: The evolution and technical history of German submarines*. London: Arms and Armour Press, 1981.

Sarty, Roger. *War in the St. Lawrence: The Forgotten U-Boat Battles on Canada's Shores*. Toronto: Allen Lane, 2012.

Simpson, William. *The Second Reich: Germany, 1871–1918*. Cambridge: Cambridge University Press, 1995.

Spindler, Arno. *Der Krieg zur See 1914–1918: Handelskrieg mit U-Booten Volume 5*. Frankfurt: E.S. Mittler & Sohn, 1966. This book is the first and last word in German source material on WWI U-boats. The work is a detailed summary of all U-boat war logs during the conflict, and was written by a retired German admiral who started his career as an officer before and during WWI. It is only available in the German language and can be difficult to translate due to the use of an older form of German script called Stettin.

Tennent, A.J. *British Merchant Ships Sunk by U-Boats in World War One*. Cornwall: Periscope Publishing, 2006.

Terraine, John. *Business In Great Waters: The U-boat Wars 1916–1945*. South Yorkshire: Pen & Sword Military, 2009.

Thomas, Lowell. *Raiders of the Deep*. Garden City, NJ: Doubleday, Doran, & Co., 1928.

Tucker, Spencer. *The Great War 1914–18*. Indianapolis: Indiana University Press, 1998.

Tucker, Spencer, ed. *World War I Encyclopedia*. Santa Barbara, CA: ABC-CLIO.

Vincent, C. Paul. *The Politics of Hunger: The Allied Blockade of Germany, 1915–1919*. Athens, Ohio: Ohio University Press, 1985.

Index

Aconit 178
aerial patrols 30–31
Allenby, Gen. Sir Edmund (General) 47
Ambrose Channel Lightship 152
American and Canadian naval defenses 91–95, 121–122
Arabic 23
Atlas Werke (shipbuilders) 45, 196

Baltic Sea 10–11, 18, 36
Bauer, Hermann (Kommodore) 42, 44, 176, 184
Bell, USS 140
Benson, William (Admiral) 16, 30, 32, 92, 181
British blockade 6, 9, 11, 19, 21, 26, 28, 81, 171
British Grand Fleet 17, 31
Bugel, Kurt (Leutnant zur See) 191
Byrd, Richard (Lieutenant) 122

C24, HMS 65
Canary Islands 3, 6, 54–55, 57, 62–63, 66, 68, 70–72, 75, 82–83, 92, 117, 124, 127, 148
Cape Cod canal 118
Cape Verde Islands 70, 72, 171
Caporetto, battle of 48
cargo submarines 38–40
Cartier, HMCS 143–144
Cavell, Edith (executed nurse) 53, 196
CC1, HMCS 145
CC2, HMCS 145
Christy, Harley (Captain) 105, 107–109
Commission for the Relief of Belgium 15, 132, 204
contraband of war 10–11, 19, 55, 61, 71, 74, 82, 91, 102
convoy 7, 15–17, 20, 30–31, 34, 36, 42, 68, 71–73, 81, 86, 89, 91, 93–96, 99, 104, 106, 120, 122, 126, 128–133, 141, 145–149, 154, 157, 160, 168, 170, 172, 174–175, 177–178
cutting underwater communications cables 43–45, 74, 80, 87, 99, 100–103, 118–119, 121, 156, 162, 187, 202

Declarations of Paris and London 10, 193
Diamond Shoals Lightship 149
distant blockade 9
Dönitz, Karl (Admiral) 174–175, 177–179, 185–186
Dröscher, Otto (Kapitänleutnant) 151–153
Duke of Clarence, HMS 64

E35, HMS 75
E48, HMS 64–65, 67
Eckelmann, Erich (Korvettenkapitän) 80–81
Emden, SMS 41–42
English Channel 11
Erri Berro 62, 64, 67, 185
Espionage Act 110
Evans, David (Captain of the *Penistone*) 133–134

Feldt, Richard 84–86, 88, 100–101, 103, 106, 108, 110–113, 116–122, 125–126, 128–129, 131–138, 140–145, 147–148, 155, 162–166, 169, 172, 188, 191
Ferlicot (Commander of French armed schooners) 141
food crisis in Germany 11–13
Fort Santiago 59, 188, 197
Fort São Brás 179
Franz, Adolph (Kapitänleutnant) 157–161
Fryatt, Charles (Captain of SS *Brussels*) 53–54
Funchal 60, 63, 69, 167, 170, 188

Gansser, Konrad 3, 5–6, 51–54, 56–57, 59–62, 65–70, 75, 78, 84, 86, 127, 163, 169–170, 172
Gercke, Hermann (Korvettenkapitän) 74–76
German High Seas Fleet 10, 18, 29, 32, 35, 85, 161
Germaniawerft (shipbuilders) 45, 196
Goetting, Gernot (Korvettenkapitän) 72
Grant, Sir William Lowther (Vice-Admiral) 109, 131

218 Index

Halifax 96, 99–100, 106, 122, 126–127, 129–132, 135, 155–156, 160, 168
Hall, William Reginald (Admiral) 62, 185
Harvester, HMS 178
Hierro Island 3, 63–64, 67, 169
Hilken, Paul 111
Hochelaga, HMCS 143–144, 152
Holland 10–11, 15, 36
HS-1L flying boat 94, 115–116
Hull, USS 149

influenza pandemic 12
Iron Cross (medal) 51, 54, 86

Japanese Navy 15, 168, 174–175, 205
Jellicoe, John (First Sea Lord) 30, 183
Jouett, USS 95, 125, 131, 140–141, 200

Kaiser Wilhelm II 24, 28–31, 33–34, 39–40, 61, 67, 89–90, 99–100, 159, 161
Kamps, Heinrich 123, 166–167
Kiel 45–46, 57, 68, 71, 77, 80–81, 83–84, 86–87, 100, 171, 188, 196
Kingfisher, USS 152
Knöckel, Paul Richard 3, 54, 61–62, 121–122, 132, 134, 137–140, 142, 163, 191
Koch (Fregattenkapitän) 69
Kolbe, Constantin (Kapitänleutnant) 71
König, Paul 39–40, 184
Kophamel, Waldemar (Korvettenkapitän) 70, 148–150
Kriegsmarine 174–177

L8, HMS 164, 168
Lawrence of Arabia 47
Legate, Robert (Lieutenant) 143–145
Lenin, Vladimir 48
Liberia 74–76, 199
Ludendorff, Erich (First Quartermaster General) 26–27, 29–30, 32, 34, 49, 172, 183
Lusitania 22, 40, 92
Lutzner, Albert (Leutnant zur See) 191
Luz Blanca 129–132, 170, 190

Madeira 55, 58, 60, 63, 68–70, 80, 92, 170, 188, 197
Madrid, German embassy to 62–63, 67, 82
Magdeburg, SMS 35
Mark IV aerial bomb 94, 115, 117–118
Mark VI sea mine 166
Mata Hari 111
Mathew Luckenbach 179
McGuirk, H.F. (Lieutenant) 143–144
Meusel, Karl (Kapitänleutnant) 76–81
Michelsen, Andreas (Kommodore) 42, 44, 166, 184
Minnesota, USS 154, 206
Mitchell, Maurice (Commander) 62, 64
Möltenort U-boat Memorial 187

Naos Bay 3, 5, 63, 66–69, 163, 165, 170
Nauen 35, 37, 58, 60, 62, 66–67, 70–71, 73, 75, 80, 95–96, 99–100, 102, 110–112, 121, 148, 162–164, 167, 195
Nauset Beach 113–115, 117, 143, 165, 167–168, 187
naval defenses in the Canaries and Azores Islands 54–55
Naval Overseas Transportation Service 15, 145
neutral shipping 10–11, 14–15
Niemann, Ernst (Head Engineer) 191
Norddeutscher Lloyd 104
North America (German attacks in WWII) 175–176, 179
North America (German decision to attack in WWI) 32–34, 89–91
North Sea 10–11, 18, 30, 50, 80
northern mine barrage 162–163, 165, 169
Nossa Senhora da Paz Sanctuary 187

Orleans, Massachusetts 113, 117–120, 163, 168, 170, 175, 187, 202

Pola (U-boat base) 51, 69, 197
Portugal (hospital ship) 51, 53
Pour le Mérite (medal) 51, 126, 184–185
prize rules 25, 28, 34, 55, 91, 96, 173
protected war grave 168

R-9 seaplane 94, 116–117
radio direction finding 31, 36
Rave, Ortwin (Korvettenkapitän) 83
Reinhold, Arthur 170
Room 40 36–37, 44, 57, 65, 69, 74, 85, 91, 95, 97, 100, 155, 164
Rose, Hans 39–40, 45, 184
Rotterdam 10
Royal House Order of Hohenzollern (medal) 51, 185

saboteurs 38, 108, 110
sailing ships (diverted to western Atlantic) 92
San Diego, USS 105–106, 108–110, 123, 125, 132, 162, 168–170, 187, 189
Scheer, Reinhard (Admiral and his u-boat building program) 34, 171–172, 183
Schlemm, Martin (Doctor) 142, 191
Sharif Faisal (Rebel leader) 47
Sims, William (Admiral) 16, 37, 91, 93, 96, 100, 157, 181
Skagen, Denmark 164–165, 207
Stringham, USS 150
Studt, Ferdinand (Korvettenkapitän) 154–157, 161
submarine blockade zone 11, 16, 19, 22, 31, 33–34, 71, 89–90, 112, 147, 171
submarine chasers 17, 95, 100, 119, 130–131, 152
Sussex 25

Index

Taranaki 65
Taylor, Danforth 117
Taylor, F.H. (Lieutenant Commander) 64–66, 145
Ticonderoga, USS 154, 157–159
torpedo 5–6, 15, 25, 43, 45, 53, 57, 64–65, 67, 72–73, 75–76, 78–80, 82, 86, 91, 96, 99, 107, 110, 117, 123, 129–130, 133–134, 146, 148–149, 151–153, 156, 158, 160, 165, 170, 179
Tortuguero 101, 170, 189
TR 22, HMCS 143
TR 32, HMCS 143
Treaty of Brest-Litovsk 48
Treaty of Bucharest 47
Triumph 136–142, 163, 169, 190
Trotsky, Leon 48
Turner, Arthur Harold 101

U-1, SM 148
U-2, SM 148
U-8, SM 51
U-19, SM 76
U-30, SM 86
U-33, SM 51–53, 169
U-35, SM 42
U-38, SM 42
U-40, SM 65, 145
U-49, SM 54
U-50, SM 54
U-53, SM 89, 91
U-62, SM 42, 73, 75
U-91, SM 42
U-117, SM 42, 115, 117, 123, 148, 151–154, 156, 192, 206
U-139, SM 42, 160–161, 163, 173, 192, 207
U-140, SM 42, 121, 123, 147, 149–151, 154, 160, 206
U-141, SM 42, 161, 192
U-151, SM 42, 70–71, 89, 95–101, 103, 148, 151, 171, 192
U-152, SM 71–72, 157–159, 163–164, 207
U-153, SM 72–75, 199
U-154, SM 73–76, 166
U-155, SM 76–81, 138, 154–157, 159, 206
U-157, SM 3, 42, 46, 62–64, 66, 71–72, 81–83, 124, 129, 138, 192
U-161, SM 163
U-444 178
U-523 179
U-527 178

U-701 175–176
U-boat officer's school 86
U-Bremen 39
U-Deutschland 39–40, 89, 101, 121, 154
U-Kreuzer design flaws and weaponry 40–41, 43–45
UB-94, SM 163–164
United States Coast Guard Lifesaving Stations 93–94, 114–115, 153, 175
United States Lighthouse Service 93, 200
United States Navy 12, 15–16, 130–131, 152
United States Ship Protection Committee 92
United States Shipping Board 14, 15–19, 193
United States Weather Bureau 93
unrestricted submarine warfare 19, 22–31, 33–34, 40, 89, 112

Valentiner, Max (Kapitänleutnant) 63, 66–67, 69–70, 75, 81–82, 185
Virginia Beach 175–176
von Arnauld de la Perière, Lothar (Kapitänleutnant) 126, 160–161, 163
von Bethmann-Hollweg, Theobald (German Chancellor) 26, 28, 182
von Capelle, Eduard (Minister of the Marine) 25–26, 182
von Hindenburg, Paul (Field Marshal) 26–27, 30, 34, 172, 182
von Holtzendorff, Henning (Admiral) 23–26, 28, 30, 32–34, 89–90, 100, 112, 182
von Ingenohl, Friedrich (Admiral) 22, 182
von Luxburg, Karl (Count) 99, 200
von Nostitz und Jänckendorff, Heinrich (Korvettenkapitän) 96–98, 155, 185
von Tirpitz, Alfred (Admiral) 21, 24–25, 181
vorkampff-Laue, Arnold (Kapitänleutnant) 86–87, 191

Walke, USS 133
Weimar Republic 16, 194
Wilhelmshaven 45, 196
Wilson, Woodrow 13, 25, 29, 93
wolfram ore 62, 64, 66
Wood, Spencer (Rear-Admiral) 118
Wunderwaffe (wonder weapons) 50

Yorktown, USS 132

Zeppelin 36
Zimmermann telegram 29, 185